Law Society of Ireland

Insolvency Law

Law Society of Ireland

Insolvency Law

General Editor

Joanne Wright

Authors

Nicholas Comyn	Barry O'Neill
Niamh Counihan	Michael Quinn
Bill Holohan	Doug Smith
Julie Murphy-O'Connor	

Bloomsbury Professional

Published by
Bloomsbury Professional
Maxwelton House
41–43 Boltro Road
Haywards Heath
West Sussex
RH16 1BJ

Bloomsbury Professional
The Fitzwilliam Business Centre
26 Upper Pembroke Street
Dublin 2

ISBN: 978 184766 104 3
© Law Society of Ireland 2009

British Library Cataloguing-in-Publication Data
A catalogue record for this book is available from the British Library

FSC
www.fsc.org
MIX
Paper from
responsible sources
FSC® C020438

Typeset by Marie Armah-Kwantreng, Dublin, Ireland
Printed and bound in Great Britain by Hobbs the Printers Ltd, Totton, Hampshire

ABOUT THE AUTHORS

Nicholas Comyn is a partner in Ronan Daly Jermyn, Cork. He practises in the area of corporate and commercial law with a particular focus on insolvency and has vast experience in all aspects of commercial agreements. He has been involved in most major liquidations, receiverships or examinerships in the Munster area over the last twenty years. He also advises a number of multinational pharmaceutical companies. Nicholas has lectured for the Law Society on insolvency for twenty years. He is an associate member of the Institute of Arbitrators and has lectured on and published several articles on commercial law issues. He obtained a BA in Economics and a Masters of Civil Law from UCD. He holds a Diploma in European Law. He qualified as a solicitor in 1970. In 2006 he was recommended as a leading lawyer in the *Chambers Global-Client's Guide*, *Legal 500* and the *European Legal Experts*.

Niamh Counihan, BCL, graduated from University College Cork in 2000 and completed a stage in the European Court of Justice. She joined Matheson Ormsby Prentice in 2000 and is an associate in the firm's Corporate Restructuring and Insolvency Law Group. Niamh provides specialist advice to companies, shareholders, directors, financial institutions, creditor groups, liquidators, receivers and examiners on contentious and non-contentious corporate restructuring and insolvency matters. Niamh is a member of INSOL and the Irish Society of Insolvency Practitioners. She lectures on the professional practice courses of the Incorporated Law Society of Ireland in relation to corporate restructuring and insolvency law.

Bill Holohan, BCL, LLB, FCILS, FCI Arb, AM (CEDR), the Senior Partner of Holohan Solicitors, is qualified as a solicitor, a Commissioner for Oaths, a Notary Public, a Chartered Arbitrator, a CEDR Accredited Mediator, an Irish Trade Mark Agent and an EU Community Trade Mark Practitioner. Bill is co-author of a number of books on bankruptcy law and practice, leasing, international civil procedures, insolvency law and the rescue of companies.

He is the Legal Advisor to the Irish Franchise Association, as well as being an Executive Committee Member. He is also an Executive Committee Member of the Irish Maritime Law Association, as well as being a Titulary Member of the Comité Maritime International. He is a Founder Member and Committee Member of the Irish Society of Insolvency Practitioners and is a Consultant on Insolvency to the Law School of the Law Society of Ireland and has acted as Internal Examiner for the Law Society Examinations on the subject of insolvency. In 2007 he was awarded the 'Franchise Person of the Year' Award, awarded by the Members of the Irish Franchise Association, the only service professional ever to be so recognised by the industry. He is a director of 16 limited liability companies, as well as being a shareholder, director and company secretary of the Aura Leisure group of companies.

Julie Murphy-O'Connor, LLB, graduated from Trinity College Dublin in 1995, and completed a stage in the Council of the European Union, DG XIV, where she worked on the then evolving Cross-Border Insolvency Regulation. She joined Matheson Ormsby Prentice in 1996, where she is a partner in the Corporate Restructuring and Insolvency Law Group. She has been involved in most major liquidations, receiverships and examinerships in Ireland of recent years, and numerous cross-border insolvencies and restructurings. Julie has been recommended by international legal directories as one of Ireland's leading insolvency and restructuring lawyers. Julie has contributed to a number of domestic and international publications on both insolvency and litigation-related matters. She has lectured on insolvency law at the Continuing Legal Education seminars of the Incorporated Law Society of Ireland and of the Dublin Solicitors Bar Association, and on the professional practice courses of the Incorporated Law Society of Ireland. She is an accredited mediator, and a member the Irish Insolvency Group and INSOL Europe.

Barry O'Neill is a partner in Eugene F Collins, Solicitors. Barry has wide-ranging specialist experience in dealing with the legal aspects of corporate and insolvency issues. He has lectured on numerous occasions to the Law Society, to the main professional accountancy bodies and to the International Bar Association. He is one of the compilers of the *Combined Companies Acts*.

Michael Quinn is a partner at William Fry, Solicitors, practising in all aspects of insolvency and corporate recovery. He has extensive experience in advising liquidators, receivers, examiners and others affected by the insolvency process including investors, financial institutions, creditors and directors and officers of companies encountering financial difficulties. He has lectured and tutored in the area of business law at the Law Society, the Irish Centre for Commercial Law Studies and the Irish Centre for European Law. Michael is a past President of INSOL Europe, the European Insolvency Practitioners Association, and past Chairman of the Irish Society of Insolvency Practitioners.

Doug Smith is a Partner in the Corporate Recovery Group of Eugene F Collins, Solicitors. He has a broad range of experience in the area of commercial law and specialist knowledge of corporate restructuring and insolvency law. He represents companies in financial difficulty, creditors of companies in financial difficulty, insolvency/restructuring office holders and the executives of companies in financial difficulty. He is involved in most significant Irish restructuring and insolvency cases in one capacity or another. He has also been involved in cross-border restructurings and insolvencies. He is highly recommended by international legal directories as an expert in the area of restructuring and insolvency law (see *Legal 500* and *Plc Which Lawyer?*). He has a BA and LLB from University College Galway and is a solicitor. He is a member of IBA (section on insolvency restructuring and creditors rights), INSOL, the UK Insolvency Lawyers' Association and the Irish Society of Insolvency Practitioners. He is a regular lecturer and tutor on corporate restructuring and insolvency law matters with the Law Society of Ireland. He has spoken at conferences organised by professional bodies and other organisations including the IBA.

Joanne Wright qualified as a solicitor in England in 1999. Joanne holds an LLB from Warwick University and a Post Graduate Certificate in Higher Education from Nottingham Trent University. She practised in Commercial Litigation before becoming a Senior Lecturer at Nottingham Law School. Since August 2007 Joanne has been the Course Manager responsible for the Law Society's Business Law courses. Joanne was admitted to the Roll of Solicitors in Ireland in 2009.

CONTENTS

About the Authors v
Contents vii
Table of Cases xi
Table of Legislation xvii

Chapter 1   Introduction to Insolvency – Overview

Michael Quinn

1.1   Introduction 1
1.2   Corporate insolvency procedures 2

Chapter 2   Proof of Debt and Rules as to Priorities

Julie Murphy-O'Connor

2.1   Realisation and distribution of assets 7
2.2   Rules as to priorities 8
2.3   Priority of payments in liquidation 12
2.4   Priorities in a receivership 16
2.5   Priorities in an examinership 16

Chapter 3   Compulsory Liquidations

Niamh Counihan

3.1   Introduction 17
3.2   Jurisdiction to compulsorily wind up companies 17
3.3   *Locus Standi* to petition the court 17
3.4   Commencement of a winding up 18
3.5   Procedure 18
3.6   Who can act as liquidator? 21
3.7   Impact of liquidation on the officers of the company 21
3.8   Appointment of the liquidator 22
3.9   Examiner's Office sitting 24
3.10   First sitting of the court 24
3.11   Proof of debt 25
3.12   Official liquidator's remuneration 27
3.13   Discharge of the liquidator 27
3.14   CRO filings 27

Chapter 4   Liquidators' Duties and Powers

Niamh Counihan

4.1	Introduction	29
4.2	Liquidators' qualifications	29
4.3	Liquidators' duties	29
4.4	Liquidator's powers	33
4.5	Asset-swelling measures	40

Chapter 5   Members' Voluntary Liquidations

Nicholas Comyn

5.1	Voluntary winding up: overview	45
5.2	Members' voluntary winding up	46
5.3	Who may be appointed liquidator	50
5.4	Can there be a 'solvent' creditors' voluntary winding up?	51
5.5	Consequences of voluntary winding up: ss 254–255 of CA 1963	51

Chapter 6   Creditors' Voluntary Liquidations

Nicholas Comyn

6.1	When does a creditors' voluntary winding up take place?	53
6.2	Is the company insolvent?	53
6.3	Can the company continue to perform existing contracts even though it is insolvent?	53
6.4	What happens to employees?	53
6.5	Assets – can creditors with reservation of title move their goods?	53
6.6	Moneys received	54
6.7	Steps to be taken to wind up as a creditors' voluntary winding up	54
6.8	Rules of the Superior Courts	57
6.9	Creditors' meeting	58
6.10	Issues post-liquidation	61
6.11	Provisions applicable to every voluntary winding up	62
6.12	Representing a creditor at a meeeting of creditors	64
6.13	Representing the company	64

Chapter 7   General Concepts of Receiverships

Bill Holohan

7.1	Introduction	67
7.2	How and when receivers are appointed	68
7.3	Powers, duties and functions of a receiver	69
7.4	Receiver as agent of company/debentureholder	74
7.5	Notification/publication	74
7.6	Effect of a receiver's appointment	74

7.7   The receiver's position when appointed 75

7.8   Council Regulation (EC) No 1346/2000 77

Chapter 8   Advising Parties Involved in a Receivership

Bill Holohan

8.1   Advising the various parties 79

8.2   Advising the potential receiver 80

8.3   Advising the receiver when appointed 84

8.4   Director of Corporate Enforcement 87

8.5   Advising contractors and suppliers 88

8.6   Advising creditors 89

8.7   Advising a liquidator appointed to the company 90

8.8   Advising directors 93

8.9   Advising shareholders/guarantors 94

8.10   Advising employees 95

8.11   Sale of the company/assets by a receiver 97

8.12   Checklist for assessing the validity of an appointment 97

8.13   Checklist of practical points to consider when advising
        the potential receiver   98

8.14   Checklist when purchasing from liquidator or receiver 98

Chapter 9   Alternatives to Winding Up

Doug Smith

9.1   Examinerships 101

9.2   Schemes of arrangement and compromises:
        ss 201–204 and 279 of CA 1963 115

Chapter 10   Duties and Liabilities of Directors of Insolvent Companies

Julie Murphy-O'Connor

10.1   Introduction 117

10.2   Fraudulent and reckless trading 117

10.3   Failure to keep proper books of acount 120

10.4   Fraudulent preferences 121

10.5   Duty of directors to act in the interests of creditors 123

10.6   Misfeasance 123

10.7   Restriction and disqualification 124

10.8   Advising directors of insolvent companies 125

Chapter 11   Restriction and Disqualification of Directors

Julie Murphy-O'Connor

11.1   Restriction 127

11.2   Application 128

11.3 Defending a restriction application 128
11.4 Obligations of a non-executive director 130
11.5 Legal costs 132
11.6 Costs of investigation 133
11.7 Relief from restriction 134
11.8 Consequences of a restriction order 134
11.9 Disqualification 136
11.10 Costs 136
11.11 Automatic disqualification 136
11.12 Disqualification at the discretion of the court 137
11.13 Applicants 138
11.14 Time limits 138
11.15 Period of disqualificaion 138
11.16 Enforcement of restriction and disqualification orders 139

Chapter 12   Personal Insolvency: Bankruptcy

Barry O'Neill

12.1 Introduction 141
12.2 Bankruptcy proceedings 143
12.3 The debtor's position 147
12.4 Arrangements with creditors outside/prior to bankruptcy 148
12.5 After bankruptcy 150
12.6 Winding up by a trustee 151
12.7 Composition after bankruptcy 151
12.8 Receivers and managers 152
12.9 Estates of persons dying insolvent 152
12.10 EU Insolvency Regulation 153

Chapter 13   International and Cross-Border Insolvency

Michael Quinn

13.1 Introduction 155
13.2 Extra-territorial effect of Irish insolvency appointments and orders 155
13.3 Effect in Ireland of foreign insolvency proceedings 157
13.4 International rules on cross-border insolvencies 157
13.5 Council Regulation (EU) No 1346/2000 on Insolvency Proceedings 158
13.6 Scope of the Regulation 159
13.7 Jurisdiction and 'main' proceedings 159
13.8 Recognition of insolvency proceedings 161
13.9 *Lex concursus* 163
13.10 Secondary insolvency proceedings 164
13.11 Information and treatment of creditors 165
13.12 Public policy 166
13.13 Conclusion 166
Index 169

TABLE OF CASES

A

ABC Coupler and Engineering Ltd (No 5), re [1990] 1 WLR 702 .... 3.11.1

Airline Airspace Ltd v Handley Page Ltd [1970] 1 All ER 29 .... 8.5, 8.11.1

Alexander Hull and Co Ltd v O'Carroll Kent and Co Ltd
[1955] 18 ILTR 70 .... 7.1.1, 8.2.5

American Express International Banking v Hurley [1986] BCLC 52 .... 7.4

Angelis v Algemene Bank Nederland (Ireland) Ltd
(High Court, 4 June 1974) 7.1.1, 8.2.5

Anglo-Moravian Hungarian Junction Railway Co ex parte Watkin
(1875) 1 Ch D 130 .... 4.4.4.1

Antigen Holdings Ltd [2001] 4 IR 600 .... 9.1.20

Ardmore Studios (Ireland) Ltd v Lynch [1965] IR 1 .... 7.4

AV Sorge & Company Limited [1986] BCLC 490 .... 6.7.4

B

Bacal Contracting v Modern Engineering [1980] 2 All ER 655 .... 7.3.2.4

Balbradagh Developments Limited and the Companies Acts 1963–2007,
in the matter of [2008] IEHC 329 .... 6.9

Barings plc (No 5): Secretary of State for Trade and Industry v Baker & Ors, re
[1999] 1 BCLC 433 .... 11.4

Betarose Limited, Forrest v Harrington, re
(Ex Tempore, High Court, 12 January 2006) 11.15

Birchport Limited (High Court, 2 December 2008) 9.1.20

Boyd, re (1885) 15 LR Ir 521 .... 10.4

British Eagle International Airlines Limited v Air France [1975] 2 All ER 390 .... 2.2.2

Brook Cottage, re [1976] NI 78 .... 4.3.6

Business Communications Ltd v Baxter & Parsons
(High Court, 21 July 1995) 11.3.2, 11.9

C

Camoate Construction Ltd (In Liquidation), re [2005] IEHC 346 .... 11.3.2

Capital Finance Ltd v Stokes [1968] IR 573 .... 8.7.6

Casey v Irish Intercontinental Bank [1979] IR 364 .... 7.3.1

CB Readymix Limited (In Liquidation) Cahill v Grimes [2002] IR 372 .... 6.11, 11.15

Centrebind Ltd, re [1966] 3 All ER 880 .... 5.2.6

CHA Limited (In Liquidation) [1999] 1 IR 437 .... 6.11

Chartbusters Limited (High Court, 9 April 2009) 9.1.14

Circle Network (Europe) Ltd (15 February 2001) 9.1.9

City Car Sales Ltd (In Receivership and Liquidation), re [1995] 1 ILRM 221 .... 7.7.3

Cladrose, re [1990] BCLC 204 .... 11.15

Clare Textiles Limited, re [1993] 2 IR 213 .... 9.1.11

Clare Textiles Ltd, re (High Court, 7 May 1992) 9.1.21

Clawhammer Limited, re [2005] IEHC 85 .... 11.15

Clayton's Case [1816] 1 Mer 572 ....8.7.8

Colm O'Neill Engineering Services Limited, re [2004] IEHC 83 ....11.3.2

Columbian Fireproofing Ltd, re [1910] 2 IR 120 ....8.7.7

Comhlucht Paipear Riomhaireachta Teo v Údarás na Gaeltachta
    [1990] ILRM 266 ....3.11.1, 6.11

Competitive Insurance Company Limited v Davies Investments Limited
    [1975] 3 All ER 254 ....4.3.2

Computstore Limited (in Voluntary Liquidation), in the matter of
    (22 February 2005) 6.7.4

Cornish Manures Limited, re [1967] 1 WLR 807 ....6.10

Corran Construction Co Ltd v Bank of Ireland Finance [1976–7] ILRM 175 ....10.4

Costello Doors Limited, re (High Court, 21 July 1995) 11.4

Creation Printing Co Ltd, Crowley v Northern Bank Finance Corp Ltd, re
    [1981] IR 40 ....6.2

Cuckmore Brick Co Ltd v Mutual Finance Ltd [1971] 2 All ER 633;
    [1971] Ch 949 ....7.3.4

Cyona Distributors Limited, re [1967] 1 Ch 889 ....10.2.2

D

Daly & Co Ltd, re (1887–88) 19 LR Ir 83 ....10.4

Daniels v Anderson [1995] 16 ACSR 607 ....11.4

Davis (SI) and Co. [1945] ch 402 ....4.4.4.2

Dempsey v Bank of Ireland [1985] IESC 6 ....2.2.2

Desmond v Glackin (No 2) [1993] 3 IR 67 ....13.12

Digital Channel Partners Ltd, Kavanagh v Cummins & Ors, re [2004] 2 ILRM 35 .....11.5

Don Bluth Entertainment Limited, re [1994] 3 IR 141 ....9.1.11

Donovan v Landys Ltd [1963] IR 441 ....10.2.2

Dowling v Lord Advocate [1963] SLT 146 ....6.9

Duignan v Carway [2002] IEHC 10 ....11.3.2

Dunleckney Limited, in re [1999] IEHC 109 ....11.3.2

E

EB Tractors Limited, re (High Court of Justice in Northern Ireland,
    21 March 1986) 10.2.1

Eden Park Construction Limited, re [1994] 3 IR 126 ....9.1.11

Euro Chick Ireland Limited, in the matter of 6.11

Eurofood IFSC Limited Case C–341/04, ECJ 2/5/2006 ....13.7

F

Falcon RJ Developments Limited, re [1987] BCLC 437 ....6.9

Fate Park Limited [2009] IEHC 375 ....9.1.12

Favon Investments Co. Ltd (In Liquidation) [1993] 1 IR 87 ....5.2.1, 6.11

Fennell v Frost & Ors [2003] IEHC 15 ....10.7, 11.2.1

Foster Parks Ltd Indenture Trusts, re [1966] 1 WLR 125 ....8.10.1

FP & CH Matthews Ltd, re [1982] 2 WLR 495 ....10.4

Frederick Inns Limited, in re [1991] ILRM 582 ....4.5.4, 10.5

G

Gallium Limited, re [2009] 2 ILRM 11 .... 9.1.9

Gasco Ltd (In Liquidation), re [2001] IEHC 20 .... 11.3.2

Gaslight Improvement v Terrell [1870] LR 10 EG 168 .... 8.7.9

Gertzenstein Limited, re [1936] 3 All ER 341 .... 4.1

Glow Heating Limited v Eastern Health Board [1988] IR 110 .... 2.2.2, 6.11

GMT Engineering Ltd, Luby v McMahon & Egan, re [2003] 4 IR 133 ...... 11.5

Griffiths v Secretary of State for Social Services [1974] QB 468 .... 8.10

GWI Ltd, re (High Court, 16 November 1987) 3.11.1, 6.11

Gye v McIntyre [1990–1991] 171 CLR 609 .... 2.2.2

H

Hand v Blow [1901] 2 Ch 721 .... 8.6.2

Hayes Homes Limited (In Voluntary Liquidation) and
  Liam J Irwin Collector General, in the matter of [2004] IEHC 124 .... 6.7.2.1

Hefferon Kearns Ltd, re [1993] 3 IR 191 .... 10.2.2

Hendy Lennox (Industrial Engines) Ltd v Grahame Puttick Ltd
  [1984] 2 All ER 152 .... 2.2.3.3

Holidair (High Court, 6 May 1995) 9.1.20

Holohan v Friends Provident and Century Life Office [1966] IR 1 .... 7.3.1, 7.3.4

Hunting Lodges Ltd, re [1985] ILRM 75 .... 10.2.1, 11.4

I

Industrial Development Authority v Moran [1978] IR 159 .... 7.3.5

Industrial Services Company (Dublin) (in Liquidation), in the matter of
  [2002] IEHC 57 .... 3.8.5, 4.5.5

Irish Oil and Cake Milk Ltd (High Court, 27 March 1984) 8.8.2

Irish Provident Assurance Company Ltd, re [1913] IR 352 .... 10.6

J

Jetmara Teoranta [1992] 1 IR 147 .... 9.1.20

Johnson (B) and Co (Builders) Ltd, re [1955] All ER 775 .... 7.3.4

Jones v Gunn [1997] 2 ILRM 245 .... 10.5

K

Kelleher v Continental Meats Ltd (High Court, 9 May 1978) 10.4

Kelly's Carpet Drome Limited (No 2), re (High Court, 13 July 1984) 10.2.1

Kill Inn Motel Limited, re [1978–1987] III ITR 706 .... 4.5.1

Kinsela v Russell Kinsela Pty Ltd (1986) NSWLR 722 .... 10.5

Knowles v Scott [1891] 1 Ch 717 .... 4.3.1

Kruppstahl AG v Quitmann Products Ltd [1982] ILRM 551 .... 2.2.3.3

Kushler (M) Ltd, re [1943] 2 Ch 481 .... 8.7.9

L

La Moselle Clothing Ltd v Soualhi [1998] 2 ILRM 345 .... 11.3.2

Le Chatelaine Thudichum Limited (In voluntary Liquidation) v Conway
  [2008] IEHC 349 .... 4.5.2

Lycatel (Ireland) Limited [2009] IEHC 264 .... 3.5.1.7
Lyn Rowan Enterprises Ltd [2002] IEHC 90 .... 11.1

M

M & R Electrical Ltd, re (High Court, 30 July 1985) 6.9
Mack Trucks (Britain) Ltd, re [1976] 1 All ER 977 .... 8.10.1–8.10.3
Manning Furniture Ltd, re, 1 ILRM 13 .... 7.3.1
Matthers Ltd (FP and CH), re [1982] 1 All ER 339 .... 8.7.9
McCarthy v Mooreview Developments Ltd 8.10
McGowan v Gannon [1983] ILRM 516 .... 7.3.1
Mehigan v Duignan [1997] 1 IR 340 .... 4.5.8.2, 10.3
Mitek Holdings Limited & Ors v Companies Act [2005] IEHC 160 .... 11.6
Mont Clare Hotels Ltd, re (In Liquidation) Ray Jackson v Pauline Mortell
    and Others (High Court, 2 December 1986) 10.6

N

Naiad Limited (In Voluntary Liquidation), in the matter of
    (High Court, 13 February 1995) 5.3, 6.7.2, 6.9, 6.11
National Irish Bank, The Director of Corporate Enforcement v D'Arcy, re
    [2005] IEHC 333 .... 11.12–11.15
Newhart Developments Ltd v Co-operative Commercial Bank Ltd [1978] QB 814 ... 8.8.2
Northside Motor Co Ltd, re (High Court, 25 July 1985) 10.4
Noyek & Sons Limited [1989] ILRM 155 .... 6.11

O

O'Keefe v Ferris and Others [1997] 3 IR 463 (SC) 13.12
Oakthorpe Holdings (In Voluntary Liquidation) v Registrar of Companies
    [1987] IR 632 .... 6.11
OBG Limited v Allan [2008] 1 AC 1 .... 4.3.2
Outdoor Advertising Services Limited, re [1997] IEHC 201 .... 11.3.1

P

Patrick and Lyon Ltd, re [1933] Ch 786 .... 8.7.7, 10.2.1
Peachdart Ltd, re [1983] 2 All ER 204 .... 2.2.3.3
Pye (Ireland) (High Court, 12 November 1984; Supreme Court, 11 March 1985) 9.2.2

R

R v Grantham [1984] 3 All ER 166 .... 10.2.1
Reiman, re 20 Fed Cas 490 .... 12.1.1
Rendall v Conroy [1897] 8 QLJ 89 .... 4.4.4.3
Riviera Insurance Limited [2009] IEHC 183 .... 3.5.1.1
RMF (Ireland) Ltd Kavanagh v Riedler & Ors, re [2004] IEHC 334 .... 11.4

S

Sarflax Ltd, re [1979] Ch 592 .... 10.4
Sevenoaks Stationers (Retail) Limited, re [1991] Ch 164 .... 11.15

Shannon Granary Ltd (In Voluntary Liquidation), re
  (High Court, 22 November 1990) 6.9
Somers v Allen [1984] ILRM 43 .... 2.2.3.3
Springline Ltd (In Liquidation), re [1999] 1 ILRM 15 .... 3.11.1
Squash (Ireland) Limited, re [2001] 3 IR 35 .... 11.3–11.3.2
Standard Chartered Bank Ltd v Walker [1982] 3 All ER 938 .... 7.3.1, 8.9
Station Motors Ltd v Allied Irish Bank Ltd [1985] IR 756 .... 10.4
Staunton (FE) (No 2), re [1929] 1 ER 180 .... 8.7.7
Stokes and McKiernan Ltd, re (High Court, 12 December 1978) 2.2.3.3
Sugar Distributors Ltd v Monaghan Cash and Carry Ltd [1982] ILRM 399 .... 2.2.3.3

T

Taylor (Assignees of) v Killeleagh Flax Spinning Co (1869–70) IRCL 120 .... 10.4
Taylor (Assignees of) v Thompson (1869–70) 10.4
Tempany v Royal Liver Trustees [1984] ILRM 273 .... 6.11
Thos Mortimer Ltd, re (1925) [1965] 1 Ch 187 .... 8.7.8
Timberlands Limited, re (1979) 4 ACLR 259 .... 4.4.4.3
Tipperary Fresh Foods Limited (In Liquidation) v Companies Act
  [2005] IEHC 153 .... 11.6
Titan Transport Logistics Limited (In Voluntary Liquidation), re
  (High Court, 19 February 2003) 6.9
Traffic Group Limited, re [2008] 2 ILRM 1 .... 9.1.9, 9.1.20
Truck and Machinery Sales Ltd v Marubeni Komatsu Ltd [1996] IR 12 .... 3.5.1.6
Tuskar Resources plc [2001] IR 668 .... 9.1.2, 9.1.9–9.1.9

U

Union Accident Insurance Co Ltd, re [1972] 1 All ER 1105 .... 3.7
United Bars Ltd v Revenue Commissioners [1991] 1 IR 396 .... 7.3.1
Universal Private Telegraph Company (1870) 23 LT 884, 19 WR 297 .... 4.4.4.1
USIT World plc, re [2005] IEHC 285 .... 11.3.1, 11.5

V

Van Hool McArdle Ltd v Rohan Industrial Estates Ltd [1980] IR 237 .... 4.3.6, 4.4.4.4
Vantive Holdings, in the matter of [2009] IESC 68 .... 9.1.9
Vehicle Imports Limited, re [2000] IEHC 90 .... 11.4
Visual Impact and Displays Limited (In Liquidation) [2003] 4 IR 451 .... 11.5

W

West Mercia Safetywear Ltd v Dodd [1988] BCLC 250 .... 10.4
Western Counties Construction Limited v Whitney Town Football
  and Social Club [1993] The Times, 19 November 3.2
Wheeler (M) and Co Ltd v Warren [1928] Ch 840 .... 7.3.2.1
Whiterock Quarries Ltd, re [1937] IR 363 .... 3.7
William C Leitch Bros Limited, re [1932] 2 Ch 71 .... 10.2.1
WMG (Toughening) Limited, re [2001] 3 IR 113 .... 3.5.1.1
Wogan's (Drogheda) Ltd (No 3), re (High Court, 9 February 1993) 9.1.2, 9.1.21

Worldport Ireland Limited (In Liquidation), in the matter of [2005] IEHC 189 3.8.5, 4.5.5
Wreck, Recovery and Salvage Company (1880) 15 Ch D 353 .... 4.4.4.2

X

Xnet Information Systems Limited (In Voluntary Liquidation) [2004] IEHC 82 .... 11.7

Y

Yeovil Glove, re [1965] Ch 148 .... 8.7.8

TABLE OF LEGISLATION

Statutes

Amendment Act of 1999 .... 9.1.6

Auctioneers and House Agents Act 1967 .... 12.1.3

Bankruptcy (Ireland) Amendment Act 1872 .... 1.1

Bankruptcy Act 1914
  s 44 .... 8.7.9

Bankruptcy Act 1988 .... 1.1, 3.11.2, 12.1.2, 12.2.2, 12.9
  s 2 .... 9.1.1, 9.1.2, 9.1.9
    (2) 9.1.9
  7 (1) 12.1.3
  8 .... 12.3
  11 .... 12.2.2.2, 12.2.2.3
  12 .... 12.2.1
  15 .... 12.3.1
  16 .... 12.2.2.3
  16B 12.2.2.3
  18 .... 9.1.17, 9.1.20
    (3) 9.1.6
  19 .... 9.1.20
  20 .... 9.1.14
  21 .... 9.1.2
  22 .... 9.1.17
    (5) 9.1.20
    (6) 9.1.20
  23 (4A) 9.1.17
  24 .... 6.11, 9.1.20
    (3) 9.1.20
    (4) 9.1.20
      (c) (ii) 9.1.19
  25A 9.1.18
  25B 9.1.19
  26 .... 9.1.20
  29 .... 9.1.21
    (1) 9.1.11
    (3) 9.1.21
    (3A) 9.1.11
    (4) 9.1.21
  38 .... 12.7
  39 .... 12.7.1
  44 (1) 12.5.1
  45 .... 12.5.1
  51 .... 2.2.4, 12.2.1
    (2) 12.2.1
  73 .... 12.8

Bankruptcy Act 1988 (contd)
    s 75 ....2.1.3, 3.11.2
      76 ....2.1.3, 3.11.2
      81 ....12.2.1
      87–109 ....12.4.1
      89 ....12.4.1
      105 ....12.1.3
      117 ....12.9
      123 ....12.5.2
      142 ....13.3
        (1) 13.3
  Sch 1 ....2.1.3, 2.2.2

Bills of Sale (Ireland) Acts 1879–83 ....2.2.3.1

Capital Gains Tax Act 1975
  Sch 2 ....2.3.3.1

Central Bank Act 1971
    s 28 (1) 12.1.3

Civil Liability Act 1961 ....3.11.2

Companies Act 1963 ....1.2.1, 3.6, 9.2, 9.2.2
    s 3 (1) 9.1.1
        (2) 9.1.1
        (3) 9.1.2
        (3A) 9.1.2
        (3B) 9.1.2
        (5) 9.1.1
        (6) 9.1.7
      3A 9.1.2
        (8) 9.1.2
      4 ....9.1.9
      4A 9.1.4
      5 (1) 9.1.6, 9.1.20
        (2) 9.1.6
      5A 9.1.16
      6A 9.1.7
      7 ....9.1.11
        (5A) 9.1.14
        (5C) 9.1.14
      8 ....9.1.11
      9 ....9.1.12
        (1) 9.1.12
        (2) 9.1.12
      10 ....9.1.11
        (2) 9.1.2
      11 ....9.1.11
      12 ....9.1.10
      13
        (6) 9.1.15
      25 ....9.1.20

Companies Act 1963 (contd)

s 98 .... 1.2.4, 2.4, 7.3.1, 8.6.3, 8.7.4, 9.1.7

　99 .... 2.2.3.1, 2.2.3.3, 8.1.2

　106 .... 8.1.2

　107 .... 7.5, 8.3.3, 8.3.4, 8.4.1

　131(3) 4.4.5.4

　139 .... 9.1.17

　14 .... 4.5.1

　140 .... 4.5.7.2

　155(5) 4.5.7.2

　183 .... 12.5.1

　183A 12.5.1

　201 .... 9.2, 9.2.4, 9.2.5

　　(3) 9.2.1

　205 .... 9.1.6, 9.1.13

　206–50 .... 1.2.3

　208 .... 3.3, 5.2.5

　213 .... 1.2.3, 3.3

　　(a)–(g) 3.3

　　(c)–(f) 3.3

　　(e) 3.3, 3.5.1

　　(f) 3.3

　214 .... 3.5.1, 3.5.1.1, 3.5.1.2

　　(a) 3.5.1.1, 3.5.1.6

　215 .... 3.3

　　(g) 3.3

　218 .... 2.2.2, 3.5.1.7, 3.8.5, 4.5.5

　219 .... 4.4.6

　220 .... 3.5.1.7

　　(1) 3.4

　　(2) 3.4

　221 .... 3.8.2, 4.3.3.2

　222 .... 2.1.2, 4.4.6

　224 .... 3.8.6, 3.10

　226 .... 3.5.2, 4.4.1

　227 .... 3.8.1, 4.3.3.2

　228(d) 3.12, 4.4.5.5

　229 .... 4.4.6

　　(1) 4.3.2

　231 .... 3.1, 3.8.7, 4.4.2

　　(1) 4.3.5.2, 4.4.3, 4.4.5, 6.11, 6.13

　　　(b) 4.4.4.2

　　　(d) 4.4.5.1

　　　(e) 4.4.5.1

　　　(f) 4.4.5.1

　　(1A) 4.4.4.4

　　(2)(h) 4.4.4.3

　　(3) 4.4.4.4

　　　(d) 4.4.5.2

　　　(e) 4.4.5.2

　　　(f) 4.4.5.2

Companies Act 1963 (contd)

s 232 ....3.8.7, 4.3.3.2, 4.3.5.2, 4.4.2
  233 ....3.8.7, 6.9
  236 ....4.4.6
  244A 4.4.6
  245 ....4.4.6, 13.8.1
  245A 4.4.6
  246 ....4.4.6
  247 ....4.4.6, 13.8.1
  250 ....13.3
  251 ....5.1, 10.8
    (1) 5.1
      (b) 5.2.4
      (c) 5.4, 6.1, 6.7, 6.7.3
  252 ....4.3.3
  253 ....5.1, 5.5, 6.1, 6.7.3
  254 ....5.1, 5.3, 5.5, 6.3
  255 ....5.5
  256 ....1.2.1, 5.2, 5.2.3
    (3) 5.2.3
    (11) 5.2.4, 5.4
  256–264 ....1.2.1
  257(4)(c) 3.3
  258 ....4.4.5.5
    (1) 5.2.4
    (2) 4.4
  258–64 ....5.2
  259 ....5.2.5
  260 ....5.2.5, 6.10
    (3) 5.2.5
  261 ....4.3.4
    (1) 4.3.3.1
  262 ....4.3.5.1, 5.2.5
    (1) 4.3.3.1
  263 ....5.2.7
    (2) 4.3.3.1
    (3) 4.3.3.1
  264 ....4.3.3.1
  265 ....6.1
  265–73 ....1.2.2
  266 ....5.2.6, 6.1, 6.7, 6.7.2.1, 6.8, 6.9
    (1) 6.7.2
    (2) 6.7.2.1, 6.9
    (3) 6.7.1, 6.9
      (1) 6.9
      (a) 6.7.1
      (b) 6.9
    (4) 6.7.1, 6.9
    (5) 6.7.3
  266–268 ....10.8
  267 ....6.11
    (3) 6.9

Companies Act 1963 (contd)

s 268 .... 4.3.5.1, 4.4.2

  (1) 6.9

  (2) 6.9

 269 .... 4.4, 4.4.5.2, 6.10

  (1) 4.4.5.5

  (2) 4.4.5.2

  (3) 4.4.5.2, 6.10

 270 .... 6.10

 271 .... 6.10

 272 .... 4.3.3, 6.10

  (1) 4.3.3.3

 273 .... 4.3.3, 6.1, 6.10

  (2) 4.3.3.3

  (3) 4.3.3.3

 274 .... 6.11

 275 .... 2.1.2, 2.2.1, 2.2.2, 3.11.2, 5.4, 6.11

 275–282 .... 6.11

 276 .... 3.1, 4.3.5.1, 4.4.5, 4.4.5.2, 4.4.5.4, 6.11, 6.13

  (1)(a) 4.4.5.1

    (b) 4.4.5.3

 276A 5.1, 6.7.3, 6.11

 277 .... 6.11

  (2) 5.3

 278(1) 4.3.3

 279 .... 6.11

  (1) 9.2.5

 280 .... 4.3.5.1, 5.2.1, 5.2.3, 6.11

  (3) 6.11

 281 .... 6.7.4, 6.11

 282 .... 6.11

  (D) 4.4.6

 282A 6.11

 282B 4.4.6, 6.11

 282C 4.4.6, 6.11

 283 .... 2.1.3

 283–313 .... 1.2.3

 284 .... 2.1.3, 2.2.2, 2.2.4, 3.11.2

  (2) 12.2.1

 285 .... 2.3, 2.3.3, 5.1, 8.6.3, 8.10.3

  (2) 2.3.3.2

    (a) 2.3.3.1

      (iii) 2.3.3.2

  (11) 2.3.3.2

 286 .... 4.5.3, 6.6, 8.2.3, 8.7, 8.7.9, 10.4, 13.8.1

  (3) 10.4

  (5) 10.4

 288 .... 4.5.6, 8.2.3, 8.7, 8.7.5, 8.7.6, 13.8.1

  (1) 4.5.6, 8.7.5

 290 .... 4.4.6

  (1) 4.4.6

 292 .... 3.8.3, 4.3.3

Companies Act 1963 (contd)

s 297 ....9.1.2, 10.2.1, 13.8.1, 13.12
   297A 4.5.8.1, 9.1.2, 10.2.2, 10.3, 10.7
     (1) 10.2, 10.2.2
     (2) 10.2.2, 10.4
       (b) 10.2.2, 10.8
     (3) 10.2.2
     (4) 10.2.2
     (6) 10.2.2
     (8) 10.8
   298 ....10.6, 13.8.1
   299 ....4.3.2, 4.4.7
   300 ....3.6, 4.2
     (a) 5.3
   300A 3.6, 4.2
     (3) 5.3
   301(1) 6.9
   303 ....3.8.4
     (1) 4.3.3, 6.13
   305 ....5.2.7
   310 ....6.10
   314 ....7.2.1, 7.7.2, 8.2.1
   314–23 ....7.1.2
   315 ....7.2.1, 8.2.1, 8.3.7, 12.5.1
     (2) 7.7.2, 8.3.7
     (5) 7.7.2
   316 ....7.7.1, 8.9
     (2) 8.5, 8.10
   316A 7.3.4
   317 ....7.3.2, 8.3.4
     (1) 7.6.1
     (2) 7.6.1
   318 ....7.7.3, 8.2.4
     (1) 8.2.4
     (2) 8.2.4
   319 ....7.5, 8.3.4, 8.3.6, 8.8.1
     (2A) 8.3.4, 8.4.1
     (7) 7.5, 7.7.4, 8.4.1
     (A) 7.5
   319–20 ....8.8.1
   320 ....7.5, 7.6.1, 8.8.1
   321 ....7.3.1
   322 ....8.7.9
     (1)(b) 8.3.6
   322A 8.3.8
     (1) 7.7.4
     (2) 7.7.4
   322B 8.3.8
   322C 8.3.7
     (1) 7.7.4
     (2) 7.7.4
   324 ....3.2

Companies Act 1963 (contd)
s 325 .... 3.2
345 .... 3.2
Pt VII 7.1.2

Companies (Amendment) Act 1982
s 9 .... 1.2.1, 5.2, 5.2.2
10 (a) 2.3.3.2
(b) 2.3.3.2
(c) 2.3.3.2
(d) 2.3.3.2

Companies (Amendment) Act 1990 ....Chapter 9, 9.1.10, 10.2
s 8 .... 13.12
10 .... 2.3
29 .... 2.3, 3.11.1
33 .... 10.2.2
36 .... 13.3

Companies Act 1990 .... 4.5.7.1, 8.7.9, 13.12
s 12 .... 3.3
26 .... 4.4.4.4
(1)(a) 8.7.6, 10.4
29 .... 4.4.4.4
128 .... 1.2.1, 5.2, 5.2.1, 5.2.3, 5.4
(8) 5.2.3
129 .... 5.2.6
131 .... 6.13
(2)(a) 4.4.5.4
(5) 5.2.4
133 .... 5.1, 6.7.3
134 .... 2.3.3
139 .... 4.5.2, 13.8.1
140 .... 4.5.7.1, 8.7.6, 10.4, 13.8.1
141 .... 4.5.7.1, 4.5.7.3, 13.8.1
142 .... 10.6
144–45 .... 7.1.2
146 .... 5.3
149 .... 11.1
150 .... 4.3.3, 4.4.7, 10.7, 11.1, 11.2.1, 11.2.2, 11.3.2,
11.4, 11.5, 11.6, 11.7, 11.13, 11.15
(2) 11.4
(4B) 11.5, 11.6
152 .... 11.7
154 .... 10.7, 11.2.1
160 .... 4.4.7, 10.7, 11.9, 11.13, 11.15
(1) 11.11
(a) 11.12
(1A) 11.11
(2) 11.9, 11.12
(9A)–(9B) 11.10

Companies Act 1990 (contd)

s 161 .... 11.11

    (1) 11.16.1

163(2) 11.16.2

    (3) 11.16.2

164(1) 11.16.1

    (4) 11.16.2

165(1) 11.16.2

168 .... 11.16.2

169 .... 11.11

170 .... 7.2.1, 8.2.1

170–79 .... 7.1.2

172 .... 7.3.4

175 .... 8.3.8

176 .... 8.3.8, 8.7.9

177 .... 8.3.7

178 .... 4.5.2

180 .... 4.5.2

202 .... 4.5.8.2, 10.3, 11.12

203 .... 4.5.8.2, 13.8.1

204 .... 4.5.8.2, 10.3, 13.8.1

251 .... 4.5.2, 10.2, 11.2.1, 13.8.1

297A 11.12

Pt VI 7.1.2

VII 11.1, 11.2.1, 13.8.1

VIII 7.1.2

Companies (Amendment) (No 2) Act 1999 .... Chapter 9, 13.12

s 5 .... 9.1.9

Companies (Amendment) Act 2003

s 57 .... 6.7.1

Companies Acts 1963–2006 .... 3.2, 4.1

Companies Acts 1963–2009 .... 1.2, 5.2.4, 5.2.7, 6.7.2.1, 6.7.3

Company Law Enforcement Act 2001 .... 6.9, 11.2.2, 11.10, 11.13

s 41 .... (1)(c) 11.2.2

42 .... 11.11, 11.12

    (f) 11.10

47 .... 6.9

49 .... 6.11

51 .... 4.4.7, 11.5

52 .... 7.1.2

    (a) 7.5, 7.7.4, 8.4.1

    (b) 7.5, 8.3.4, 8.4.1

53 .... 7.1.2, 8.4.2

54 .... 11.2.1

55 .... 4.4.6, 7.1.2

56 .... 6.9, 11.2.2, 11.5

    (1)–(2_ 4.3.3

57 .... 8.4.2

58 .... 7.1.2

Conveyancing Act (Ireland) 1634
   s 10 .... 4.5.1

Conveyancing Act 1881
   s 19 .... 7.1.1, 8.2.2
      24 .... 8.2.2
      46 .... 7.3.5

Corporation Tax Act 1976
   s 145
       (5) 2.3.3.1
      151 .... 2.3.3.1

Electoral Act 1923 .... 12.5.1

Finance Act 1976
   s 14 .... 2.3.3.2

Health Contributions Act 1979
   s 6 .... 23.3.2
      15 (1) 23.3.2

Income Tax Act 1967
   s 132 .... 2.3.3.2
      550 .... 2.3.3.1

Insurance Intermittent Unemployment Act 1942 .... 2.3.3.2

Investment Funds, Companies and Miscellaneous Provisions Act 2005
   s 72 .... 5.2.4

Investment Funds, Companies and Miscellaneous Provisions Act 2006
   s 11 .... 11.6
      (2) 11.10

Irish Bankrupt and Insolvent Act 1857 .... 1.1, 12.1.2

Liability for Defective Products Act 1991 .... 7.3.4

Minimum Notice and Terms of Employment Act 1973 .... 2.3.2, 2.3.3.2
   s 13 .... 2.3.3.2

Protection of Employment (Employers' Insolvency) Acts 1984–2001 .... 8.10.1

Protection of Employment Act 1977 .... 8.10

Redundancy Payments Act 1967
   s 28 .... 2.3.3.2
      42 .... 2.3.3.2

Redundancy Payments Act 1979 .... 2.3.3.2
   s 2 .... 2.3.3.2
      3 .... 2.3.3.2
      14 .... 2.3.3.2

Redundancy Payments Acts 8.10.3

Sale of Goods Act 1893 .... 2.2.3.1

Social Welfare (Consolidation) Act 1993
   s 15 (2) 2.3

Social Welfare Acts 1952–1961 ....2.3.3.2

Supreme Court of Judicature Act (Ireland) 1877 .... 7.1.1

Unfair Dismissals Act 1977 ....2.3.2, 2.3.3.2
  s 12 (i) 2.3.3.2

Value Added Tax Act 1972
  s 21 ....2.3.3.1

Other Legislation

Corporate Insolvency Regulations (SI 333/2002) 13.6

European Communities (Protection of Employees' Rights
  on Transfer of Undertakings) Regulations 2003 (SI 131/2003) 8.10, 8.10.4

European Communities (Protection of Employment) Regulations 2000 (SI 488/2000) 8.10

Protection of Employment Act 1977 (Notification of
  Proposed Collective Redundancies) Regulations 1977 (SI 140/1977) 8.10

Protection of Employment Order 1996 (SI 370/1996) 8.10

Rules of the Superior Courts
  Ord 74 .... 1.2, 2.1.3, 3.5
       r   7 ....3.5.1.2
          12 ....3.5.1.2, 4.4.4.2
          15 ....3.5.1.5
          16 ....3.5.1.5
          32 ....4.4.4.2
          39 ....4.4.4.4
          42 ....12.5.1
          50–53 ....6.9
          56 ....6.8
          57 ....3.8.7
          58–83 ....6.8
          59 ....6.9
          64 ....6.9
          65 ....3.8.7, 6.9
          66 ....6.9
          68 ....6.9
          69 ....6.9
          71 ....6.9
          72 ....6.9
          73 ....6.9
          74–75 ....6.7.2.1
          77 ....6.7.2.1
          79 ....6.9
          82 (1) 6.7.2.1
          91 ....4.4.6
          95 ....3.11.3
          97 ....3.11.4
          102–111 ....3.11
          117–123 ....4.4.6
          128 ....2.3, 2.3.1, 3.11.1
              (2) 3.12

Rules of the Superior Courts (contd)

Ord 74 (contd)

      r 130 .... 4.3.3.3

         (b 3.9

         129 .... 6.9

    75 .... 1.2

    75A 1.2

      r 4 (3) 9.1.2, 9.1.3

         (4) 9.1.5

        5 (1) 9.1.5

         (2) 9.1.5

        18 .... 9.1.17

        21 .... 9.1.22

        22 .... 9.1.21

    Appendix M 3.9

Rules of the Superior Courts (No 3) 1989 (SI 79/1989) 12.2.2

Supreme Court and High Court Fees Order 2008 (SI 200/2008) 4.4.4.2

European Legislation

Council Directive 2001/23/EC 8.10, 8.10.4

Council Regulation 1346/2000/EC 3.2, 7.8, 12.10, 13.1, 13.4, 13.5

  Art 1 .... 13.5, 13.6

    2 .... 13.6, 13.7.1

    3 .... 13.7

    3.1 .... 13.7

    3.2 .... 13.7.1

    3.4 .... 13.7.1

    4 .... 13.9

    5 .... 13.9.1

    6 .... 13.9.1

    7 .... 13.9.1

    8 .... 13.9.1

    9 .... 13.9.1

    10 .... 13.9.1

    11 .... 13.9.1

    13 .... 13.9.1

    16 .... 13.8

    20 .... 13.11

    21 .... 13.8

    24 .... 13.8

    26 .... 13.12

    31 .... 13.10

    32 .... 13.10

    33 .... 13.10

    39 .... 13.11

  Ch III 13.10

Directive 2001/24/EU 13.6

Directive 2002/74/EC of the European Parliament and of the Council 2.3.2

Directive 2001/17/EC 13.6

Regulation 2001/44/EC 13.8
  Art 1.2 .... 13.5

Hague Convention
  Art 4 .... 5.2.1

United Kingdom

Insolvency Act 1986
  Pt III 7.1.1

CHAPTER 1

INTRODUCTION TO INSOLVENCY – OVERVIEW

Michael Quinn

1.1   Introduction

The study of bankruptcy and insolvency laws dealt historically with the traditional remedies available to creditors, such as enforcement of debt recovery on a collective basis, realisation of a defaulter's assets for the benefit of creditors, and the penalisation of recalcitrant debtors (which, historically, included even terms of imprisonment). Trends in this area of commercial and legal practice now focus on more positive concepts, such as the rehabilitation of the debtor. The so-called 'rescue culture' aims at recovery and reconstruction, with the principal benefits being the saving of value for all stakeholders, whether they are investors, creditors or employees, hence the importance of such procedures as examinership. At the same time, recent developments in corporate insolvency law are designed to curb the activities of those who abuse the concept of limited liability, to penalise those who perpetrate such abuses and to protect third parties from the effects of repetition, through such measures as restriction and disqualification of directors.

To understand the benefits that can be achieved by the orderly conduct of insolvency and corporate rescue procedures, it is necessary to develop a knowledge of the basic remedies and procedures available. Therefore, this book covers all forms of insolvency law and practice, namely bankruptcy, liquidation, receivership and examinership.

This chapter is an introduction to the basic concepts of insolvency. You may already have encountered some of these when studying company law. However, the laws governing insolvency are a blend of company law, banking law, equity and trusts, property law and other aspects of commercial law generally. If acting for a liquidator, receiver or an examiner, you will invariably encounter numerous other areas of regulatory, commercial and contract law, largely because many companies which are insolvent and which are subjected to the formal processes discussed in this text are, almost by definition, in default in their obligations to third parties and frequently in their statutory or regulatory obligations.

Most frequently in commercial practice, one will encounter the insolvency of limited liability companies. The term 'bankruptcy' is used in this jurisdiction to describe insolvency procedures relating to natural persons or partnerships of natural persons. The principles of bankruptcy were originally governed by specific bankruptcy statutes, mainly the Irish Bankrupt and Insolvent Act 1857 and the Bankruptcy (Ireland) Amendment Act 1872. Each of these and several other statutes relating to bankruptcy were repealed and replaced in Ireland by the Bankruptcy Act 1988, which is now the principal source of law. This text includes a separate chapter dedicated to bankruptcy law and procedure. However, it should be noted that many of the principles which govern the winding up of insolvent companies are based on traditional concepts of bankruptcy law.

Typically you will only encounter bankruptcy cases in the following situations:

(a) where a person trades commercially in his own right or in a partnership, as distinct from doing so through a limited liability company, and the business venture fails;

(b) cases where directors and officers become personally liable for the debts of a company and are unable to meet those debts, leading ultimately to personal bankruptcy. This can arise under specific provisions of the Companies Acts which identify the exceptional circumstances in which personal liability would be imposed on directors and officers, notably liability for fraudulent or reckless trading, or failure to keep proper books and records. The other common such circumstance arises where directors or officers or others may have given personal guarantees in favour of third parties in respect of the debts of a company and default on the guarantee; or

(c) 'consumer debt' cases, typically arising from inability to meet repayments on credit card accounts, personal loan defaults etc.

In bankruptcy practice there is no direct equivalent of the concept of a liquidator or receiver, who in corporate insolvency practice will generally be an accountant in private practice appointed to the office of a liquidator or receiver. Where the High Court makes an order adjudicating a person a bankrupt, the affairs of the bankrupt are administered by the Official Assignee in Bankruptcy, who is an officer of the High Court and in the full-time employment of the Courts Service.

1.2   Corporate insolvency procedures

Formal insolvency and winding-up procedures applicable to companies are:

(a) voluntary liquidation (which includes members' voluntary liquidation and creditors' voluntary liquidation);

(b) compulsory liquidation;

(c) receivership; and

(d) examinership.

Company insolvencies are governed by the Companies Acts 1963 to 2009, the Rules of the Superior Courts, Orders 74, 75 (SI 15/1986), and Order 75A (SI 147/1991), and case law.

There are two tests for establishing insolvency:

(a) the 'cash flow' test, which requires showing that the company is unable to pay its debts as they fall due for payment; and

(b) the 'balance sheet' test, which depends on showing that the value of the company's assets is insufficient to meet its liabilities, including (for certain statutory purposes) contingent and prospective liabilities.

These separate tests have different applications and implications, depending on the particular statutory provision being applied.

This book contains separate chapters relating to each of the four areas listed above and deals with a number of subjects that apply to more than one form of insolvency procedure. These include such topics as the rules of priority among creditors in a winding up and the remedies available to liquidators in respect of certain pre-liquidation transactions or conduct.

One of the best ways to describe liquidation is that it is a form of 'collective debt collection'. The French use the apposite expression 'procédures collectives'. The company is in default towards its creditors – unable to pay its debts as they fall due for payment – and the core functions of a liquidator are to take possession of and realise all the assets of the defaulting company and to distribute the proceeds of that realisation among the admitted creditors in accordance with the priorities set by law. The other very important duties and powers of a liquidator are for the most part directed to this core function. They concern such objectives as establishing that all of the assets have been traced and realised for the benefit of creditors, and that creditors are not treated unfairly or unequally as a consequence of actions or transactions perpetrated prior to the liquidator's appointment. The liquidator has certain powers to set aside preferences, to challenge certain pre-liquidation transactions and to investigate the conduct of directors, officers and others. Where appropriate, the liquidator must pursue persons who may be personally liable for debts of the company. His functions in relation to the restriction and disqualification of directors are based on the objective of protecting other parties who might be exposed to repeated business failures by the same persons.

After the liquidator has concluded the realisation of assets, and distribution of dividends, and complied with investigation and reporting obligations, he will make a final return to the Registrar of Companies, following which the company will be dissolved.

We now turn to the different forms of insolvency process for companies. The first distinction to note is between voluntary and compulsory liquidation. The term 'voluntary' denotes a liquidation which is commenced on the company's own initiative. The company is placed in liquidation by resolution of the shareholders. A *members'* voluntary liquidation is a solvent winding up. A *creditors'* voluntary liquidation occurs where the company is insolvent. The term 'compulsory liquidation' denotes a winding up which is commenced by order of the court. Here the company is invariably, but not necessarily in certain circumstances, insolvent.

1.2.1 Members' voluntary liquidation

This is a form of company winding up that is distinct from an insolvency procedure. It arises where the members of a solvent company decide for their own commercial reasons to wind up the company voluntarily and distribute its assets. To avail of this procedure, the company must be solvent and the creditors' debts must be paid in full.

A members' voluntary liquidation can be distinguished from a creditors' voluntary liquidation by the fact that in a members' voluntary winding up, the directors must complete and file with the Registrar of Companies a statutory Declaration of Solvency. This is a sworn declaration to the effect that the company will be able to pay its debts in full within a period not exceeding 12 months from the commencement of the liquidation.

The provisions specifically applicable to a members' voluntary liquidation are ss 256–264 inclusive of the Companies Act 1963, as amended by s 9 of the Companies (Amendment) Act 1982 and s 128 of the Companies Act 1990. In this book references to 'CA 1963' are references to the Companies Act 1963 (as amended).

The winding up commences when the shareholders at a duly convened EGM pass a Special Resolution to wind up the company voluntarily and appoint a liquidator. All or the majority of the directors must swear a Declaration of Solvency within 28 days prior to this general meeting. A Statement of Assets and Liabilities is exhibited to the Declaration. A report by an independent person must be appended to the Statement of Assets and Liabilities, to the effect that in the opinion of the directors the company will be able to pay its debts in full within 12 months, and that the statement of the company's assets and liabilities embodied in the Declaration of Solvency is reasonable. Under s 256, the independent person is a person qualified to be an auditor to the company, and usually is the auditor.

The directors' powers cease on the appointment of the liquidator save where the company in general meeting or the liquidator sanctions the continuance of those powers. The liquidator is answerable to and reports to the members of the company.

1.2.2 Creditors' voluntary liquidation

This form of liquidation arises where a company is insolvent and unable to pay its debts. It is referred to as 'voluntary' because the shareholders, frequently on the recommendation of the board of directors, resolve to place the company in liquidation without being compelled (from a legal point of view) to do so by a third party, such as a creditor. The procedure is governed by ss 265–73 of CA 1963.

In this form of liquidation, the directors are responsible for the preparation of an estimated statement of the company's affairs setting out its assets and liabilities.

The legal process of a creditors' voluntary winding up commences by a resolution by the members that the company be wound up voluntarily. This meeting will invariably be preceded by board meetings which decide to initiate the process (see **Chapter 6** on creditors' voluntary winding up), but it is the passing of the shareholder resolution which places the company in liquidation. At the same time, the members also pass a resolution appointing a liquidator and the directors' powers cease (unless continued by decision of the Committee of Inspection (see (d) below) or resolution of the creditors). A meeting of the creditors must be held the same day or the day after the day on which the resolution is passed. The creditors' meeting must be advertised at least 10 days in advance in two daily newspapers circulating in the district where the company has its registered office or principal place of business, and notified in writing to all creditors of the company.

The creditors' meeting must be chaired by a director of the company. The business of the meeting is as follows:

(a)   The Statement of Affairs is presented to all creditors in attendance. Questions on the Statement are addressed to the chairman of the meeting.

(b)   The liquidator appointed by the company must attend and report to the creditors on any actions he has taken since his appointment.

(c)   Creditors may confirm the appointment of the liquidator nominated by the company or alternatively they may elect their own nominee as liquidator, in which case the creditors' nominee prevails.

(d)   A Committee of Inspection comprising representatives of creditors and members of the company may also be appointed.

At the end of this meeting, the company will be in creditors' voluntary liquidation and a liquidator will have been appointed. The liquidator is answerable to and reports to the creditors of the company.

1.2.3 Compulsory liquidations

Section 213 of CA 1963 prescribes the circumstances in which the High Court can order the winding up of a company. The most frequent such case is where a company is unable to pay its debts as they fall due or where it is just and equitable that the company be wound up. In this text, compulsory liquidation is examined principally in the context of insolvency.

Sections 206–250 inclusive and ss 283–313 inclusive of CA 1963 govern compulsory liquidations.

A petition to the court for a winding-up order may be presented by one or more of the following parties:

(a)   one or more creditors with undisputed debts;

(b)   the company itself, if authorised by the special resolution of members; or

(c)   a member of the company (subject to certain conditions).

Of these three, the most common is the creditors' petition grounded on failure to pay a liquidated amount.

On hearing the petition, the court may dismiss it, adjourn it or make a winding-up order. A winding-up order places the company in liquidation and appoints the Official Liquidator.

After the presentation of a petition and before the hearing, the court can, on sufficient urgency being shown, appoint a provisional liquidator for the purposes of continuing the company's business or protecting its assets pending the hearing.

In a court liquidation, the liquidator acts at all times under the auspices of the High Court. A liquidator appointed by the court is an officer of the court and is called an 'Official Liquidator'.

1.2.4 Receivership

Although most receiverships in true legal form are merely a method of enforcing security, and as such not a 'collective procedure', receivership is in practice frequently treated as a form of insolvency procedure.

A receiver is appointed on foot of a debenture or charge which confers on a secured creditor the power in defined circumstances, usually including default by the borrower, to appoint its own receiver for the purposes of realising the assts secured by the debenture.

Irish law provides for several different types of receivership (including the appointment of a receiver by the court). However, the most common type occurs where a secured creditor (usually a lending institution) appoints a receiver under contractual powers granted by the company in a debenture or charge. The debenture is a contractual document and all the powers of the debentureholder and of the receiver are governed by this document except for a small number of statutory provisions. Such a receiver's appointment extends only over assets which have been charged.

The appointment of the receiver does not change the legal status of the company. Although the directors cease to control the assets over which the receiver has been appointed, their normal powers and duties continue in respect of any other assets and liabilities of the company. Where the receiver is appointed under a floating charge over all or substantially all the assets and undertaking of a company, the practical effect is to vest full management powers in such receiver, to the exclusion of the directors.

Receivership is a temporary condition affecting a company which, unlike liquidation, does not necessarily lead to the company's dissolution. After a receiver has been discharged, the directors resume their normal functions in relation to all of the company's affairs, unless a liquidator has been appointed in the meantime. In practice, many receiverships result ultimately in the dissolution of the company, whether or not following liquidation.

Most modern debentures confer the power to appoint a receiver with power to manage the company, that is, to continue the management of the business of the company.

The principal function of the receiver is to realise the charged assets and distribute the proceeds to the holder of the charge, subject to any other valid charges and priorities. If a receiver is appointed on foot of a floating charge as distinct from a fixed charge, he must pay the claims of creditors whose claims would be preferential in a winding up, in priority to the claim of the debentureholder (CA 1963, s 98).

A receiver and liquidator may act concurrently in respect of the same company, but a liquidator is precluded from taking possession of or dealing with those assets under a receiver's control. This is a consequence of the company having contracted, with the lender, by the instrument of debenture or charge, to give the appointed receiver exclusive power and control over the charged assets.

1.2.5   Examinership

This procedure is intended to facilitate the rescue of insolvent and nearly insolvent companies. It enables the company to petition the High Court for a period of 70–100 days 'protection of the court' during which time its creditors are restrained from exercising their rights to pursue claims, and secured creditors are prohibited from exercising their security, subject to certain protections for the priority such security affords them. The High Court appoints an examiner whose function is to formulate proposals for a compromise or scheme of arrangement between the company, its members and its creditors. Such a scheme of arrangement typically involves a combination of new investment, adjustment of the rights of members, compromise of creditors' claims and payment of dividends to creditors thereby providing an outcome more favourable for members and creditors as a whole than a winding up of the company. The company continues to trade during the protection period and the directors remain in control of and responsible for the day-to-day operations of the company. If the scheme of arrangement is confirmed by the court, it becomes binding on the company and all its members and creditors. If it is successfully implemented by the company, the company resumes its ordinary 'life' after the process, with its affairs restructured by the process. If a scheme is not confirmed by the court or successfully implemented, the protection of the court is withdrawn and liquidation or receivership invariably follows.

Not all companies are suitable for examinership. Before appointing an examiner, the court must be satisfied that there is reasonable prospect of the survival of the company, and that the appointment of an examiner will facilitate that objective.

CHAPTER 2

PROOF OF DEBT AND RULES AS TO PRIORITIES

Julie Murphy-O'Connor

2.1 Realisation and distribution of assets

2.1.1 The role of the liquidator

A liquidator's obligations are to take control of all the property and assets of the company, to realise those assets and to apply the proceeds of the realisation to the discharge as far as possible to the claims proved against the company. Where there is a deficit, the liquidator must refer to the law as to priorities.

2.1.2 Effect of winding up on creditors and third parties

Once a company goes into liquidation, the fundamental principle is that all creditors should rank *pari passu* with each other as set out in s 275 of the Companies Act 1963 (CA 1963). However there are numerous exceptions to this rule (see **2.2** below).

Once the company has gone into court/compulsory liquidation, creditors must notify the liquidator of any sums, which they claim are due to them, and the liquidator will adjudicate on the claims. In practice there is little point in continuing any legal proceedings a creditor may have by way of debt collection as the adjudication process will replace the court process at that stage. If, however, a party wants to continue court proceedings against the company in liquidation, it must apply under s 222 of CA 1963 to continue the said proceedings. Any judgment obtained will rank as an unsecured debt.

A liquidation does not affect the ability of a secured creditor to subsequently appoint a receiver pursuant to its charge. If a liquidator is appointed where a receiver has already been appointed to a company, the receiver is still entitled to act in relation to the secured assets of the company.

2.1.3 Proof of debts

In liquidation the onus of proof of an amount due lies on the creditor. The debts which may be proved in a liquidation are specified in s 283 of CA 1963. Section 284 of CA 1963 applies the rules for admitting debts for the time being in force under the law of bankruptcy to the liquidation of companies. Section 75 of the Bankruptcy Act 1988 provides that 'debts and liabilities, present or future certain or contingent, by reason of any obligation incurred by the bankrupt before the date of adjudication shall be provable in the bankruptcy.' Section 76 of the Bankruptcy Act 1988 provides that the provisions of Schedule 1 to the Act shall apply in relation to the proof of debts. Thus Schedule 1 to the Bankruptcy Act 1988 is incorporated into company law.

The rules in Schedule 1 to the Bankruptcy Act 1988 provide the procedure for valuing the debts due by the bankrupt. See also Rules of the Superior Courts (RSC) Ord 74. Not all debts are due at the date of commencement of bankruptcy. There may be a credit period before the amount is due. The debt may be contingent, as in the case of a guarantee. The claim may involve a number of payments due over a future period, such as rent.

2.2   Rules as to priorities

2.2.1   The *pari passu* rule

All debts rank equally against the assets under this rule incorporated in s 275 of CA 1963. Where debts rank equally and the assets are insufficient to meet them, the debts abate in equal proportions; that is to say, on a distribution each debt is paid in similar proportion or percentage of the amount outstanding.

However, many exceptions to the *pari passu* principle now exist, created both by contract and by law. Any party holding security will rank ahead of unsecured creditors. Certain debts are preferred by statute, and thus rank ahead of unsecured creditors although behind the holders of fixed security. Assets which are held in trust and moneys that must be set off are also unavailable for distribution by a liquidator.

2.2.2   Insolvency set off and contractual set off

As already mentioned, s 284 of CA 1963 provides that in the winding up of an insolvent company, the same rules should prevail and be observed relating to the respective rights of secured and unsecured creditors and to the debts provable and to the valuation of annuities and future and contingent liabilities as are in force for the time being under the laws of bankruptcy.

Rule 17 of Schedule 1 of the Bankruptcy Act 1988 provides: 'Where there are mutual credits or debts as between a bankrupt or any person claiming as a creditor, one debt or demand may be set off against the other and only the balance found owing shall be recoverable on one side or the other'.

In relation to the winding up of a company by the court, the date of presentation of the petition is the relevant date for determining the rights of set off. Therefore the debtor is not permitted to set off any pre-liquidation against any post-liquidation debts. Indeed, s 218 of CA 1963 provides 'in a winding up by the Court, any disposition of the property of the company, including things in action … made after the commencement of the winding-up shall, unless the Court otherwise orders, be void'.

In order for set off on insolvency to exist there must be mutuality. Mutuality has three aspects. The best statement of what is necessary for the requirement of mutuality in insolvency in contained in *Gye v McIntyre* [1990–1991] 171 CLR 609 at 623:

> … there are three aspects of the … requirement of mutuality. The first is that the credits, the debts, or the claims arising from other dealings be between the same persons. The second is that the benefit or burden of them lie in the same interests. In determining whether credits, debts or claims arising from other dealings are between the same persons and in the same interests, it is the equitable or beneficial interests of the parties which must be considered … The third requirement of mutuality is that the credits, debts or claims arising from other dealings must be commensurable for the purposes of set off under the section. That means that they must ultimately sound in money.

Before considering the approach of the Irish courts in applying these provisions, it is worthwhile summarising the attitude of the English courts to the equivalent provisions of English law. The English courts have taken the view that the set off provisions which apply under the English insolvency rules are mandatory in nature and it is not possible to contract out of them. Thus, upon the onset of insolvency, a contractual right of set off is displaced and is replaced by the insolvency rules. This means that, as a matter of public policy, it is not possible to contract beyond that which is permitted by the insolvency rules as this would breach the *pari passu* rule. In other words, the English courts have taken the view that so far as set off is concerned, the only exception permitted to the *pari passu* rule is that which is expressly permitted by the insolvency rules.

In Ireland, the courts have adopted a different approach, which is best demonstrated by two cases: (1) *Dempsey v Bank of Ireland* [1985] IESC 6 and (2) *Glow Heating Limited v Eastern Health Board* [1988] IR 110. The net effect of these decisions is that the Irish courts when considering the exercise of a contractual right of set off in an insolvency context will apply the principle that the liquidator cannot get a better right to the company's assets than the company itself had. Thus, if an asset is subject to a contractual right of set off, that right of set off remains exerciseable notwithstanding the commencement of a liquidation.

Therefore, the only way, for example, a debtor might succeed in a claim of set off of a pre-liquidation debt against a post-liquidation debt would be if they had a pre-existing and enforceable contractual right of set off which would override the insolvency set off provisions mentioned above.

The *Glow Heating* case concerned a clause in a construction agreement whereby moneys paid by the employer to a main contractor under a retention clause were made subject to an obligation to pay sub-contractors directly in certain circumstances. It was stressed by Costello J that s 275 of CA 1963 should 'not be interpreted as meaning that every contract is void by which a party to it obtains rights over a company's assets superior to those given to ordinary creditors under the section'. Such an interpretation, Costello J opined, would mean, for example, that retention of title clauses in contracts for the sale of goods, and clauses in building contracts conferring rights on building owners over retention moneys, would be void – which is obviously not the case. He said that *British Eagle International Airlines Limited v Air France* [1975] 2 All ER 390 in no way conflicts with the well established principle 'that the liquidator takes the company's property subject to liabilities which affected it in the company's hands'.

It was held that the clause in question in that case did not contravene s 275 of CA 1963 because, on a correct analysis, it could not be regarded as part of a contract for the disposal of assets of the company. Instead, the clause imposed 'a contingent liability on an asset of the main contractors, the moneys in the retention fund, namely a liability to suffer a reduction in the event of a specified default on the contractor's part.' The liquidator took the retention fund subject to that very liability.

In the unreported Supreme Court case of *Dempsey v Bank of Ireland*, what was at issue was whether the bank was entitled to enforce a contractual right to appropriate a sum by way of debit, notwithstanding the winding up. Henchy J was at pains to point out that the claim was not one to prove a debt in the winding up, but rather to recover by means of a direct debit pursuant to a contractual arrangement:

> ... to say that when the liquidator takes over, the assets of the company vest in him, is a less than complete statement of the legal position. The general rule is that he only acquires such title to the assets as the company had – no more, no less. He cannot take any better title to any part of the assets than the company had. This means that he takes the assets subject to any pre-existing enforceable right of a third party in or over them. If that were not so, equities, liabilities and contractual rights validly and enforceably created while the assets were in the hands of the company would be unfairly swept aside and an unjust distribution of the assets would result.

Henchy J quoted the following passage from *Halsbury's Laws of England*, 4(3), para 594:

> The general rule is that the trustee in bankruptcy takes no better property to title than the bankrupt himself had. The bankrupt's property passes to the trustee in the same plight and condition in which it was in the bankrupt's hands, and is subject to all the equities and liabilities which affected it in the bankrupt's hands, to all dispositions which have been

validly made by the bankrupt, and to all rights which have been validly acquired by third persons at the commencement of the bankruptcy.

In the *Dempsey* case the right in question was originally a contingent one and it was to the effect that if the bank was called on before 31 March 1983 by the trustee to pay €75,000, while it would be bound to do so, it could reimburse itself by debiting Eurotravel's account with that sum. When the trustee called on the bank to pay €75,000 on 29 March 1983 and the bank became immediately bound to make that payment, Eurotravel's accounts in the bank became actually rather than contingently subject to the bank's right to debit. It was in that state of contractual liability that those accounts passed to the liquidator on 11 April 1983. Immediately before the liquidator took over on that date, the bank was entitled to pay the €75,000 and entitled to recover it by debiting it against Eurotravel's accounts.

2.2.3   Retention of title

2.2.3.1 *Purpose*

Generally where goods are sold and delivered to a buyer, title is considered to pass even if the purchase price is not immediately paid by the buyer. However, the Sale of Goods Act 1893 gives the parties in a sale of goods contract freedom to determine by contract when title should pass, facilitating retention of title (ROT) clauses. The seller may, by the terms of the contract, reserve title in the goods until certain conditions are fulfilled by the buyer. In such cases, notwithstanding delivery of the goods to the buyer, the property in the goods does not pass to the buyer until the conditions imposed by the seller are fulfilled.

It is therefore important for the seller of goods to insert a term into the contract of sale between himself and the buyer providing that property in the goods is not to pass from the seller to the buyer until a specified condition is fulfilled. Such a proprietary interest protects the seller in the event of the insolvency of the buyer and also provides a direct remedy if the buyer fails to pay the purchase price.

The specified condition may be:

(a)   that the purchase price for the goods in question must be paid in full (simple ROT clause); or

(b)   that the buyer must discharge all indebtedness to the seller – not confined to the goods in question (all sums due / current account ROT clause).

The retention of title clause is therefore used by the supplier of goods to retain ownership in goods supplied by him to the buyer or at least to give himself some form of interest in those goods, in order to protect himself against the buyer's insolvency by giving himself some priority over the general body of unsecured creditors.

There are other conditions which a seller will often attempt to incorporate into the clause, and which will not always be upheld as effective. These are dealt with below. Questions as to the validity and scope of such clauses generally only arise when and if the buyer becomes insolvent. The liquidator or receiver will generally resist any attempt by suppliers to enforce their retention of title claim and will usually challenge the validity of any such clause. The arguments usually used to invalidate such clauses will be:

(a)   that the clause has not been properly incorporated into the contract of sale between the buyer and seller and so the buyer is not bound buy it; and/or

(b)   even if it has been properly incorporated, it is invalid for some reason, for example because it is attempting to create a charge over the buyer's assets and is therefore void because it has not been registered within 21 days of its creation under s 99 of CA 1963 as amended (or if granted by an individual under the Bills of Sale (Ireland) Acts 1879–83 in the Central Office of the High Court within seven days of its execution).

2.2.3.2 *Incorporation*

In order to successfully rely on an ROT clause, the seller must first be able to show that it was properly incorporated into the contract of sale between the buyer and the seller, and so is binding on the buyer.

It is a general principle of contract law that a party is not bound by a term of the contract unless he knew or ought to have known of its existence at the time he entered into the contract, and the other party took all reasonable steps to bring it to his notice.

The best way of ensuring this is to write to the buyers informing them of the introduction of the ROT clause and obtain an acknowledgment and acceptance from each of them.

Courts will also consider factors such as the knowledge and prior experience of the parties, and documents involved and any previous dealings between them. For example, where the clause is clearly printed on all invoices from the seller to the buyer, and there has been a history of dealing between the parties, then the case law at present would support an argument that the term has been incorporated into the contract of sale.

2.2.3.3 *Validity*

The validity of an ROT clause will depend on (a) the type of clause used by the seller, and (b) the facts of each case (ie what happened to the goods once they came into the possession of the buyer).

There are a number of different types of clauses and circumstances which may arise:

(a) A simple retention of title clause does not prevent the buyer from reselling or using the goods before payment. Where the goods have been sold on and are no longer in the possession of the seller, then the ROT clause will be of no use to the seller. However, where a buyer has sold on the goods to a sub-purchaser subject to a retention of title provision, then unless and until the sub-purchaser has paid the price of the goods, the seller is entitled to claim the goods as his property in the hands of the sub-purchaser.

(b) A 'proceeds of sale clause' purports to acknowledge that a buyer can bona fide sell the goods to a third party, but provides that the proceeds of those sales are to be held in trust for the seller. This type of clause has been held in the UK to constitute a charge which is void if not registered under the Companies Acts. However, there is Irish case law to the effect that the seller will be allowed to trace into the proceeds of sale provided a fiduciary relationship exists giving the seller the equitable right to trace into the proceeds of sale of the goods supplied (*Re Stokes and McKiernan Ltd* (High Court, 12 December 1978) and *Sugar Distributors Ltd v Monaghan Cash and Carry Ltd* [1982] ILRM 399). It is important however to confirm one's tracing rights to the proceeds of sale of goods which have been supplied and not to claim rights to trace the proceeds of sale of both the goods supplied and those in which they have been incorporated if subsequently manufactured, as this has been held to create a charge which would be registerable pursuant to s 99 of CA 1963 (*Kruppstahl AG v Quitmann Products Ltd* [1982] ILRM 551). Another problem in practice is identifying the proceeds as having derived from those goods.

(c) Where the goods in question have been incorporated into other goods so as to lose their identity (for example where resin was sold and then used by the buyer in the manufacture of chipboard before it was paid for), then the ROT clause will not be effective (*Borden (UK) Ltd v Scottish Timber Products Ltd* [1979] 3 All ER 961).

(d) Where the goods in question, although identifiable, have been used in the production of other goods in a manner in which they cannot be extracted or removed from the end product (for example leather used by the buyer in the production of handbags), then the ROT clause will not be effective (*Re Peachdart Ltd* [1983] 2 All ER 204).

(e)   Where the goods are incorporated into other goods before payment, but are readily identifiable and removable, then the ROT clause is effective (for example engines which are incorporated into a generator and which can be removed simply by undoing a number of bolts) (*Hendy Lennox (Industrial Engines) Ltd v Grahame Puttick Ltd* [1984] 2 All ER 152; *Somers v Allen* [1984] ILRM 43).

(f)   A 'products retention of title clause' provides that until such time as the goods are paid for, the title in products manufactured from the goods, even where mixed with other goods not subject to the retention of title clause, will rest in whole or in part with the seller. Case law to date suggests that such a clause will be held to constitute a charge, and will be void if not registered.

2.2.4   Judgment mortgages

Any judgment mortgage which has been registered within three months of the passing of a resolution for a voluntary winding up or the date of the presentation of the winding-up petition where a company is wound up by order of the court is invalid (CA 1963, s 284 as amended by s 51 of the Bankruptcy Act 1988).

2.3   Priority of payments in liquidation

In every liquidation, the priority in which claims are paid is broadly as follows:

(a)   Remuneration, costs and expenses of an examiner which had been sanctioned by court under s 29 of the Companies (Amendment) Act 1990 are paid in full before any other claim, secured or unsecured, in any receivership or winding up of the company.

(b)   Fixed chargeholders (assets which are subject to a fixed charge belong to the security holder and not to the company and, accordingly, whether or not the liquidator deals with them is at the behest of the secured creditor).

(c)   Expenses certified by an examiner under s 10 of the Companies (Amendment) Act 1990 rank after the claims of fixed charge holders (Companies (Amendment) Act 1990, s 29(3)).

(d)   Costs and expenses of the winding up (priorities in relation to costs in a liquidation are set out in RSC Ord 74, r 128).

(e)   Fees due to the liquidator.

(f)   Any claim under s 16(2) of the Social Welfare (Consolidation) Act 1993, ie any sum deducted by an employer from the remuneration of an employee in respect of an employment contribution due by the employer and unpaid by the employer shall not form part of the assets of a limited company in a winding-up. A sum equal to that deducted shall be paid into the Social Insurance Fund ahead of all preferential debts (super preferential claim).

(g)   Preferential debts, eg rates and taxes, wages and salaries (CA 1963, s 285).

(h)   Floating charges rank in the order of their creation.

(i)   Unsecured debts ranking *pari passu* with each other.

(j)   Deferred debts ranking *pari passu* with each other.

Within each ranking, all claims in one category receive full payment before any remaining proceeds are distributed to creditors in the following category. When proceeds are insufficient to meet the claims of one category in full, payments for that category are pro-rated.

2.3.1 Costs in a court liquidation

Priorities in relation to costs in a court liquidation (see **2.3(d)** above) are set out in RSC Ord 74, r 128. These are the fees and expenses properly incurred in preserving, realising or getting in the assets, and such payments are made in the following order of priority:

(a) Costs of the petition, including costs of any person appearing on the petition whose costs are allowed by the court.

(b) Costs and expenses of any person who makes or concurs in making the company's statement of affairs.

(c) The necessary disbursements of the official liquidator, other than expenses properly incurred in preserving, realising or getting in the assets hereinbefore provided for.

(d) The costs payable to the solicitor for the official liquidator.

(e) The remuneration of the official liquidator.

(f) The out-of-pocket expenses necessarily incurred by the Committee of Inspection (if any).

No payments in respect of bills or costs, charges or expenses of solicitors, accountants, auctioneers, brokers or other persons, other than payments for costs, charges or expenses fixed or allowed by the court, shall be allowed out of the assets of the company unless they have been duly fixed and allowed by the Examiner or the Taxing Master as the case may be.

2.3.2 Protection of Employees (Employers Insolvency) Acts 1984–2004

Under provisions of the Acts, which implement Directive 2002/74/EC of the European Parliament and of the Council, the payments of certain debts to employees under contracts or under the provisions of protective legislation arising from employers' insolvencies are guaranteed out of the Insolvency Payments Scheme and payments are made from the Social Insurance Fund. This scheme was formerly known as the Redundancy and Employers Insolvency Fund. Where the employer is a company, for the purposes of the application of the Acts, 'insolvency' includes the appointment of a receiver on behalf of any debentureholder secured by a floating charge, the commencement of a voluntary winding up or the commencement of a compulsory winding up. The principle debts for which payment is guaranteed are as follows:

(a) arrears of wages of up to eight weeks;

(b) the amount of any award by the Employment Appeals Tribunal of compensation under the Minimum Notice and Terms of Employment Act 1973;

(c) arrears of holiday pay for a period of holiday not exceeding eight weeks; and

(d) awards of compensation under the Unfair Dismissal Act 1977.

Any debt calculated by reference to remuneration is subject to a limit of €600 per week. For the purposes of administration of payment of the guaranteed sums in a liquidation, the liquidator is the 'relevant officer' and he arranges for the submission of statements of claim on prescribed forms to the fund which is administered by the Insolvency Payments Section of the Department of Enterprise, Trade and Employment. The Acts also contain provisions guaranteeing the payment of certain unpaid contributions to occupational pension schemes of insolvent companies. Where any payment out has been made from the Social Insurance Fund to employees, the Minister for Enterprise, Trade and Employment is subrogated to those employees' preferential rights as creditors in the winding up of the company.

2.3.3   Preferential debts (see 2.3(g) above)

Under s 285 of CA 1963 certain debts must be paid out of the realised assets of a company in liquidation after the costs, charges and expenses of the liquidation have been paid but prior to the claims of creditors secured by registered floating charge and the unsecured creditors.

Section 134 of the Companies Act 1990 introduces a provision which limits preferential status to those of the liabilities listed below at **2.3.3.1** and **2.3.3.2** which are notified to or become known to the liquidator within six months after advertisement by the liquidator for claims in two daily newspapers. If the assets are insufficient to pay the preferential debts in full, then the debts abate in equal proportions.

Where the company is ordered to be wound up by order of the court, the phrase 'relevant date' in the lists set out at **2.3.3.1** and **2.3.3.2** means:

(a)   the date of the appointment of a provisional liquidator; or

(b)   if no provisional liquidator has been appointed, then the date of the winding-up order;

unless in either case the company had commenced to be wound up voluntarily before that date.

Where, prior to the date of the appointment of a provisional liquidator or the date of a winding-up order the company had passed a resolution for the winding up of the company, the 'relevant date' means the date of the passing of that resolution.

In these circumstances, the following are preferential debts.

2.3.3.1   *Rates and taxes*

Rates and taxes which are preferential debts are defined as follows:

(a)   Local rate: any amount due at the relevant date and having become due and payable within 12 months before that date (CA 1963, s 285(2)(a)(i)).

(b)   Assessed taxes: unpaid amount assessed on the company up to 5 April next before the relevant date and not exceeding in the whole one year's assessment (but inclusive of any interest chargeable thereon) (CA 1963, s 285(2)(a)(ii)).

(c)   Capital gains tax (to 5 April 1976) (CA 1963, s 285(2)(a)(ii); Income Tax Act 1967, s 550; Capital Gains Tax Act 1975, Sch 2, para 15).

(d)   Corporation tax (including tax on capital gains with effect from 6 April 1976 (CA 1963, s 285(2)(a)(ii); Income Tax Act 1967, s 550; Corporation Tax Act 1976, s 145(5)).

(e)   Income tax deducted from payments (CA 1963, s 285(2)(a)(ii); Corporation Tax Act 1976, s 151; Value Added Tax Act 1972, s 21).

2.3.3.2   *Wages and salaries*

Wages and salaries which are deemed to be preferential debts are as follows:

(a)   The amount due in respect of services of a clerk, servant, workman or labourer in the four months next before the relevant date subject to a maximum of £2,500 in any case (CA 1963, s 285(2)(a), (b), (c) and s 285(3); Companies (Amendment) Act 1982, s 10(b)).

(b)   The whole or proportionate part of a lump sum payable under contract to a farm labourer at the end of a year of hiring (CA 1963, s 285(4)).

(c)   'Wages' including any remuneration in respect of the period of holiday or absence from work through good cause (CA 1963, s 285(11); Companies (Amendment) Act 1982, s 10(d)).

(d)   All accrued holiday remuneration (CA 1963, s 285(2)(d)).

(e) Advances to pay wages/salaries: any person who has advanced money to a clerk, servant, workman or labourer for the payment of wages, salaries, accrued holiday remuneration, absence from employment due to ill health or pursuant to any scheme or arrangement for the provision of superannuation benefits to or in respect of such workers is preferred to the extent to a maximum of £2,500 per employees for the four-month period prior to the relevant date before the payments have been made (that is, the same rights as those of the employee concerned) (CA 1963, s 285(6); Companies (Amendment) Act 1982, s 10(c)).

(f) Social welfare contributions: all amounts due in respect of contributions payable during the 12 months next before the relevant date by the company as employer of any persons under the Insurance Intermittent Unemployment Act 1942 or the Social Welfare Acts 1952 to 1961 (CA 1963, s 285(2)(e)).

(g) Deductions by a company from payment to employees, sub-contractors and individuals not in insurable employment.

(h) Any amounts due to the Revenue Commissioner in respect of deductions made (or which should have been made) during the period or periods falling within the period of 12 months before the relevant date from:

    i. Salary or wages of employees in respect of income tax (PAYE) together with interest thereon, the Youth Employment Levy (from 6 April 1982) and the Income Levy (from 6 April 1983);

    ii. Payments to subcontractors (where the company in liquidation is the principal contractor) (CA 1963, s 285(2)(a)(iii); Income Tax Act 1967, s 132; Finance Act 1976, s 14); and

    iii. Payments in respect of health contributions (CA 1963, s 285(2)(a)(iii); Income Tax Act 1967, s 132; Health Contributions Act 1979, ss 6 and 15(1)).

(i) Workman's compensation: all amounts including costs due to an employee in respect of compensation or liability for compensation in so far as they have not been effectively covered by insurance (CA 1963, s 285(2)(f)).

(j) Accidents: all amounts due in respect of damages and costs to an employee in connection with an accident in the course of employment in so far as they have not been effectively covered by insurance (CA 1963, s 285(2)(g)).

(k) Sickness schemes: all sums due to an employee arising out of any scheme or arrangement for the provision of payments to an employee while he is absent from employment due to ill health (CA 1963, s 285(2)(h); Companies (Amendment) Act 1982, s 10(a)).

(l) Unfair dismissals: all compensation payable under the Unfair Dismissals Act 1977 by the company to an employee (Unfair Dismissals Act 1977, s 12(i)).

(m) Minimum notice: all compensation payable to an employee under the Minimum Notice and Terms of Employment Act 1973 (Minimum Notice and Terms of Employment Act 1973, s 13).

(n) Redundancies: contributions to the redundancy fund (other than employers' weekly redundancy contributions to which s 28 of the Redundancy Payments Act 1967, as amended, applies) payable by the company during the 12 months before the commencement of the winding-up order (Redundancy Payments Act 1967, s 42; Redundancy Payments Act 1979, ss 3, 14 and 22).

(o) Any lump sum (or portion of a lump sum) payable by the company under the Redundancy Payments Act 1979 or reclaimed by the redundancy fund (but subject to the 60 per cent rebate recoverable or deductible, as the case may be, from the fund).

2.4   Priorities in a receivership

In a receivership, the receiver must realise the assets subject to the fixed and floating charge provided for in the debenture deed. Basically the same priorities apply in a receivership as have already been listed in relation to liquidations. Section 98 of CA 1963 imposes a positive duty on the receiver to pay preferential creditors out of the proceeds of sale of floating charge assets in advance of payment to the security holder.

A receiver will not be concerned with charges ranking after the charge on foot of which he was appointed and nor will he deal with unsecured creditors. Any surplus after the chargeholder has been paid its debt, and the receiver's costs and expenses have been paid, goes back to the company (or to the liquidator if one has been appointed).

2.5   Priorities in an examinership

There are no formal priority rules in the examinership procedure. As the company continues to trade, it may pay debts arising during the examinership period. Where it cannot pay a debt arising, the examiner has the power to certify a debt as necessarily incurred by the company and should the examinership ultimately fail, and the company go into liquidation, certified liabilities rank before other creditors (with the exception of fixed-charge holders) and the examiner's remuneration ranks above all other creditors (including fixed-charge holders).

CHAPTER 3

COMPULSORY LIQUIDATIONS

Niamh Counihan

3.1   Introduction

A compulsory or official liquidation will arise where the High Court is petitioned to have the company compulsorily wound up. The principal differences between voluntary liquidations (which are dealt with in **Chapters 5 and 6**) and liquidations commenced by court order (which are referred to in this chapter as court liquidations) are that, in the case of court liquidations, liquidators are required to obtain leave of the court (or a committee of inspection, if appointed) under s 231 of the Companies Act 1963 (CA 1963) before exercising many of their powers. In voluntary liquidations no such leave of the court (or a committee of inspection, if appointed) is required (however, see s 276 of CA 1963, which requires voluntary liquidators to obtain the consent of the members in the case of members' voluntary liquidations and the committee of inspection or, if there is no such committee of inspection, the creditors' approval before exercising certain powers). The Examiner of the court exercises a supervisory role in relation to court liquidations. A court-appointed liquidator is described as an official liquidator.

3.2   Jurisdiction to compulsorily wind up companies

The companies which the High Court has jurisdiction to wind up are those which are formed or registered under the Companies Acts 1963–2006, former Companies Acts (CA 1963, s 324 and s 325) and unregistered companies (CA 1963, s 345 and see also *In Western Counties Construction Limited v Whitney Town Football and Social Club* [1993] The Times, 19 November). In certain circumstances, the Irish courts also have jurisdiction to wind up foreign companies, formed or registered abroad (see **Chapter 13** in relation to the application of Council Regulation (EC) No 1346/2000 of 29 May 2000 on insolvency proceedings).

3.3   *Locus Standi* to petition the court

Those who are entitled to petition the court to have a company wound up are:

(a)   The company itself (see s 213(c)–(f) of CA 1963 for the grounds on which a company can petition for its own winding up).

(b)   A creditor of the company (see s 213(c)–(f) of CA 1963 for the grounds on which a creditor can petition to wind up a company).

(c)   A contributory (see s 208 of CA 1963 which defines 'contributory') or a member (see s 213(a)–(g) of CA 1963 for the grounds on which a member or contributory can petition to wind up a company. Please note s 215 of CA 1963 which restricts a contributory's right to present a petition).

(d)   The Director of Corporate Enforcement (the 'DCE') (see s 12 of the Companies Act 1990 (CA 1990).

(e)   The Registrar of Companies (see s 213(h) and (i) of CA 1963).

Section 215(g) of CA 1963 provides that the only person with *locus standi* to petition for the winding up of an investment company on the grounds that such is just and equitable (CA 1963, s 213(f)) is the trustee of an investment company (the person nominated by the Irish Financial Services Regulatory Authority under s 257(4)(c) of CA 1990).

Court liquidation occurs where a creditor or the company itself petitions the court for an order seeking the winding up of the company and appointing a liquidator. In the case of insolvent companies the usual ground relied upon is that the company is 'unable to pay its debts' (CA 1963, s 213(e)) although an insolvent company may also be wound up on the basis that it is just and equitable that the company should be wound up (CA 1963, s 213(f)). This chapter deals with insolvent court liquidations on foot of the company's or a creditor's petition that the company be wound up by order of the High Court.

3.4   Commencement of a winding up

A court liquidation is deemed to commence at the time of the presentation of the petition for the winding up (CA 1963, s 220(2)). Presentation of the petition takes place when the petition is filed in the Central Office of the High Court and the registrar allocates a date for the hearing of same, unless a voluntary liquidator has previously been appointed, in which case the liquidation is deemed to have commenced at the date of the passing of the resolution for the winding up of the company (CA 1963, s 220(1)).

3.5   Procedure

Please see Order 74 of the Rules of the Superior Courts (the 'RSC') in relation to the procedural requirements in respect of a creditor's petition. A summary of the procedures is outlined below.

3.5.1   Creditor's petition

Most creditors' petitions are based on the ground that the company is unable to pay its debts as they fall due for payment, ie insolvent (see **Chapter 1** in relation to insolvency tests generally and s 214 of CA 1963).

Section 214 of CA 1963 assists creditors in proving that a company is unable to pay its debts in certain circumstances. A petition may be presented under s 213(e) of CA 1963 on the ground that the company is unable to pay its debts and inability to pay its debts can be established by reason of one of the following specified events pursuant to s 214 of CA 1963:

(a)   if a creditor, by assignment or otherwise, to whom the company is indebted in a sum exceeding €1,269.74 then due, has served on the company, by leaving it at the registered office of the company, a demand in writing requiring the company to pay the sum so due, and the company has for three weeks thereafter neglected to pay the sum or to secure or compound for it to the reasonable satisfaction of the creditor; or

(b)   if execution or other process issued on a judgment, decree or order of any court in favour of a creditor of the company is returned unsatisfied in whole or in part; or

(c)   if it is proved to the satisfaction of the court that the company is unable to pay its debts, and in determining whether a company is unable to pay its debts, the court shall take into account the contingent and prospective liabilities of the company.

Where a creditor can rely on grounds (a) and (b) above, there is a presumption that the company is unable to pay its debts, and the court ought to grant the petition. Ground (c) may be a faster method of proving insolvency and can be useful where a creditor has evidence of insolvency. The court has discretion to refuse to order to wind up a company. Please see paragraph 25.058 of Courtney, *The Law of Private Companies* (2nd edn, 2002) and MacCann and Courtney, *Companies Acts 1963–2006*.

3.5.1.1   *The demand letter*

The '21-day letter' or notice of intention to liquidate (the 'Notice') referred to in s 214(a) of CA 1963 is the most common way in which a creditor can prove that a company is unable to pay its debts. The Notice should be served by hand on the debtor's registered office and, in the event that the debtor's trading address is different to that of its registered office address, a copy of the Notice should be sent by ordinary pre-paid post to the trading address (see *In Re WMG (Toughening) Limited* [2001] 3 IR 113 and *In the matter of Riviera Insurance Limited* [2009] IEHC 183). Pursuant to s 214 of CA 1963, if a debtor fails to pay on foot of the Notice (within 21 days of the date thereof), the debtor is deemed to be unable to pay its debts. The amount owed must be at least €1,269.74 and should be a valid undisputed debt.

3.5.1.2   *Issuing a petition*

Pursuant to s 214 of CA 1963, if a debtor fails to pay on foot of the Notice (within 21 days of the date thereof), the debtor is deemed to be unable to pay its debts and the creditor can present a petition (see RSC Order 74, r 7 which sets out the details to be included and the form of the petition and verifying affidavit) to wind up the company. The petition is verified by affidavit to which the petition, which has duly been presented, is an exhibit. In the case of a creditor's petition the creditor's financial or credit controller is usually the deponent (RSC Order 74, r 12). The registrar dealing with the matter in the Central Office of the court allocates a hearing date for the petition at the time of its presentation in the Central Office. The date fixed by the registrar must allow the petitioner sufficient time to advertise the petition in accordance with the registrar's directions, usually in two national daily papers and *Iris Oifigiúil*.

3.5.1.3   *Service of the petition (RSC Order 74, r 11)*

It is advisable that the petition and affidavit be served on the company's registered office (and trading address / solicitor's office if relevant) as soon as the petition is issued and in any event prior to advertising.

3.5.1.4   *Advertising the petition (RSC Order 74, r 10)*

The petition is required to be advertised in two daily national newspapers (as directed by the Central Office) and *Iris Oifigiúil* at least seven days in advance of the hearing thereof.

3.5.1.5   *Proceeding with the hearing of the petition to have a liquidator appointed*

As mentioned at **paragraph 3.5.1** above, it should be noted that the power vested in the court to wind up a company is a discretionary one. The petitioner must also nominate a suitable candidate to act as official liquidator. The official liquidator appointed by the court is usually nominated by the petitioner and is required to indicate his written consent in advance.

It is recommended that a booklet of petition papers should be lodged with the Central Office of the High Court on the Thursday prior to the petition hearing to allow the relevant judge review the papers in advance of the petition hearing:

(a)   The petitioner must ensure that all necessary proofs are in order to ensure that the petition will be considered by the court.

(i)   Affidavit of service in relation to service of the petition papers on the company.

(ii)   Ensure advertisements have been placed and vouch same in the Central Office of the High Court in advance of the petition hearing.

(iii)   Obtain a letter of consent to act from the official liquidator. It is also necessary for an affidavit of suitability to be sworn, usually sworn by the solicitor independent of the solicitor whom the official liquidator, when appointed, will retain.

(b)   It is necessary to lodge a list of creditors/contributories who have served upon the petitioner, notices of intention to appear with the registrar when the matter is called (see RSC Order 74, rr 15 and 16).

All creditors and contributories are entitled to be heard and creditors/contributories who intend to appear at the petition hearing should notify the petitioner in advance. Any interested party will usually request a copy of the petition papers following the advertisement of the petition.

3.5.1.6   *Defending a winding-up petition*

The debtor could of course challenge the petition and would have to establish that it had a *bona fide* defence to defend the petition. In order to defend a petition the company may try to argue that, where the petitioner purports to seek the winding up of the company as a creditor, the petitioner is not a creditor and therefore does not have *locus standi* to seek an order winding up the company or that the debt is the subject of a *bona fide* dispute. These bases for opposing a winding-up petition amount in practice to the same thing (see *Truck and Machinery Sales Ltd v Marubeni Komatsu Ltd* [1996] IR 12).

Because of the potentially damaging effect of a winding-up petition on the business of a debtor company, where the debtor has a *bona fide* dispute in relation to the alleged debt upon which the petition is based, the debtor company may obtain an interim or interlocutory injunction restraining the petitioner from advertising the petition or, if advertisement has already taken place, proceeding with the petition.

In the case of a creditor relying on the deeming provision (CA 1963, s 214(a)), the debtor company must be in a position to establish that there is no undisputed debt in a sum in excess of €1,269.74. In the event that there is such an undisputed amount, the debtor company will have the option either to pay the undisputed amount or lodge the undisputed amount in court.

Please see paragaphs 25.066–25.075 of Courtney, *The Law of Private Companies* (2nd edn, 2002) for further discussion.

3.5.1.7   *Other creditors*

In the event that the petitioning creditor for whatever reason does not proceed with the petition, it is open to another creditor to take over the petition (see *In the matter of Lycatel (Ireland) Limited* [2009] IEHC 264). This is of significant importance if the first petitioning creditor has been paid its debt (either in full or in part by way of a settlement of the debt) and the company is subsequently wound up. In the event of a winding-up order being made, the commencement of the winding up relates back to the time when the petition was presented in the Central Office of the High Court (CA 1963, s 220). Section

218 of CA 1963 covers all dispositions of a company's property made between the presentation of the petition and winding-up order, and provides that all dispositions of a company's assets after the commencement of the winding up are void, unless the court orders otherwise.

3.5.2 Company's petition

The company itself can petition for a winding up. The procedure is similar to the creditor's petition to wind up the company. However, petitions of this nature are less common than creditors' voluntary liquidations because, ordinarily, the company will elect for a voluntary liquidation as it is usually more cost effective. There are however instances where a court liquidation is preferable to a creditors' voluntary winding up (see below in relation to provisional liquidators).

The company (or indeed a creditor) can apply on an *ex parte* basis for the appointment of a provisional liquidator pending the petition hearing. The court may, and frequently does, appoint a provisional liquidator after the presentation of the petition. A provisional liquidator is generally appointed on the basis of evidence presented to the court of the necessity for the appointment in order to protect the assets of the company, which are in imminent danger of dissipation. The provisional liquidator's powers are limited to those afforded to him by the court (CA 1963, s 226). Subject to the court's directions, the provisional liquidator can then trade the business pending the hearing of the winding-up petition. Assets can be immediately secured by the provisional liquidator to prevent creditors availing of 'self-help' remedies. Please see **Chapter 4** in relation to the powers of provisional liquidators. The goodwill of the business might be preserved to facilitate the sale of the assets post liquidation.

3.6   Who can act as liquidator?

CA 1963 does not prescribe who can be appointed liquidator. However there are a number of grounds upon which individuals are disqualified from appointment as liquidator (see s 300 and s 300A of CA 1963) but, to date, there is no licensing system or requirement, either in the case of court-appointed or voluntary liquidators, that they possess any specific academic or professional qualifications.

3.7   Impact of liquidation on the officers of the company

The liquidator is 'the executive officer appointed by the court for the purpose of winding up proceedings' (*per* Johnston J in *Re Whiterock Quarries Ltd* [1937] IR 363 at 366). See also *Re Union Accident Insurance Co Ltd* [1972] 1 All ER 1105 at 1113, where Plowman J observed that 'the liquidator assumes and the directors usually lose, the functions and authority which they previously held'. It is clear from the judgment of Plowman J that the necessity to use the word 'usually' was due to the fact that the directors may retain some powers whilst a provisional liquidator stands appointed such as, for example (and as was the case here), the power to retain lawyers to defend the winding-up petition on the company's behalf.

The directors and officers have however a duty to co-operate with the liquidator in the conduct of the liquidation. From the appointment of the liquidator, it is only the liquidator who can act for and on behalf of and in the name of the company, in liquidation.

3.8   Appointment of the liquidator

As mentioned above, an official liquidator is appointed by order of the High Court. Following his appointment there are statutory and procedural requirements which are summarised below. Before he does anything, a liquidator must ensure he is validly appointed and it is his solicitor who should check on the procedures set out above.

3.8.1   Advertising the Official Liquidator's appointment

The official liquidator's appointment must be advertised in the newspapers where the petition was advertised and *Iris Oifigiúil* within 21 days of his appointment (CA 1963, s 227).

3.8.2   Filings in the Companies Registration Office (the 'CRO')

The liquidator must file notice of his appointment/an attested copy of the winding-up order in the CRO (CA 1963, s 221).

3.8.3   Service of notice of appointment

The official liquidator must serve notice of his appointment on the sheriff of the county where the company's registered office is located (CA 1963, s 292).

3.8.4   Correspondence

Pursuant to s 303 of CA 1963, where a company is being wound up, every invoice, order for goods or business letter issued by or on behalf of the company or a liquidator of the company must contain a statement that the company is being wound up. A company in court liquidation will have the words 'In Liquidation' after its name.

3.8.5   Serving the winding-up order on the company's bankers

The liquidator must ensure that the company's bank accounts are 'ruled' (see s 218 of CA 1963 and *In the matter of Industrial Services Company (Dublin) (In Liquidation)* [2002] IEHC 57 and *In the matter of Worldport Ireland Limited (In Liquidation)* [2005] IEHC 189).

3.8.6   Serving the winding-up order on the company and its officers (if required)

If the petitioner is not the company, a copy of the winding-up order should be immediately served on the company at its registered office address. A copy of the winding-up order must also be served on the company's officers who were directed by way of the winding-up order to make out and file statements of affairs pursuant to s 224 of CA 1963.

3.8.7   Creditors' and Contributories' Meeting

The liquidator may need to convene a creditors' and contributories' meeting for the purposes of determining whether a committee of inspection (COI) should be formed.

At the petition hearing (or thereafter) the court might direct the liquidator to convene a meeting of the company's creditors and contributories for the purposes of considering whether a COI should be formed pursuant to s 232 of CA 1963.

The COI is a committee of creditors and members (whose appointment is determined by the court following the meetings of the company's creditors and contributories) who assist the liquidator in the conduct of the liquidation. As outlined in **Chapter 4**, the exercise of some of the official liquidator's powers require the consent/sanction of the High Court or the COI. In other words, the COI can sanction the exercise by the official liquidator of any powers which require the consent of the court (CA 1963, s 231). The COI must comprise of no more than eight members (up to five may be appointed by the creditors and three may be appointed by the company).

The proceedings applicable to the COI are set out in s 233 of CA 1963, which states that:

(a) the COI can meet as often as it sees fit (or as often as the liquidator feels is necessary);

(b) the liquidator, or any committee member, can convene a meeting; and

(c) the COI may act by majority of those committee members present (so long as a majority of the members of the committee are present at the meeting for quorum purposes).

The COI cannot act unless a majority of the members are present at the meeting (CA 1963, s 233(3)). Therefore, where a majority is not present, the liquidator must adjourn the meeting (the liquidator has the power to do so under RSC Order 74, r 65), and reconvene it for another day. The liquidator must inform members by ordinary post of the reconvened meeting, giving no less than seven days' notice (RSC Order 74, r 57).

3.8.8 Issue the notice to proceed in the Examiner's office of the High Court

As mentioned above, all court liquidations are supervised by the Examiner of the court and indeed, in some instances, an application to the court itself is required in relation to the exercise of certain powers of the liquidator (please see **Chapter 4** for further details). The liquidator is obliged to bring the liquidation before the Examiner by issuing a notice to proceed. In order to proceed before the Examiner, the following must be lodged in the Examiner's Office:

(a) notice to proceed with five copies with appropriate notice parties thereon (that is, others who attended the hearing of the petition);

(b) affidavit of service of notice to proceed on the various parties who attended in court on the hearing of the petition and on the company;

(c) copy petition;

(d) copy verifying affidavit;

(e) copy winding-up order;

(f) copies of any affidavits referred to in the winding-up order (such as affidavit of service and affidavit verifying suitability);

(g) letter to the Examiner advising as to whether any court orders were made between the presentation and hearing of the petition and subsequent to the winding-up order;

(h) draft bond or an affidavit dispensing with the requirement to enter into a bond on the basis that the official liquidator's professional indemnity insurance is sufficient;

(i) recent company search;

(j) copy statement of affairs, if available;

(k) evidence of service of the winding-up order on the following parties:

    (i) the company,

    (ii) the Registrar of Companies,

    (iii) the Central Bank of Ireland,

    (iv) the directors, and

    (v) the sheriff,

(l)   original newspaper and *Iris Oifigiúil* advertisements;
(m) authorisation to open bank account(s), duly completed by the official liquidator;
(n)   letter of consent to act from the official liquidator;
(o)   authorisation to appoint a solicitor, duly completed by the official liquidator;
(p)   affidavit of suitability; and
(q)   report of official liquidator (which if possible should include an estimated outcome and an estimated timescale to the completion of the liquidation).

3.9   Examiner's Office sitting

Once the above-mentioned documents have been filed with the Examiner, the notice to proceed will be issued for a date that usually pre-dates the first return date in court. All parties who appeared at the petition hearing are required to be served with the notice and an affidavit as to the service of the notice to proceed is then required for the Examiner's Office sitting.

After the initial sitting before the Examiner, the Examiner:

(a)   considers all necessary proofs referred to above;
(b)   considers the official liquidator's first report and might suggest amendments to the report in advance of the first court sitting (referred to below);
(c)   counter-signs the authorisation to appoint a solicitor, duly completed by the official liquidator;
(d)   counter-signs the authorisation to open bank account(s), duly completed by the official liquidator;
(e)   sets the dates up to which, each year, the official liquidator is required to account to the Examiner (RSC Order 74, r 130(b) and No 45 of Appendix M of the RSC); and
(f)   usually adjourns his consideration of the liquidation from time to time (this is a practice that has also been adopted by the court itself, which, in recent years, has taken to adjourning the winding-up order for further consideration until the final application seeking the dissolution of the company).

3.10   First sitting of the court

At the first sitting at which the winding-up order is considered further by the court, the judge taking the Examiner's List in the court will usually:

(a)   consider the official liquidator's first report and in particular the estimated outcome and estimated timescale to completion (often, as the liquidator will only have been appointed a matter of weeks and investigations are ongoing, it is not possible to give firm estimates);
(b)   award the petitioner (or any other party who appeared at the petition hearing) its costs, such costs to be taxed in default of agreement;
(c)   refer the level of the bond into which the official liquidator is required to enter to the Examiner or give the liquidator liberty to dispense with the requirement to enter into a bond on the basis that the official liquidator's professional indemnity insurance is sufficient; and
(d)   consider whether the officers of the company have complied with their obligations to make out and file a statement of affairs in relation to the company pursuant to s 224 of CA 1963. If not, the judge is likely to adjourn the further consideration of the matter periodically pending the filing of same. It is sometimes necessary for the liquidator to issue a motion for attachment and committal in respect of the officers' obligations in this regard.

If the above-mentioned matters are all dealt with at the first hearing, the court is likely to adjourn the further consideration of the liquidation for one year and periodically thereafter, depending on the specific issues in the liquidation.

3.11 Proof of debt

The Examiner's most substantial input into the liquidation process occurs at the time when the liquidator has realised all of the company's assets and wishes to make a payment of a dividend to the creditors. The process of proof of creditors' claims is initiated by the Examiner and set out in RSC Order 74, rr 102–111. Clearly, the procedure is only necessary in circumstances where there are sufficient moneys to pay a dividend to creditors, whether preferential creditors only or preferential and unsecured creditors. The costs and expenses of liquidation (summarised below) take precedence over creditors' claims.

3.11.1 Priority of payment

Please see **Chapter 2** in relation to the priorities generally.

The order of priority of payment of costs and expenses in court liquidations is set out in RSC Order 74, r 128 as follows:

(a) fees and expenses properly incurred in realising or getting in the assets;
(b) where the company has previously been wound up voluntarily, the remuneration, costs and expenses of the voluntary liquidator;
(c) the petitioner's costs and the costs of all persons awarded their costs in respect of the hearing of the petition;
(d) costs in relation to the preparation of the statement of affairs;
(e) the costs and necessary disbursements of the liquidator;
(f) the liquidator's solicitors' fees;
(g) the liquidator's own remuneration; and
(h) the out of pocket expenses incurred by the COI, if any.

Section 29 of the Companies (Amendment) Act 1990 (the '1990 Amendment Act') should be noted as it gives the remuneration and expenses of an Examiner priority over all other claims (including the liquidator's remuneration and expenses (*Re Springline Ltd (In Liquidation)* [1999] 1 ILRM 15), whether secured or unsecured, in a receivership or in winding up: The necessary disbursements of the liquidator may include rent on leasehold property where the liquidator has adopted the lease (see *Re GWI Ltd* (High Court, 16 November 1987 and *Re ABC Coupler and Engineering Ltd (No 5)* [1990] 1 WLR 702)) or the costs awarded against the company to a successful litigant in respect of an action brought against the company whilst in liquidation or on the company's behalf by the liquidator (see *Comhlucht Paipear Riomhaireachta Teo v Údarás na Gaeltachta* [1990] ILRM 266).

3.11.2 Claims which are admissible to proof

Section 275 of CA 1963 sets out the basic rule which applies in the liquidation of a company with regard to the satisfaction of its liabilities. It provides that the property of an insolvent company should be applied in satisfaction of its liabilities *pari passu*. This is known as the *pari passu* rule. There are exceptions to this rule. For example, any party holding security will rank ahead of unsecured creditors and certain debts are preferred by statute and thus rank ahead of unsecured creditors although behind the holder of fixed security. In addition to these exceptions, there are also specific rules dealing with set-off in a liquidation. Please see **paragraph 2.2.2** in relation to set-off.

Section 284 of CA 1963 provides that in the winding up of an insolvent company, the same rules should prevail and be observed relating to the respective rights of secured and unsecured creditors and to the debts provable and to the valuation of annuities and future and contingent liabilities as are in force for the time being under the laws of bankruptcy relating to the estates of persons adjudged bankrupt, and all persons who in any such case would be entitled to prove for and receive dividends out of the assets of the company may come in under the winding up and make such claims against the company as they respectively are entitled to by virtue of s 284.

The rules which apply in the case of the bankruptcy of individuals are found in the Bankruptcy Act 1988. Section 75 of the Bankruptcy Act 1988 provides that debts and liabilities, present or future of certain or contingent, by reason of any obligation incurred by the bankrupt before the date of adjudication and claims in the nature of unliquidated damages for which the bankrupt is liable at that date by reason of a wrong within the meaning of the Civil Liability Act 1961, are provable in the bankruptcy. Section 76 of the Bankruptcy Act 1988 provides that the provisions of the First Schedule to the Act apply in relation to the proof of debts. The net effect of these provisions is that in the liquidation of a company the rules which apply are the same as those which apply in the bankruptcy of an individual.

Please see pp 505–506 and 517–520 of MacCann and Courtney, *The Companies Acts 1963–2006* for further discussion.

3.11.3 Advertising for creditors (RSC Order 74, r 95)

If there are sufficient assets in a liquidation to pay a dividend for creditors, the official liquidator places advertisements in a prescribed form signed by the Examiner or Assistant Examiner in the daily newspapers in which he is directed to place them by the Examiner or Assistant Examiner. The advertisements indicate the date upon which the adjudication by the Examiner or Assistant Examiner is to take place. This date is usually a week or two after the deadline specified in the advertisements for receipt of claims.

3.11.4 Adjudication of claims

After the deadline has passed, the official liquidator is required to swear an affidavit specifying those claims which, in his view, should be admitted and those in respect of which further proof is required. In the event that the Examiner or Assistant Examiner dealing with the matter is of the view that any claim or claims require further proof, he or she will direct the liquidator to serve notices to prove on the creditors in question specifying an adjourned date upon which these creditors are required to attend and prove their claims and also indicating that they are required to file an affidavit in support of their claims.

The better view appears to be that, when filing his affidavit (RSC Order 74, r 97) indicating whether creditors' claims should be admitted or should be required to be proved further, the liquidator should take account of claims of which he is aware but in relation to which no formal claim pursuant to the advertisements placed in the newspapers has been received.

The outcome of the adjudication will be set out in a certificate drafted by the Examiner. If, ultimately, a creditor does not prove his claim to the satisfaction of the Examiner or Assistant Examiner dealing with the case, the court may order, on the application of the liquidator, that the creditor in question be excluded from the benefit of any distribution. A creditor who is not satisfied with the outcome of the adjudication as set out in a certificate of the adjudication may appeal the matter to court.

3.12   Official liquidator's remuneration

A court-appointed liquidator is required to obtain court approval before payment of his own remuneration out of the company's assets (CA 1963, s 228(d)). The official liquidator's remuneration and his expenses are determined by the court at the hearing of the liquidator's application for final orders in relation to the liquidation. It is the practice, however, for liquidators to apply at least once in the course of the liquidation for a payment on account of fees and expenses.

Expenses such as the official liquidator's legal costs also require court approval and such costs are required to be taxed by the Taxing Master (RSC Order 74, r 128(2)) in the absence of an order dispensing with the requirement to tax same. If there is a shortfall in respect of the official liquidator's fees and expenses, the court might measure the official liquidator's legal fees and dispense with the requirement to have legal fees taxed.

An application for the payment out of the liquidator's fees and expenses is issued by way of notice of motion and grounded upon an affidavit of the liquidator (which usually exhibits a report setting out the status of the liquidation together with a summary of the work done by reference to the fees sought). The largest materially affected creditor is required to be put on notice. The motion papers are firstly lodged for checking in the Examiner's Office prior to the motion being issued in the Examiner's Office and the Central Office.

3.13   Discharge of the liquidator

When a court-appointed liquidator has carried out all of his functions, he is required to apply to the court for final orders which will include an order discharging him as liquidator. This application is issued by way of notice of motion and grounded upon an affidavit of the liquidator (which usually exhibits a report setting a summary of all work carried out in the liquidation together with, if the liquidator is also seeking liberty to pay out of the assets of the company his fees and expenses, a summary of the work done by reference to the fees sought). The largest materially affected creditor is required to be put on notice. The motion papers are first lodged for checking in the Examiner's Office prior to the motion being issued in the Examiner's Office and the Central Office.

Discharge occurs only after the liquidator has made all payments which he is required to make pursuant to the final orders of the court and after the Examiner of the court has filed in the Central Office of the court a certificate as to due disposal of the assets of the company. The final order and the certificate of due disposal must be filed in the CRO. If a bond has been entered into, the bond is required to be vacated in the Central Office of the High Court.

3.14   CRO filings

In addition to the matters set out above in connection with the notice to proceed in the Examiner's Office, if the liquidation is not concluded within two years of commencement, the liquidator is required to file in respect of each year thereafter an account in the CRO.

CHAPTER 4

LIQUIDATORS' DUTIES AND POWERS

Niamh Counihan

4.1   Introduction

There are four types of liquidator: members' voluntary liquidator, creditors' voluntary liquidator, official liquidator and provisional liquidator. Liquidators are fiduciaries of the company to which they are appointed (*Re Gertzenstein Limited* [1936] 3 All ER 341). All liquidators are appointed for the purpose of winding up the affairs of the company, which involves the realisation and distribution of a company's assets in accordance with law. The purpose of this chapter is to consider a liquidator's duties and powers. Liquidators' duties and powers derive principally from the Companies Acts 1963–2006 (the 'Companies Acts') and the Rules of the Superior Courts (the 'RSC').

Please see generally chapter 26 of Courtney, *The Law of Private Companies* (2nd edn, 2002) and chapter 1 of Forde, Kennedy and Simms, *The Law of Company Insolvency* (2008).

4.2   Liquidators' qualifications

The Companies Acts do not prescribe who can be appointed liquidator of a company. Rather ss 300 and 300A of the Companies Act 1963 (CA 1963) specify persons who are *not* qualified for appointment as liquidator.

4.3   Liquidators' duties

4.3.1   Fiduciary duties

Liquidators owe fiduciary duties to the company, as opposed to individual creditors in the discharge of their statutory obligations and duties (*Knowles v Scott* [1891] 1 Ch 717). As mentioned at paragraph 1–96 of Forde, Kennedy & Simms, *The Law of Company Insolvency* (2008), liquidators' 'fiduciary duties also include not taking unfair advantage of, or profiting from their office and avoiding all undue conflicts of interest. The only gain that liquidators may make from their office is whatever remuneration has been authorised; they have no right to retain any other profit which fell to them in the course of their duties'. For example, a liquidator cannot make a secret profit, and if he does will have to account for it. Breach of fiduciary duty can result in the liquidator being deprived of his remuneration as well as having to compensate the company (*Re Gertzenstein Limited* [1936] 3 All ER 341).

4.3.2   General duties

In general terms a liquidator must:

(a)   take possession of the company's property;

(b)   insure the assets of the company;

(c)   serve notice on all employees still employed and process employee claims in respect of their unpaid entitlements with the Department of Enterprise, Trade and Employment;

(d)   take possession of the books and records of the company and the company's seal;

(e)   change the registered office to that of the liquidator's address;

(f)   write to banks asking for any balances and ensure that the company's accounts are ruled;

(g)   open his own bank account; and

(h)   carry out filing and returns in the Companies Registration Office (the 'CRO') and with the Revenue Commissioners.

Liquidators have a duty to investigate the company's affairs and to ascertain the full extent of its assets and liabilities. An official liquidator must 'take into his custody or under his control all the property and things in action to which the company is or appears to be entitled' (CA 1963, s 229(1)).

If an official liquidator comes across any wrongdoing, he must bring the matter to the court's attention. Where it appears in a court or a voluntary winding up that any past or present officer or member of the company has been guilty of a criminal offence in relation to the company, the liquidator must report the matter to the Director of Public Prosecutions (the 'DPP') (CA 1963, s 299).

In the event that liquidators intermeddle with other persons' property, such as selling chattels which are subject to retention of title rights (see paragraph **2.2.3**), they may be liable to such persons for trespass or conversion (*OBG Limited v Allan* [2008] 1 AC 1). In addition, if liquidators intermeddle with trust property, liquidators may be held liable as constructive trustees (*Competitive Insurance Company Limited v Davies Investments Limited* [1975] 3 All ER 254).

Liquidators are also subject to the same general duty of care, to avoid negligently causing reasonably foreseeable loss, as are all others who are involved in a company's affairs.

4.3.3   Administrative/procedural statutory duties

Every liquidator has certain filing obligations with the CRO and advertising requirements which are referable to the type of liquidation in question. In summary, the liquidator must:

(a)   file notice of his appointment in the CRO (CA 1963, s 278(1));

(b)   ensure that the resolution to wind up is filed in the CRO (CA 1963, s 252) together with (in the case of a creditors' voluntary winding up) a certified copy of the resolutions of the creditors;

(c)   serve notice of his appointment on the sheriff (CA 1963, s 292);

(d)   ensure that the words 'In Liquidation' or 'In Voluntary Liquidation' appear on all letters, invoices and orders (CA 1963, s 303(1));

(e)   in the context of an insolvent liquidation a liquidator must within six months of his appointment and thereafter at intervals prescribed by the Director of Corporate Enforcement (the 'DCE'), report to the DCE in the prescribed form (see Company Law Enforcement Act 2001, s 56(1)), unless excused from doing so by the director, and between three and five months later the liquidator must apply to have the directors restricted (Company Law Enforcement Act 2001, s 56(2) and Companies Act 1990, s 150); and

(f)   hold statutory meetings (CA 1963, ss 272 and 273).

4.3.3.1 *Members' winding up*

In a members' voluntary winding up, the liquidator must:

- (a) hold a general meeting within three months of the end of each year of the liquidation (CA 1963 s 262(1));
- (b) produce an account of his dealings at the end of each year;
- (c) file that account within seven days in the CRO (CA 1963, s 261(1));
- (d) hold a general meeting at the end of the liquidation, which is to be advertised 28 days in advance in two daily newspapers (CA 1963, 263(2));
- (e) produce and file a copy of his final account (CA 1963, 263(3)); and
- (f) fulfil alternative provisions where the liquidator is of the opinion that the liquidation must be continued as a creditors' voluntary winding up (CA 1963, s 264).

4.3.3.2 *Compulsory liquidation*

In a compulsory liquidation, the official liquidator must:

- (a) advertise his appointment in the Companies Registration Office Gazette within 21 days of his appointment (CA 1963, s 227);
- (b) file notice of his appointment / a true certified copy of the winding-up order in the CRO (CA 1963, s 221 and s 227) within 21 days of his appointment;
- (c) serve the winding-up order on the company and its officers (if required);
- (d) convene a creditors' and contributories' meeting for the purposes of determining whether a committee of inspection (COI) should be formed (CA 1963, s 232); and
- (e) file the final order and the certificate of due disposal in the CRO to dissolve the company from the register of companies.

4.3.3.3 *Creditors' winding up*

In a creditors' winding up, the liquidator must:

- (a) hold a general meeting of the company and the creditors within three months of the end of each year of liquidation (CA 1963, s 272(1));
- (b) produce an account of his acts and dealings at the end of each year of the liquidation;
- (c) file that account within seven days in the CRO (CA 1963, s 272(1));
- (d) hold a general meeting of the company and the creditors at the end of liquidation, to be advertised 28 days in advance in two daily newspapers (CA 1963, s 273(2));
- (e) produce at meetings and file an account of his dealings in the CRO (CA 1963, s 273(3)); and
- (f) if the liquidation continues for more than two years, file a statement of account within 30 days of the expiration of such two-year period and every year thereafter file an account of his dealings in the CRO (RSC Order 74, r 130).

4.3.4 Statutory duties to members

Liquidators owe many statutory duties to members of a company. In particular, as mentioned in **Chapter 5**, a members' voluntary liquidator is obliged to call a meeting of the company's creditors if he is of the opinion that the company will not be able to meet its debts in full within the time specified in the directors' declaration of solvency (CA 1963, s 261).

4.3.5   Statutory duties to creditors

Liquidators owe many duties to creditors. When a company is insolvent, its creditors are the beneficiaries of the company's assets. A creditors' voluntary liquidator and an official liquidator are obliged to apply the assets of the company in accordance with the rules of priorities as discussed in detail at **Chapter 2**. Please see paragraph 26.021 of Courtney, *The Law of Private Companies* (2nd edn, 2002).

4.3.5.1   *Creditors' voluntary liquidation*

If a COI is formed pursuant to s 268 of CA 1963, the liquidator is under an obligation to seek the approval of the COI in respect of the exercise of the powers set out in s 276 of CA 1963, as explained in greater detail below. Please also see **paragraph 6.9**, which sets outs the procedural requirements in relation to the convening of and conduct of COI meetings.

The liquidator is under a duty to call a meeting of creditors of the company at the end of the first year of the winding up and within three months from the end of each succeeding year (s 262 of CA 1963). The liquidator is obliged to lay before these meetings an account of his acts and dealings and of the conduct of the winding up during the preceding year and within 7 days to send a copy of such account to the registrar of companies. Any creditor or contributory in a voluntary winding up may apply to court to determine any matter concerning the liquidator's exercise of his functions (CA 1963, s 280), including applying to hold him liable for wrongdoing.

4.3.5.2   *Compulsory liquidation*

As explained at **Chapter 3** above, the court might direct that an official liquidator convene a meeting of the company's creditors and contributories for the purposes of determining whether or not an application is to be made to the court for the appointment of a COI (CA 1963, s 232). Where a COI has been appointed, it will act in conjunction with a liquidator. A COI in a court liquidation can sanction the exercise by the liquidator of any of the powers which require the sanction of the court (CA 1963, s 231(1)). An official liquidator should not exercise any of the powers outlined in s 231(1) without first obtaining the liberty of the High Court or the COI.

4.3.6   Liquidator's duty to realise assets

As mentioned at **paragraph 4.1** above, one of the liquidator's primary duties and powers is to collect in the company's assets. In the context of the realisation of corporate assets, Courtney indicates at paragraph 27.004 of Courtney, *The Law of Private Companies* (2nd edn, 2002) that the duties of liquidators may be seen to include:

- taking possession of all corporate assets, and protecting them, pending the distribution of the proceeds in accordance with law;
- pursuing all assets which in law or in equity belong to the company, but which may be in possession of others;
- realising claims for compensation and damages against wrong-doing corporate officers and others who owe the company money; and
- realising and liquidating all assets so as to have the proceeds available for distribution in accordance with law.

It is the duty of the liquidator to secure the best price reasonably obtainable for the company's assets (*Van Hool McArdle Ltd v Rohan Industrial Estates Ltd* [1980] IR 237). If the property is to be sold at a price below the best possible available, an injunction may be obtained by a creditor or contributory restraining the sale (*Re Brook Cottage* [1976] NI 78).

4.4   Liquidator's powers

The company's directors' powers generally cease on the appointment of a liquidator. On the appointment of a members' voluntary liquidator, the powers of the company's directors cease, save as the company in general meeting or the liquidator approves their continuance (see s 258(2) of CA 1963). The powers of a company's directors cease on the appointment of a creditors' voluntary liquidator save as the COI or, if there is no COI, the creditors, sanction the continuance thereof (s 269 of CA 1963). As outlined in **Chapter 3**, the appointment of a provisional liquidator and an official liquidator also displaces the powers of the directors, save that the directors have the power to challenge the winding-up order.

4.4.1   Powers of provisional liquidators

In the first place, if a provisional liquidator is appointed pending the hearing of the winding-up petition (as referred to in greater detail at **Chapter 3**), the provisional liquidator's powers are limited to those afforded to him by the court in the order appointing him as provisional liquidator (CA 1963, s 226). On the application of the appointment of the provisional liquidator, it is common for the petitioner to list the powers that it thinks that the provisional liquidator should have. Such powers might include the power to:

(a)   take possession of the company's assets;
(b)   open a bank account;
(c)   insure assets and hire security for such purposes;
(d)   retain or dismiss employees;
(e)   continue trading the company's business;
(f)   licence the trading of the company's business to third parties; and/or
(g)   sell assets up to a certain *de minimus* amount.

In the event that the provisional liquidator requires additional powers pending the hearing of the winding-up petition and his confirmation as official liquidator (if so appointed), it is open to the provisional liquidator to apply to court for liberty as may be required. Such an application is often made *ex parte* and grounded upon an affidavit sworn by the provisional liquidator. In certain instances, the provisional liquidator will put, or be required by the court to put, the largest materially affected creditor on notice of the application.

4.4.2   Powers of official liquidators

The exercise of some of the official liquidator's powers require the consent of the court, or of the COI (CA 1963, s 231) if one is appointed (see s 232 of CA 1963 for the appointment of the COI in a compulsory liquidation and s 268 of CA 1963 for the appointment of a COI in the context of voluntary liquidations). An official liquidator is an officer of the court and he is subject to the control and supervision of the court and the Examiner's Office of the High Court. Official liquidators can apply to court for directions in relation to the conduct of the liquidation.

4.4.3   Powers which require court/COI sanction

Pursuant to s 231 (1) of CA 1963 the consent of the High Court or the COI is required in advance of an official liquidator:

(a)   bringing/defending any action/legal proceeding in the debtor's name;
(b)   carrying on the business of the debtor;

(c)   appointing a solicitor;

(d)   paying any class of creditors in full;

(e)   compromising/settling any creditors' claims/debtors' claims; and

(f)   compromising with creditors or with shareholders in respect of calls, appointing a solicitor, carrying on the business and bringing/defending actions.

It should be noted that it is open to any creditor or shareholder to apply to the court in relation to the exercise or proposed exercise of these powers. An application by the official liquidator to the High Court in relation to the exercise of any of the above-mentioned powers is by way of notice of motion or on an *ex parte* basis grounded upon affidavit sworn by the liquidator. Such applications are heard in public. In determining whether or not to grant leave to exercise all or any of the above-mentioned powers, the court or the COI, as the case may be, must have regard to whether the exercise of that power is in the best interest of those creditors or contributories of the company who have a real interest in the assets of the company.

4.4.4   Powers exercisable without court/COI sanction

Other powers (set out below and which speak for themselves) are exercisable by the official liquidator without the need to obtain the sanction of the court or the COI:

(a)   sell the company's assets;

(b)   act in the name of the company in liquidation;

(c)   deal with the estate in bankruptcy of all contributories;

(d)   draw, accept, make or endorse any bill of exchange or promissory note in the name of and on behalf of the company in liquidation;

(e)   borrow money on the security of the assets of the company in liquidation;

(f)   take out, in his name, letters of administration to any deceased contributory;

(g)   give security for costs;

(h)   appoint an agent to do any business which the official liquidator is unable to do himself; and

(i)   do all such other things as may be necessary for the winding up of the company in liquidation and distributing its assets.

Some of the powers mentioned above are dealt with in greater detail below.

4.4.4.1   *Appointing a solicitor*

In appointing a solicitor to advise him in the context of the liquidation, a liquidator is obliged not to employ someone whose independence may be unduly conflicted (*Re Universal Private Telegraph Company* (1870) 23 LT 884, 19 WR 297). The solicitor's fees are a cost of the winding up and, accordingly, have priority over other debts, including the liquidator's own remuneration. The liquidator is, however, not personally responsible for those costs and is entitled to be indemnified out of the assets of the company in respect of same (*Re Anglo-Moravian Hungarian Junction Railway Co* ex parte Watkin (1875) 1 Ch D 130).

4.4.4.2   *Carrying on the business*

Official liquidators are authorised to 'carry on the business of the company so far as it may be necessary for the beneficial winding up thereof' (CA 1963, s 231(1)(b)). In order for an official liquidator to obtain the liberty of the High Court to continue the business of the company, he must be able to demonstrate to the satisfaction of the court that trading the company's business is necessary for the beneficial winding up of the company. For example, if trading the business for a period of time post-liquidation would result in net realisations for the company, it is likely that a court would make an order granting the official liquidator liberty to continue to trade the business. In addition, it may be necessary to preserve the goodwill associated with the business (to secure a sale of the company's business going forward). Such applications may be made on an *ex parte* basis, but the court normally directs that creditors be put on notice, such as the Revenue Commissioners, which is usually the largest materially affected creditor.

In carrying on the business of the company, the official liquidator will be under a duty to closely monitor the affairs of the company and if he forms a view that it is no longer beneficial for the winding up of the company, to therefore cease carrying on the business of the company. It should be noted that carrying on the business must be with a view to winding up the company, not with a view to its continuance (*Re Wreck, Recovery and Salvage Company* (1880) 15 Ch D 353).

There are several other specific powers which are ancillary to carrying on the business of the company, such as, to draw, accept, make or endorse any bill of exchange or promissory note in a company's name and to appoint an agent to do any business which the liquidator himself cannot do.

From the official liquidator's perspective, it is also important to note that debts incurred by the liquidator for this purpose rank in priority over other debts, because they are costs of the liquidation as outlined at **Chapter 3** above (*Re Davis (SI) and Co.* [1945] Ch 402).

In carrying on the business of the company, it may be more expedient from the official liquidator's perspective to obtain the liberty of the High Court to use a float/trading account, which does not require each cheque to be countersigned by the examiner of the High Court. Pursuant to RSC Order 74, r 32 an official liquidator is obliged to open bank accounts in the name of the company in liquidation, with the official liquidator and the examiner of the High Court being co-signatories on the account (RSC Order 74, r 12). Court duty of 4% is payable on the net realisations (Supreme Court and High Court Fees Order 2008 (SI 200/2008), Pt 3, No 23). From the official liquidator's perspective, it is, perhaps, less time consuming if a trading account is opened and all receipts are lodged in the trading account and payments discharged out of the trading account, with the net balance being transferred to the official liquidator's bank account (opened with the Examiner of the High Court) at the end of the period of trading.

4.4.4.3 *Appointing an agent*

A liquidator can appoint agents to act on his behalf under s 231(2)(h) of CA 1963. However, he is not entitled to delegate his discretional matters that require the exercise of professional judgement (*Rendall v Conroy* [1897] 8 QLJ 89; *re Timberlands Limited* (1979) 4 ACLR 259). In addition, an official liquidator is not entitled to receive payment in respect of tasks delegated that should have been performed by him.

4.4.4.4 *Sale of assets – restrictions*

The RSC provide that the official liquidator may not directly or indirectly purchase any part of the company's assets save by leave of the court and any such purchase made without leave is capable of being set aside on the application of any creditor or contributory of the company (RSC Order 74, r 39).

The limitations imposed on sales to officers of the company should also be borne in mind. Section 231(1A) provides that an liquidator of a company must not sell 'a non-cash asset which is of requisite value to anyone who was an officer of the company in the three years before the winding up, unless at least fourteen days' notice of the liquidator's intention is given to all the creditors who are known to him. An officer here includes a 'connected person' within the meaning of s 26 of CA 1990 and a 'shadow director'. A 'non-cash asset' and requisite value in this context have the same meaning as that in the rules regarding substantial property transactions between the company and any of its directors (CA 1990, s 29).

The purpose of s 231(1A) of CA 1963 is to prevent liquidators selling the company's assets below market price to former officers of the company. It does not apply to every sale of assets to a former officer. It applies:

(a)   to sales by private contract and not to sales by public auction;

(b)   only if the asset is a 'non-cash asset' of the 'requisite value'; and

(c)   if the purchaser or one or more of the purchasers (a) has been an officer within the three years prior to the commencement of the winding up or (b) is connected with such an officer within the meaning of s 26 of CA 1990.

Whilst creditors are required to be given fourteen days' notice of the proposed sale, there is no prescribed remedy for an aggrieved creditor. It would, however, be open to the aggrieved creditor to make an application to court for relief under s 231(3) of CA 1963.

As mentioned above, it is the duty of the official liquidator to secure the best price reasonably obtainable for the company's assets (*Van Hool McArdle Ltd v Rohan Industrial Estate Ltd* [1980] IR 237).

4.4.5   Powers of voluntary liquidators

The powers of voluntary liquidators are set out in s 276 of CA 1963, which provides that:

1. The liquidator may:

(a)   in the case of a members' voluntary winding up, with the sanction of a special resolution of the company, and, in the case of a creditors' voluntary winding up, with the sanction of the court or the committee of inspection or (if there is no such committee) a meeting of the creditors, exercise any of the powers given by paragraphs (d), (e) and (f) of subsection (1) of section 231 to a liquidator in a winding up by the court;

(b)   without sanction, exercise any of the other powers by this Act given to the liquidator in a winding up by the court;

(c)   exercise the power of the court under this Act of settling a list of contributories, and the list of contributories shall be prima facie evidence of the liability of the persons named therein to be contributories;

(d)   exercise the power of the court of making calls; and

(e)   summon general meetings of the company for the purpose of obtaining the sanction of the company by resolution or for any other purpose he may think fit.

4.4.5.1   *Powers of the members' voluntary liquidator which require approval*

Pursuant to s 276(1)(a) of CA 1963 a members' voluntary liquidator can only exercise the following powers with the sanction of a special resolution of the company:

(a)   to pay any class of creditor in full (CA 1963, 231(1)(d));

(b)   to make any compromise or arrangement with creditors or persons claiming to be creditors (CA 1963, s 231(1)(e)); and

(c)   to compromise all calls and liabilities to calls, between the company and a contributory (CA 1963, 231(1)(f)).

4.4.5.2   *Powers of the creditor's voluntary liquidator which require approval*

The court, COI or the company's creditors must give their consent, under s 276 of CA 1963, before a creditors' voluntary liquidator can:

(a)   pay any class of creditor in full (CA 1963, s 231(d));

(b)   compromise any claim presented by a creditor (CA 1963, s 231(e)); and

(c)   compromise any claim in relation to the company (CA 1963, s 231(f)).

Further powers given to the COI in relation to the liquidator are set out in s 269 of CA 1963, enabling the COI to:

(a)   fix the level of remuneration paid to the liquidator;

(b)   determine whether the liquidator should continue the business of the company; and

(c)   determine whether the powers of the directors should continue (CA 1963, s 269(3)).

The level of remuneration paid to the liquidator is a matter to be agreed by the COI. However, where the remuneration has been agreed by the COI, it is still open to challenge by any 'creditor or contributory' pursuant to s 269(2) of CA 1963. This provision allows such contributory/creditor who believes the level of remuneration to be excessive 28 days to apply to court and have the court fix the level of remuneration to be paid to the liquidator.

4.4.5.3 *Powers of a voluntary liquidator which do not require approval*

Pursuant to s 276(1)(b) of CA 1963, a voluntary liquidator has the following powers without the sanction of the court, COI or creditors or of the members by special resolution:

(a)   bring/defend any action/legal proceeding in the debtor's name;

(b)   carry on the business of the debtor;

(c)   appoint a solicitor;

(d)   sell company assets;

(e)   act in the name of the company in liquidation;

(f)   deal with the estate in bankruptcy of all contributories;

(g)   draw, accept, make or endorse any bill of exchange or promissory note in the name of and on behalf of the company in liquidation;

(h)   borrow money on the security of the assets of the company in liquidation;

(i)   take out, in his name, letters of administration to any deceased contributory;

(j)   give security for costs in any proceedings commenced by the company or by him in the name of the company;

(k)   appoint an agent to assist him;

(l)   do all such other things as may be necessary for the winding up of the company in liquidation and distributing its assets;

(m)   exercise the power of court to settle a list of contributories;

(n)   exercise the power of the court in making calls; and

(o)   summon general meetings of the company for the purpose of obtaining the sanction of the company by resolution or for any other purpose he may think fit.

Pursuant to s 280 of CA 1963, a voluntary liquidator can apply to court for directions in relation to any issues arising in the conduct of the liquidation.

4.4.5.4 *Restrictions on the exercise of powers by a voluntary liquidator*

Section 131(2)(a) of CA 1990 provides that a liquidator who is appointed by the members at the initiation of a creditors' voluntary liquidation cannot exercise the powers granted to him by s 276 of CA 1963 before the creditors' meeting is held. However, there are certain limited exceptions and a liquidator is entitled pursuant to s 131(3) of CA 1963 to:

(a)   take into his custody or under his control all the property to which the company is or appears to be entitled;

    (b)   dispose of perishable goods and other goods the value of which is likely to diminish if they are not immediately disposed of; and

    (c)   do all such other things as may be necessary for the protection of the company's assets.

4.4.5.5 *Remuneration*

    (a)   *Provisional and official liquidators*
As outlined in **Chapter 3** above, the remuneration of the official liquidator is subject to the approval of the court (CA 1963, s 228 (d)).

    (b)   *Members' voluntary liquidators*
As outlined in **Chapter 3** above, the members at general meeting set the remuneration of the liquidator (CA 1963 Act, s 258).

    (c)   *Creditors' voluntary liquidators*
As outlined in **Chapter 3**, the COI or, if there is no COI, the creditors, fix the remuneration of the liquidator (CA 1963, s 269(1)).

4.4.6 Specific powers

An official liquidator and creditors' voluntary liquidator have a number of specific statutory powers given to them for the purposes of causing the assets of the company to be collected and preserved for the benefit of the company's creditors and to examine the conduct of the company's affairs. A brief overview of the statutory powers is set out below:

    (a)   An official liquidator may require a number of parties concerned with the company to 'pay, deliver, convey, surrender or transfer to [him] any money, property, books or papers' they possess, to which the company is *prima facie* entitled (RSC Order 74, r 91) and any money or bills, notes or other securities received by the official liquidator must promptly be paid or deposited with the bank (RSC Order 74, rr 117–123).

    (b)   Pursuant to s 236 of CA 1963, the official liquidator can avail of a procedure for obtaining possession of property that belongs to the company and which is being held by any shareholder, trustee, receiver, banker, agent or officer of the company. The court may order that person to 'pay, deliver, convey, surrender or transfer '... any money, or property, books, or papers in [their hands] to which the company is prima facie entitled'. In the event that there is a dispute in relation to the ownership, these powers do not extend to same. However, the official liquidator would, at the very least, be entitled to review the documentation, or obtain physical custody of the items under s 229 of CA 1963, pending a determination in relation to the dispute as to ownership.

    (c)   Pursuant to s 247 (in the context of a court liquidation) and s 282(D) (in the context of a creditors' voluntary liquidation) of CA 1963, provision exists for securing the arrest and detention of any contributory or officer who is about to abscond or to conceal any of his property so as to avoid being examined about the company's affairs or to avoiding payment of calls. It is open to a creditor of the company and 'any interested person' to obtain leave of the court in this regard. However, there is a heavy burden of proof on the applicant to establish probable cause for obtaining an order in this regard.

    (d)   Under s 55 of the Company Law Enforcement Act 2001, it is possible to obtain a *mareva*-type order prohibiting any officer of the company from removing assets from the state or from reducing them below a specific value. The parties who can make an application in this regard include the liquidator, as well as the company, any director, any member, any creditor, a receiver and the DCE. Pursuant to s 55, an order may be granted where the applicant has established that it has a 'substantive civil cause of action' against the party or is entitled to seek a declaration of civil liability or to claim damages against that party. In addition, there must be sufficient grounds for apprehending that the party will remove or reduce his assets so as to evade his or the company's obligations and thereby frustrate any court order.

(e) Under s 245 of CA 1963 (in the context of a court liquidation) and under s 282B of CA 1963 (in the context of a creditors' voluntary liquidation), the liquidator can seek to examine, under oath, a wide category of people who had dealings with the company. The court may summon before it any person who it knows or suspects possesses company property or is indebted to the company and any person it deems capable of giving information about the company's formation, promotion, trade, property, dealings or affairs. These persons may be required to produce any documents relating to the company that they possess (CA 1963, s 245A and CA 1963, s 282C (creditors' voluntary liquidation)). They may be examined on oath and be required to set out in a written statement an account of transactions between themselves and the company. Information obtained from these examinations frequently provides the foundation for legal proceedings. The DCE may also apply for an examination order and, in exceptional circumstances, a creditor or member may similarly do so.

(f) Section 244A of CA 1963 applies to court and creditors' voluntary liquidations. It prohibits an advisor or other third parties from withholding possession of files or documents belonging to a company by exercising a lien over them as security for unpaid fees.

(g) Under s 246 of CA 1963, the court may, in a court liquidation, require the attendance of officers of the company at certain meetings of the company's creditors/contributories or at a COI meeting.

(h) Section 219 of CA 1963 provides that no execution, attachment, sequestration, distress or execution can be put in force after the company has been put into court liquidation. (It is also worth noting that s 222 of CA 1963 also provides that no new action can be commenced against a company in court liquidation or pre-liquidation proceedings commenced, save with the leave of the court.)

(i) Section 290 of CA 1963 entitles a liquidator to disclaim onerous contracts subject to the leave of the court. For example, the assets of a company could include leasehold property held at a relatively high rent which is no longer needed but which, because of the rent and repairing and other obligations, cannot be sold. In the circumstances, the continuance of the lessee's obligations would seriously deplete the company's net assets. The purpose of disclaimer is to enable the liquidator to realise and dispose of particular assets without needlessly protracting the winding up. In addition it serves to put an end to its continuing liabilities, which would become expensive in the liquidation and thereby reduce what is available to unsecured creditors. Section 290(1) of CA 1963 sets out the property and interests that are capable of being disclaimed.

4.4.7 Policing powers/duties of a liquidator

The powers/duties of a liquidator as part of his role in connection with the policing of standards of business conduct from which creditors derive no direct benefit include:

(a) the duty to take restriction proceedings against directors of the company (CA 1990, s 150);

(b) the power to take disqualification proceedings against directors of the company (CA 1990, s 160); and

(c)   a duty, if so directed by the court, to advise both the DPP and the DCE of the commission of a criminal offence in relation to the company by a past or present officer of the company (CA 1963, s 299, as amended by Company Law Enforcement Act 2001, s 51).

4.5   Asset-swelling measures

A liquidator has an array of statutory and common law powers available to him to enable him to increase the assets of the company for the benefit of the company's creditors. Any transaction at an undervalue has the potential of being challenged by a liquidator, especially if it was entered into at a time when the company was insolvent. There are a number of remedies which a liquidator might pursue, depending on the facts of any particular case. Such remedies may be sought against the disponee, or against the officers of the company for personal liability. Please see generally, chapter 12 of Forde, Kennedy and Simms, *The Law of Company Insolvency* and chapter 27 of Courtney, *The Law of Private Companies* (2nd edn, 2002).

4.5.1   Fraudulent conveyance

Section 10 of the Conveyancing Act (Ireland) 1634 (1634 Act) provides that any conveyance of real or personal property with intent to defraud creditors is 'void' as against any person prejudiced. Section 14 of the 1634 Act exempts from the Act cases of property bona fide conveyed on 'good consideration' to a person with no notice of the intention to defraud the creditors. Transactions falling within those provisions may be voidable. The following points should, however, be noted:

(a)   it is essential that an intention to defraud creditors is established. The onus of proof is on the person seeking to have the conveyance set aside.

(b)   it is not necessary that the transferor be insolvent when the conveyance is made.

(c)   a *bona fide* purchase for value without notice is unaffected by s 10 even if the intention of the transferor was fraudulent.

(d)   the 1634 Act applies to any kind of property real or personal and is not confined to conveyances of land.

See, for example, *Re Kill Inn Motel Limited* [1978–1987] III ITR 706 where the 1634 Act was successfully invoked by a liquidator.

4.5.2   Fraudulent disposal of property

Section 139 of CA 1990 provides that where a company which has disposed of property is in liquidation, receivership or under court protection or is insolvent (but not in liquidation due to insufficiency of assets), the court may, if it considers it just and equitable, order a person to return such property where the effect of the disposal was to perpetrate a fraud on the company, its members or creditors. Section 139 is extended to receivers and examiners by s 178 and s 180 of CA 1990, respectively, and to insolvent companies not in liquidation due to insufficiency of assets by s 251 of CA 1990.

Please see generally pp 1256–1257 of MacCann and Courtney, *Companies Acts 1963–2006*. The order may be made against any person who appears to have the use, control, or possession of the property or the proceeds of sale or development thereof. Alternatively, such person may be ordered to pay a sum in respect of it to the liquidator, receiver or examiner. The court cannot make an order under s 139 unless the following six conditions are satisfied:

(a)   the company is in liquidation, receivership or under court protection or is insolvent (but not in liquidation due to insufficiency of assets);

(b)   the company has disposed of property;

(c)   the effect of the disposal was to perpetrate a fraud on the company, its creditors or members;

(d)   the disposal was not a fraudulent preference;

(e)   application for the order is made by a liquidator, receiver, examiner, creditor or contributory of the company; and

(f)   the courts (after having regard to the rights of persons who have *bona fide* and for value acquired an interest in the property disposed of) deem it just and equitable to make the order.

In the recent decision of *Le Chatelaine Thudichum Limited (In voluntary Liquidation) v Conway* [2008] IEHC 349, the High Court considered the provisions of s 139 and struck down the dispositions on the grounds that the transactions in question fell foul of s 139. The ratio of the case itself is quite limited. In this case, the liquidator of the applicant company applied for a declaration that a transfer of goods and cash to the respondent constituted a fraudulent preference or a fraudulent disposition. The respondent had engaged a South African national to manage a franchised Spar outlet. The commercial venture ran into difficulties and the applicant returned control of the premises to the respondent. The company was heavily indebted at the time. A stock take was performed and the respondent took possession of cash sums and stock. Murphy J held that the disposition in favour of the respondent had the effect of perpetrating a fraud on the applicant in depriving it of its assets and on the creditors of diminishing the pool of assets available for distribution upon liquidation.

In considering what constituted fraud for the purposes of s 139, the court referred to paragraph 27.093 of Courtney, *The Law of Private Companies* (2nd edn, 2002) and adopted it as being the correct statement of the law. The court indicated that the fraud criterion in s 139 'merely requires that the company, its creditors or members be deprived of something to which it is, or to which they are, lawfully entitled'. In *Le Chatelaine* the court held that the transactions were not bona fide as the respondent had acquired the assets knowing at the time that 'the company could not fully discharge its debts to other creditors'.

4.5.3   Fraudulent preference

Section 286 of CA 1963 provides that a fraudulent preference is a payment or disposal of the property of a company, which at the time is unable to pay its debts as they fall due, in favour of any creditor, within six months (or two years in the case of a connected party) of the commencement of a winding up, with a view to giving the creditor a preference over the other creditors. Such payment is invalid and is recoverable by a liquidator. Further information about fraudulent preferences is contained in **paragraph 10.4**.

4.5.4   Payments made by an insolvent company

In *Re Frederick Inns Limited* [1991] ILRM 582 it was held that payments made by an insolvent company in disregard of the interests of its creditors had the effect of defrauding the creditors and were thus void and illegal.

4.5.5   Post-liquidation disposition of assets

Pursuant to s 218 of CA 1963 any disposition of the property of the company made after the commencement of the winding up is void, unless the court orders otherwise. (See *In the matter of Industrial Services Company (Dublin) Ltd (In Liquidation)* [2002] IEHC 57 and *In the matter of Worldport Ireland Limited (In Liquidation)* [2005] IEHC 189.)

4.5.6   Floating charge

Section 288(1) of CA 1963 provides that a floating charge on the undertaking or property of the company created within twelve months before the commencement of the winding up is, unless it is proved the company was solvent immediately after the charge was created, invalid, except as to the amount of any cash paid to the company at the time of or subsequent to the creation of and in consideration of the charge. A floating charge will only be invalid under s 288 if the following three conditions are satisfied:

(a)   the company which granted the floating charge is in liquidation;

(b)   the floating charge was granted within the period of 12 months before the commencement of the liquidation; and

(c)   it is not proved that the company was solvent immediately after the creation of the floating charge.

Please see pp 531–532, MacCann and Courtney, *Companies Acts 1963–2006.*

4.5.7   Contribution and pooling orders

4.5.7.1   *General*

CA 1990 contains provisions which allow the High Court to make the following orders:

(a)   *Contribution order*
       In certain circumstances, in the course of the liquidation of a company, the High Court can order a related company not in liquidation to pay part or all debts of the company being wound up (see s 140 of CA 1990).

(b)   *Pooling order*
       In other circumstances, the High Court can order that in the case of two or more related companies being wound up, such liquidations are to be conducted as one (see s 141 of CA 1990).

4.5.7.2   *Contribution orders*

The court cannot make an order under s 140 of CA 1963 unless the following conditions are satisfied:

(a)   a company is in liquidation (the 'company in liquidation');

(b)   an application for an order is made by the liquidator, or a creditor or contributory of the company in liquidation;

(c)   another company (the 'related company') is related to the company in liquidation;

(d)   if the related company is a licensed bank, a copy of the application has been sent to the Central Bank of Ireland;

(e)   the court is satisfied that the circumstances giving rise to the winding up of the company in liquidation are attributable to the actions or omissions of the related company;

(f)   the court considers it just and equitable to make the order having regard to:
       (i)   the extent to which the related company took part in the management of the company in liquidation,
       (ii)   the conduct of the related company towards the creditors of the company in liquidation, and
       (iii) the effect which an order would be likely to have on the creditors of the related company; and

(g)   the grounds for making the order are not solely confined to either:
       (i)   the fact the related company is related to the company in liquidation, or

(ii) the fact that the creditors of the company being wound up have relied on the fact that the related company is or has been related to the company in liquidation.

A company is related to another company if:

(a) that other company is its holding company or subsidiary; or

(b) more than half of the nominal value of its equity share capital (as defined in s 155(5) of CA 1963) is held by the other company and companies related to that other company (whether directly or indirectly, but other than in a fiduciary capacity); or

(c) more than half the nominal value of the equity share capital (as defined in s 155(5) of CA 1963) of each of them is held by members of the other (whether directly or indirectly, but other than in a fiduciary capacity); or

(d) that other company or a company or companies related to that other company or that other company together with the company or companies related to it are entitled to exercise or control the exercise of more than one half of the voting power at any general meeting of the company; or

(e) that business of the companies have been so carried on that the separate businesses of each company, or a substantial part thereof, is not readily identifiable; or

(f) there is another company to which both companies are related.

As is apparent from above, the scope for contribution orders is wide and the court enjoys a large discretion in this regard. The liquidator or any creditor or contributory of the company that is being wound up may apply for a contribution order. If a contribution order is made against a related company, the amount of the liability thereby imposed will rank as an ordinary or unsecured liability.

4.5.7.3 *Pooling orders*

Where two or more related companies are being wound up, the court may, if it is satisfied that it is just and equitable, make an order that, subject to such terms and conditions as the court may impose, and to the extent that the court orders the companies should be wound up together as if they were one company. The court cannot make an order under s 141 of CA 1990 unless the following five conditions are satisfied:

(a) two or more related companies are in liquidation;

(b) the liquidator of any such companies makes application to the court;

(c) the court considers it just and equitable to make the order having regard to:

 (i) the extent to which any of the companies took part in the management of any of the other companies,

 (ii) the conduct of any of the companies toward the creditors of any of the other companies,

 (iii) the extent to which circumstances that gave rise to the winding up of any of the companies are attributable to the action or the omissions of any of the other companies, and

 (iv) the extent to which the businesses of the companies have been intermingled;

(d) the grounds for making the order are not solely confined to either:

 (i) the fact that the companies are related to each other, or

 (ii) that creditors of one of the companies have relied on the fact that another of the companies is or has been related to the first mentioned company; and

(e) notice of the application for the order has been served on every company specified in the application not later than the end of the eighth day before the hearing of the application.

An order under s 141 cannot affect the rights of any secured creditor of any of the companies. Unless the court orders otherwise, the claims of all unsecured creditors of the company rank equally among themselves. The parties who would be disadvantaged by the making of a pooling order will be unsecured creditors of the least insolvent of the related companies. As part of its order the court may remove any liquidator of any of the companies and appoint any person to act as liquidator of any one or more of the companies.

There is no statutory guidance on what constitutes intermingling. However, Laffoy J, in the case of *Templemore Express Couriers* (an ex tempore judgment) refused to make a pooling order in a 'phoenix situation' where the related company used the same name, staff, premises etc, as the old company.

4.5.8   Action against directors

In addition to the above-mentioned statutory and common law powers, as mentioned at **paragraph 4.4.6** above, the liquidator has additional powers, some of which involve an examination by the liquidator of the conduct of directors of the company for the purpose of establishing whether they are liable personally for the debts of the company and thereby swell the assets of the company for the benefit of the creditors.

4.5.8.1   *Fraudulent and Reckless Trading*

The provisions of the Companies Acts regarding fraudulent and reckless trading (CA 1963, s 297A) should also be borne in mind. A director, if found to be in breach of these provisions, may be held personally liable for some or all of the debts of the company. Further information on fraudulent and reckless trading is set out in **paragraph 10.2**.

4.5.8.2   *Failure to keep proper books and records*

Section 204 of CA 1990 provides that the directors of a company could be held personally liable for the debts of the company if the court finds (on an application of the liquidator) the directors' failure to keep proper books and records (pursuant to s 202 of CA 1990) has contributed to the company's inability to pay all its debts or has resulted in substantial uncertainty as to the assets/liabilities or has impeded the orderly winding up of the company. It is also a criminal offence pursuant to CA 1990 (CA 1990, s 203). See *Mehigan v Duignan* [1997] 1 IR 340, more commonly known as the *Mantruck* case.

CHAPTER 5

MEMBERS' VOLUNTARY LIQUIDATIONS

Nicholas Comyn

5.1   Voluntary winding up: overview

A company may be wound up voluntarily under s 251(1) of the Companies Act 1963 (CA 1963) in the following three circumstances:

(a)   when the period, if any, fixed for the duration of a company by its articles expires, or the event, if any, occurs, on the occurrence of which the articles provide that the company is to be dissolved, and the company in general meeting has passed a resolution that the company be wound up voluntarily;

(b)   if the company resolves by special resolution that the company be wound up voluntarily; or

(c)   if the company in general meeting resolves that it cannot by reason of its liabilities continue its business and that it should be wound up voluntarily.

Any resolution passed under any of the three headings above is called a 'resolution for voluntary winding up' and, most importantly, s 253 of CA 1963 provides that a voluntary winding up shall 'be deemed to commence at the time of the passing of the resolution for voluntary winding up'. This is the date on which the resolution is passed at a general meeting of the company. The reasons the members' and creditors' windings up are called 'voluntary winding up' is because these are decisions made by the shareholders to wind up and not decisions imposed by an outside party, that is, the court.

The first two categories in s 251 comprise the members' winding up, and the third category, the creditors' winding up. The main difference between the two types of winding up is 'solvency'. In a members' winding up, the company is in a position to pay its debts and a Declaration of Solvency has been filed within the time provided by the legislation. In the case of a creditors' winding up, the company is insolvent and not in a position to pay its debts. The powers and the duties of the liquidator are similar for both the members' and the creditors' winding(s) up but the procedures to set each in motion are different and so too is the accountability of the liquidator: in the former it is to the members, in the latter to the creditors.

The liquidator must, as in a court winding up, give his prior consent in writing to be appointed as liquidator, otherwise his appointment is of no effect (Companies Act 1990, s 133, incorporated as s 276A of CA 1963).

The purpose of a winding up is to get in the assets and distribute the money realised in accordance with their priorities as set out in s 285 of CA 1963 (as amended). Further, s 254 of CA 1963 sets out in precise terms the process of winding up:

> In the case of a voluntary winding up, the company shall, from the commencement of the winding up, cease to carry on its business, except so far as may be required for the beneficial winding up thereof, so, however, that the corporate state and corporate powers of the company shall, notwithstanding anything to the contrary in its articles, continue until it is dissolved.

5.2   Members' voluntary winding up

The sections relating to a members' winding up are s 256 (as amended by s 128 of the Companies Act 1990) and ss 258–64 of CA 1963 (as amended by s 9 of the Companies (Amendment) Act 1982). Before a members' winding up can commence, a Declaration of Solvency (Declaraton) must be filed. This Declaration must be made by the directors of the company or, where the company has more than two directors, by a majority of directors.

5.2.1   Declaration of Solvency

At a meeting of directors, the directors make a statutory declaration (sworn before a Commissioner for Oaths) to the effect that:

(a)   they have made a full enquiry into the affairs of the company; and

(b)   having made this enquiry, they have formed the opinion that the company will be able to pay its debts in full in a period not exceeding 12 months.

Sometimes one of the directors may be resident outside the UK or the state and the manner of the swearing of the statutory declaration by such person needs to be 'sworn' before a Notary Public or similar officer whose capacity or seal must be certified by a consular officer of the relevant Irish Embassy (the 'Apostille' under Article 4 of the Hague Convention). It is worth noting that for the purposes of the statement of assets and liabilities, the date of the last swearing of the statutory declaration is the date that applies.

The Declaration must be made within the 28 days immediately preceding the date of the passing of the resolution for winding up the company and must be delivered to the Registrar of Companies for registration not later than 15 days after the passing of the resolution to wind up. If these time limits are not observed and the requirements of s 128(2) of the Companies Act 1990 are not met and the resolution to wind up is passed, then the winding up will continue as a creditors' winding up. In *Favon Investments Co. Ltd (In Liquidation)* [1993] 1 IR 87 (*Favon*), where a liquidator applied for directions under s 280 of CA 1963 to correct a procedural defect in a Declaration, the court (Costello J) stated, 'the court cannot cure the defects in the procedures which were adopted ... however the court has power under s 280 to annul the resolution to wind up the company'. Essentially this is an application for directions from the court but, typically, the court will annul the resolution and permit the procedure to recommence. The application is made by Motion and Grounding Affdavit to the High Court.

5.2.2   Statement of assets and liabilities

The Declaration of Solvency must include a statement of the company's assets and liabilities as at a date not more than three months before the making of the Declaration (s 9 of the Companies (Amendment) Act 1982).

Both the Declaration and the statement are contained in Form No E1 (formerly Form No 12) of the Companies Registration Office forms and there is an excellent label attached to the form which sets out the steps to be taken. The statement of assets and liabilities should include contingent liabilities, continuing interest on an outstanding charge as well as a provision for liquidator's fees and expenses.

5.2.3   Independent report

Section 256 of CA 1963 (as amended by s 128 of the Companies Act 1990) provides that the Declaration must be accompanied additionally by:

(a)   a report made by an independent person;

(b) a statement by the independent person that he has given and has not withdrawn his written consent to the issue of the Declaration with the report attached thereto; and

(c) a copy of the Declaration attached to the notice issued by the company to convene the general meeting at which it is intended to propose the resolution to wind up.

The independent person is either:

(a) a person who is qualified to be the auditor of the company; or

(b) the auditor of the company (s 256(3) of CA 1963).

The report of the independent person shall state that in his opinion and to the best of his information and according to the explanations given to him:

(a) the opinion of the directors that the company will be able to pay its debts in full is reasonable; and

(b) the statement of the company's assets and liabilities is also reasonable (s 256(3) of CA 1963).

There is an important proviso in s 128(8) of the Companies Act 1990 that the court may, on the application of a liquidator, creditor or contributory, declare that any director who was a party to the Declaration of Solvency without having reasonable grounds for their opinion that the company be able to pay its debts in full, be personally liable for the debts of the company. The onus is on the director to prove he had reasonable grounds for his opinion.

The time limits imposed by these sections are mandatory, as pointed out by Costello J in the *Favon* case, where he stated:

> ... an application has been brought under section 280 of the Act of 1963 and orders are sought giving liberty to attach the report of the independent person (which had been omitted) to the directors' statutory Declaration of Solvency and an order directing the winding up to proceed as a members' voluntary winding up. I do not think that I have any jurisdiction to make such orders. The requirements of section 256 are perfectly clear and they are mandatory.

5.2.4 Resolution to wind up a company

The resolution of the shareholders to wind up a company as a members' voluntary winding up is a special resolution, requiring a 75 per cent majority. Section 251(1)(b) of CA 1963 provides that a company may be wound up 'if the company resolves by special resolution that the company be wound up voluntarily' and s 256(11) of CA 1963 provides that where a Declaration has been made and delivered, the winding up is referred to as a members' voluntary winding up.

It should be noted that a liquidator may apply to the High Court within seven days of his nomination as liquidator or within seven days of the day on which he first became aware of a default (in the liquidator's appointment), whichever is the later, for directions as to the manner in which the default is to be remedied (s 131(5) of the Companies Act 1990).

The following is a precedent notice convening an Extraordinary General Meeting (EGM):

Companies Acts 1963 to 2009

(Name of company) Limited

Notice is hereby given that an Extraordinary General Meeting of the above company will be held at (location) on the day of 20— (date) for the purpose of considering and if thought fit passing the following special resolutions:

1. That the company be wound up voluntarily as a members' voluntary winding up and that (proposed liquidator's name and address) be appointed liquidator for the purposes of such winding up.

2. The meeting be authorised to fix the remuneration of (name of liquidator) and to empower him to distribute *in specie* (see below).

Secretary.

Note:

A.   There is sent with this Notice a copy of the Declaration of Solvency and the consent and report of the independent person.

B.   Proxy Forms are attached.

From a practical point of view, the EGM to wind up cannot be called until after the Declaration of Solvency is sworn, as the notice convening the meeting must include a copy of the Declaration. If the EGM is held and the Declaration is sworn on the same day, the time of each should be noted, ie the Declaration must be first.

Section 258(1) of CA 1963 provides that at the EGM two matters are dealt with:

(a)   the passing of the resolution; and

(b)   the fixing of the remuneration of the liquidator (this is optional).

The form of resolution as in the notice is as follows:

> That the company be wound up voluntarily as a members' voluntary winding up and that *(name and address of liquidator)* be appointed liquidator for the purposes of such winding up and that the remuneration of *(name of liquidator)* be fixed at (€) in addition to his costs, charges and expenses and that the liquidator be empowered to distribute the assets *in specie*.

The purpose of a distribution *in specie* is to enable a liquidator to distribute assets among different shareholders and such a distribution is made at a nominal stamp duty.

From a tax point of view, a liquidator and, more particularly, the shareholder need to be aware of the capital gains tax (CGT) implications of the distribution *in specie* to the shareholders, as there is a 'double' charge, one to the company in liquidation, and another to the shareholders to whom the distribution is made.

The liquidator must also give his prior consent to act as liquidator.

There are three points to note on the passing of the resolution:

(a)   within 14 days of the passing of the resolution, notice of the resolution must be given by advertisement in the Companies Registration Office Gazette (s 72 of the Investment Funds, Companies and Miscellaneous Provisions Act 2005);

(b)   all the powers of the directors cease, except 'so far as the company in general meeting [this is distinct from a creditors' winding up] or the liquidator sanctions the continuance thereof'; and

(c)   if within 28 days after the advertisement of the resolution a creditor or creditors representing one-fifth in the number or value of the creditors apply to the court and prove to the court's satisfaction that the company will not be in a position to pay its debts within the time provided in the Declaration of Solvency, then the court may order that the liquidation should continue as a creditor's winding up. A copy of the order must be delivered within 21 days to the Registrar of Companies.

5.2.5   Sections 259, 260 and 262 of CA 1963

Under s 259 of CA 1963, a vacancy in the office of liquidator may be filled by the company in general meeting convened by any contributory (as defined in s 208 of CA 1963).

Section 260 of CA 1963 permits the liquidator to accept shares in another company as consideration for the sale of the property of the company subject to the approval of a special resolution of the company in voluntary liquidation. The reconstruction or sale permitted by this section is not binding on creditors and a liquidator must either retain sufficient funds to meet the creditors' claim or alternatively an adequate indemnity, otherwise he could be personally liable to any claim from an unpaid creditor. Section 260(3) of CA 1963 reserves rights in favour of a dissenting shareholder.

Section 262 of CA 1963 sets out the duty of the liquidator to summon a general meeting at the end of each year of the liquidation and lay an account of his acts and dealings and the conduct of the winding up during the preceding year.

5.2.6   Other matters

If after his appointment the liquidator is of the opinion that the company will not be able to pay its debts in full within the period mentioned in the Declaration of Solvency, then under s 129 of the Companies Act 1990 the liquidator must take the following steps:

(a)   Notice—

   (i)   a creditors' meeting must be held within 14 days;
   (ii)   a notice must be sent to creditors by post seven days before the meeting;
   (iii) the meeting must be advertised in *Iris Oifigiúil* and two daily newspapers at least 10 days before the meeting; and
   (iv)   the liquidator must furnish any creditor, prior to the meeting, with information that they may reasonably require, free of charge.

(b)   Meeting—

   (i)   a Statement of Affairs and list of creditors must be prepared by the liquidator and laid before the meeting; and
   (ii)   the liquidator must attend and preside at the meeting.

(c)   Resolution

The creditors' meeting replaces the original meetings under s 266 of CA 1963 and the winding up becomes a creditors' voluntary winding up and any appointment made or committee established by the creditors' meeting shall be deemed to have been made or established by that meeting.

This section (s 129 of the Companies Act 1990) was introduced largely to outlaw the effects of the decision in *Re Centrebind Ltd* [1966] 3 All ER 880 where the members of a company, which was insolvent, could appoint their own liquidator without calling a creditors' meeting.

5.2.7 Final meeting

If the liquidation continues for a period in excess of one year, the liquidator must, within three months of that year and each succeeding year, lay before a meeting of the members an account of his acts and dealings for that year.

Section 263 of CA 1963 sets out in detail the requirements for the final meeting of the company, which includes publishing the final notice in two daily newspapers. The form of notice is as follows:

> IN THE MATTER OF THE COMPANIES ACTS 1963–2009
>
> AND IN THE MATTER OF
>
> [NAME OF COMPANY]
>
> (IN VOLUNTARY LIQUIDATION)
>
> **Notice to Members of Final Meeting**
>
> NOTICE is hereby given pursuant to Sections 263 and 305 of the Companies Acts 1963 that a Meeting of the members of the above-named company will be held at [address] on [date] at [time] for the purpose of having an Account laid before them and to receive the Liquidator's report showing how the winding up of the company has been conducted and its property disposed of and of hearing any explanation that may be given by the Liquidator; and also to determine how the books and documents of the company shall be disposed of. Proxies to be used at the Meeting must be lodged with the Liquidator [name] at [address] not later than 4:00 in the afternoon of the day before the Meeting.
>
> Dated the day of 20–
>
> [Name]
>
> Liquidator
>
> [Address]

5.3   Who may be appointed liquidator

Anyone other than the following may be appointed as a liquidator:

(a)   any person who is or has been an officer or servant of the company in the past 12 months;

(b)   a body corporate – which appointment is void (s 300(a) of CA 1963);

(c)   except with the leave of the court, a parent or spouse, sister, brother or child of an officer of the company;

(d)   a partner or employee of an officer or servant of the company shall not be qualified for appointment as a liquidator (s 300(a) of CA 1963, as inserted by s 146 of the Companies Act 1990); or

(e)   the accountants' governing bodies do not permit the auditor to act as liquidator of the company.

If a liquidator becomes disqualified, as being in category (a), (c) or (d) above (category (e) is not a statutory requirement), then he must vacate his office on giving 14 days' notice to the court in a court winding up, to the company in a members' voluntary winding up and to the company and the creditors in a creditors' voluntary winding up (CA 1963, s 300A(3)). Failure to give notice or acting while disqualified will leave the liquidator open to a fine. The various institutes of the accountancy profession have also prohibited auditors of a company or members of the auditor's office from acting as liquidators of that company.

A liquidator may also be removed by the court 'on cause shown' (CA 1963, s 277(2)). '[C]ause shown' does not necessarily mean just a conflict of interest but an element of bias or *mala fides* by the liquidator *(In the Matter of Naiad Limited t/a Metal Product Fastners (In Voluntary Liquidation)* (High Court, 13 February 1995). The company continues to exist on the appointment of the liquidator and accordingly the liquidator does not assume personal liability under contracts made by him in the company's name unless the contract provides otherwise or he acts negligently. Section 254 of CA 1963 also gives the company in general meeting the power to fill a vacancy in the office of liquidator.

5.4   Can there be a 'solvent' creditors' voluntary winding up?

It is clear in s 256(11) of CA 1963, as amended by s 128 of the Companies Act 1990, that if a solvent company fails to file a Declaration of Solvency in a members' voluntary winding up, the liquidation continues as a creditors' voluntary winding up.

There has been some consideration (by the Institute of Chartered Accountants) as to whether a solvent company can be wound up as a creditors' voluntary winding up thus requiring (a) an ordinary resolution of the members and (b) no filing of a Declaration of Solvency. The argument against the right to do so is in s 251(1)(c), which provides a company may be wound up voluntarily 'if the company in general meeting resolves that it cannot by reason of its liabilities continue its business and that it be wound up voluntarily'. However, it is only where a special resolution to wind up voluntarily and a Declaration is properly filed that the liquidation is deemed a 'members' voluntary winding up'. Every other voluntary lqiuidation is a creditors' voluntary liquidation (s 256(11) of CA 1963). Further s 275 of CA 1963 gives a liquidator in every voluntary liquidation the power, after payment of the company's liabilities, to distribute the company's property 'among the members according to their rights and interests in the company'. Undoubtedly if a special resolution is passed to wind up a company voluntarily without any Declaration, then the winding up can proceed as a 'creditors' voluntary winding up'.

5.5   Consequences of voluntary winding up: ss 254–255 of CA 1963

Under s 254, the company shall from the commencement of the winding up (s 253 of CA 1963) cease to carry on its business '... except so far as may be required for the beneficial winding up thereof ...'. If carrying on the business is genuinely considered to be beneficial to the winding up, post-liquidation liabilities so incurred may be paid in priority to pre-liquidation creditors as an expense of the winding up. However, if they are subsequently found not to have been beneficial, then the position of the pre- and post- liabilities is reversed.

Under s 255, a transfer of shares after commencement of the winding up will be void unless sanctioned by the liqudiator.

CHAPTER 6

CREDITORS' VOLUNTARY LIQUIDATIONS

Nicholas Comyn

6.1   When does a creditors' voluntary winding up take place?

A creditors' voluntary winding up takes place where either:

(a)   no Declaration of Solvency has been filed (or one has been incorrectly filed); or

(b)   where the company resolves at a general meeting that it cannot by reason of its liabilities continue its business (CA 1963, s 251(1)(c)).

Section 265 of CA 1963 provides that 'Sections 266 and 273 shall apply in relation to a creditors' voluntary winding up'.

The term 'voluntary winding up' includes both a members' (see **Chapter 5**) and a creditors' winding up. In each case, s 253 of CA 1963 provides that 'a voluntary winding up' shall be deemed to commence at the time of the passing of the resolution for voluntary winding up (that is, the shareholders' resolution).

Section 266 of CA 1963 sets out the steps to be taken to wind up as a creditors' voluntary winding up and provides for a statutory period (of 10 days) before the creditors' meeting can be called and during that period, often longer, the directors are faced with commercial problems, some of which are highlighted below.

6.2   Is the company insolvent?

The legal definition of solvency is still that set out by Kenny J in *Re Creation Printing Co Ltd, Crowley v Northern Bank Finance Corp Ltd* [1981] IR 40, namely 'being able to pay one's debts as they fall due'.

6.3   Can the company continue to perform existing contracts even though it is insolvent?

Where it is for the benefit of the creditors, the company may complete or continue a contract but not otherwise. This follows the general principle of carrying on business for the benefit of the creditors after the liquidator is appointed (s 254 of CA 1963).

6.4   What happens to employees?

The employees should be laid off and given their statutory notice unless they are essential to preserve the assets or to carry on any business for the 'benefit of the creditors'.

6.5   Assets – can creditors with reservation of title move their goods?

Even though the reservation of title (ROT) clause may be valid, the directors should not let assets be removed as the liquidator has to adjudicate on claims, but creditors claiming

ROT can identify their goods and request that they be stored and not sold pending the appointment of the liquidator.

6.6   Moneys received

Once the directors are aware that the company is insolvent, and where they have decided to wind up the company, all moneys received should be put in a separate account, in trust for the liquidator, as making any payment directly to a creditor or indirectly (for example, to reduce a guarantee of a director) can leave the directors and the creditor exposed to fraudulent preference (s 286 of CA 1963).

6.7   Steps to be taken to wind up as a creditors' voluntary winding up

The steps to be taken by the directors to wind up as a creditors' voluntary winding up are set out in s 266 of CA 1963. At the initial meeting of directors at which the decision is taken to wind up the company by reason of its liabilities, the secretary is directed to convene the necessary general meeting to pass an ordinary resolution (s 251(1)(c) of CA 1963) and a meeting of creditors.

6.7.1   Statement of affairs

Section 266(3) of CA 1963 compels the directors to cause 'a full statement of the position of the company's affairs, together with a list of the creditors of the company and the estimated amount of their claims' to be presented to the meeting of the creditors.
   In general, this statement should be divided into:

(a)   assets specifically charged, their book value and their estimated realisable value;
(b)   assets not specifically charged, their book value and their estimated realisable value;
(c)   liabilities divided up as between secured creditors, preferential creditors, debentureholders and unsecured creditors; and
(d)   the anticipated net dividend should also be inserted.

A note at the end of the statement of affairs should state that the liquidator's fees have not been included. Also a note on the statement of affairs should state that some creditors claim a 'reservation of title' (if that is relevant).
   A number of further matters arise in connection with the statement of affairs:

(a)   If an accountant is employed to help prepare the statement of affairs and his fee is not paid before the company goes into liquidation, he is entitled to his fee only as an unsecured creditor after the appointment of the liquidator. However, it is possible to pay the accountant's fee in advance as a 'cost of the liquidation' but only the costs relevant to the preparation of the statement of affairs and not any other fees (eg audit) that might be due (see **6.7.4**).
(b)   The statement of affairs is the directors' estimate of the financial situation of the company (CA 1963, s 266(3)(a)).
(c)   The directors must also appoint one of the directors to preside at the creditors' meeting (CA 1963, s 266(4) 3(C)).
(d)   It is the duty of the director appointed to preside at the meeting and to attend and preside thereat (subsection (4)). If a director is in breach of this subsection, he is liable to a fine of €1,906.41 (Companies (Amendment) Act 2003, s 57).
(e)   A list of creditors' names and addresses and amounts due as up to date as possible, must be attached to and circulated with the Statement of Affairs.

(f) The Statement of Affairs is 'presented at' the meeting of creditors, that is, on the day of the meeting.

6.7.2   Convening the creditors' meeting

Section 266(1) of CA 1963 provides that a meeting of creditors must be held on the day or the day following the general meeting to wind up the company and 10 days' written notice of the meeting must be given to the creditors. The period of the notice is inclusive of weekends and bank holidays. *In the matter of Naiad Limited* (High Court, 13 February 1995), notices had been sent by post to the creditors (some situated in the UK) on 20 December 1994 for a creditors' meeting on 3 January 1995. Some of the creditors claimed, in court, that this did not comply with s 266(1) because of Christmas holidays and bank holidays. McCracken J held 'there is no doubt that these notices were sent, in the sense that they were posted, at least 10 days before the meeting, and the strict statutory provisions were complied with', although the judge noted he could take into account the timing of the meeting and of the notice.

6.7.2.1   *The form of notice and general proxy*

To the notice convening a creditors' meeting a general and special proxy allowing a creditor to appoint the Chairman of the meeting or someone else to be his proxy must be attached (the Rules of the Superior Courts 1986 (RSC), Order 74, r 77).

The format of the general proxy (as per the RSC) is:

GENERAL PROXY

IN THE MATTER OF [Name of Company] LIMITED AND IN THE MATTER OF THE COMPANIES ACTS 1963 TO 2009

I/We

Of

a Creditor, hereby appoint (1)

of

or (failing him) (2)

of

to be my/our General Proxy to vote at the Meeting of the Creditors to be held in the above matter

on day of 20— of any adjournment thereof.

Dated this day of 20—

Signed:

It should be noted that:

(a) The person appointed general proxy may be the liquidator or if there is no liquidator the chairman of the meeting, or any such persons as the creditor may appoint. The proxy form should be altered accordingly.

(b) If a firm, the firm's trading name should be signed, and the words 'by A.B. a partner in the said firm' should be added. If the appointor is a corporation, then the form must be under its common seal or under the hand of same duly authorised person in that behalf and the fact that the officer is so authorised must be so stated.

(c) The proxy form when signed must be lodged by the time and at the address stated for that purpose in the notice convening the meeting at which it is to be used (see

(d) below). If a proxy form is being signed on behalf of a company, it must be signed by an officer, eg a director or secretary, who should (a) state their capacity and (b) state, after their signature, that they are 'duly authorised'.

(d) Section 266(2) of CA 1963 provides that notice of the meeting of creditors must be advertised in two daily newspapers circulating in the district where the registered office or principal place of business of the company is situated at least 10 days before the creditors' meeting. The following is a form of notice that typically appears in the newspaper:

Companies Acts 1963–2009

[Name of Company] Limited

NOTICE is hereby given pursuant to Section 266 of the Companies Act 1963 that a Meeting of the Creditors of the above named Company will be held at [place] on [date] at [time] for the purposes mentioned in Section 266 (as amended) and Section 267 of the said Act.

By Order of the Board

Secretary

This notice can also be used when sending out the proxy forms to the creditors with the addition of the words: 'Proxy forms are enclosed with this Notice which should be completed as instructed, and returned to [the registered office of the company] not later than 4:00 pm on the day before the meeting.' RSC Order 74, r 82(1) provides that:

> every instrument of proxy shall be lodged … with the company at its registered office for a meeting under section 266 … with the person named in the notice convening the meeting to receive the same (normally the secretary of the company) not later than four o'clock in the afternoon of the day before the meting or adjourned meeting at which it is to be used.

Whether this rule was mandatory was considered in *In The Matter of Hayes Homes Limited (In Voluntary Liquidation) and in the Matter of a petition of Liam J Irwin Collector General ('the Revenue')* [2004] IEHC 124. The Revenue was a creditor and the Revenue's representative attended at the meeting. The Revenue represented more than 80% in value of the creditors at the creditors' meeting and thus would have been able to determine who would be appointed liquidator.

However, the Revenue's proxy was excluded from voting as the proxy form had not been lodged prior to 4:00 pm on the evening before the meeting (RSC, r 82(1)) even though the Revenue official produced a duplicate copy of the proxy form and a copy of the envelope posting the letter to the company at its registered office. O'Neill J held that r 82(1) was mandatory in its nature and the Revenue was not entitled to vote in the circumstances. The judge, however, exercised his discretion and wound up the company as a court winding up and appointed the Revenue's nominee as official liquidator.

It is submitted that this approach is too rigid and a fairer approach is that if an admitted creditor attends a creditors' meeting and has a valid, or a copy of a valid, proxy with him/her that the 'wishes of the creditors' should be taken into account (see **6.10**) and he/she be entitled to vote, or, if necessary, allowed to vote but with the proxy marked 'objected to' (see **6.9.1**).

(e) The general proxy which is set out in Order 74, rr 74/75, RSC must be in Form No 21 (general – see **6.7.2.1**) or Form No 22 (special).

6.7.3 Resolution to wind up the company

The resolution to wind up including the appointment of a liquidator is passed at the general meeting or extraordinary general meeting. The resolution itself is an ordinary resolution (CA 1963, s 251(1)(c)) and can be passed by a simple majority of those present in person or by proxy. The members' meeting must be held before the creditors' meeting either the day before or on the day itself. The prior written consent of the liquidator to act must be obtained, otherwise his appointment is void (CA 1963, s 276A, as substituted by s 133 of Companies Act 1990). There is one important provision under s 266(5) of CA 1963 which provides that in the event of the members' meeting being adjourned and the creditors' meeting taking place on the day or the next day, then any resolution passed at the meeting of the creditors shall take effect as if it had been passed immediately after the passing of the resolution at the adjourned meeting of the members.

The format of the resolution of the company is:

Companies Act 1963–2009

[Name of Company] LIMITED

It was resolved as an ordinary resolution that the Company cannot by reason of its liabilities continue its business and that it be wound up as a creditors' voluntary winding up and [name of Liquidator] of [address] be appointed Liquidator for the purposes of the winding up. It was noted that the Liquidator had given his prior written consent to act as Liquidator.

Once this resolution in general meeting is passed, the company is in liquidation (CA 1963, s 253).

6.7.4 Accountants' and solicitiors' fees

It will be noted that accountants' fees paid for the purposes of preparing the statement of affairs and paid prior to the appointment of the liquidator are a 'cost of liquidation' (*AV Sorge & Company Limited* [1986] BCLC 490) and not a fraudulent preference. What is the position of solicitors' costs in preparing for, and advising on, the winding up of a company? This was considered at length, in *In the Matter of Computstore Limited (in Voluntary Liquidation)* on the application of the firm of Eugene F Collins and judgment given by Laffoy J on 22 February 2005.

The net issue was whether fees and expenses due to the solicitors in respect of advices given in relation to the procedures to be followed to place the company into voluntary liquidation were 'expenses properly incurred in the winding up of the company and payable out of the assets of the company in priority to all other claims' (CA 1963, s 281). The learned judge held that the fees for advices in winding up could be paid in advance of the appointment of the liquidator but were not a cost and expense of the liquidation payable by the liquidator after his appointment, ie in priority to all other creditors. The judge's reasoning was clearly based on s 281, about which Laffoy J stated 'I am satisfied that in enacting s 281, the legislature intended that there would be a rigid temporal cut-off at the time of the passing of the resolution to wind up voluntarily'.

6.8 Rules of the Superior Courts

RSC Order 74, r 56 provides that rr 58–83 (inclusive) of Order 74 shall apply to a voluntary liquidation meeting. Unfortunately some of the Rules, such as attaching a special proxy to the notice convening the creditors' meeting, are not applicable but some are relevant to a creditors' meeting under CA 1963, s 266 as shall be shown.

6.9   Creditors' meeting

The creditors' meeting is the principle opportunity for the creditors to consider the final position of the company (the 'statement of affairs') and to quiz the director who is presiding at the meeting (CA 1963, s 266(3)(b)) as to the figures and circumstances surrounding the statement of affairs.

The purpose of the creditors' meeting is therefore to:

(a) consider the statement of affairs;
(b) appoint a liquidator other than that appointed by the company at the general meeting; and
(c) nominate members to the Committee of Inspection.

These points will be dealt with in the general context of the conduct of the creditors' meeting, some being practical in nature.

(a) It is important to ensure that a room is booked for the creditors' meeting. The notice convening the meeting must specify the place and time of the meeting (CA 1963, s 266(2)) and this is a 'cost' of the liquidation if paid in advance. In the case of *Irish Systems Ltd* (High Court) a disenchanted creditor applied to the High Court to complain that the room in which the creditors' meeting was held was too small. His application to annul the meeting was refused; the message here is be 'well prepared'.

(b) Where should the meeting be held? RSC Ord 74, r 59 provides that where a company has its registered office in the County Borough of Dublin or Cork and now Fingall it shall be held at the most convenient place in either county borough for the majority of the creditors; in every other case, it shall be held in the place most convenient to the majority of creditors.

(c) Take names of creditors as they enter the room. Where a creditor is represented by a proxy or attending in his own right and where the value of the creditor's debt becomes relevant to the appointment of a liquidator, it saves time if the creditors attending and their amounts are known before any vote is counted. It is also important to have ballot papers ready should there be a vote on the appointment of the liquidator. If there is a ballot, it is important to ensure that only those at the creditors' meeting either personally or by proxy should vote.

(d) There are no strict rules as to the manner in which the creditors' meeting is conducted, but as a director must preside (CA 1963, s 266(3)(b)) he or his solicitor should open the meeting, read the resolution passed at the members' meeting and set out the purposes for which the meeting is called and the conduct of the business of the meeting. The director must then preside at the meeting and should be in a position to answer questions on the statement of affairs.

(e) A statement of affairs must be provided. Normally, before the statement of affairs is discussed, one of the directors will read a statement setting out the reasons why the company has failed and detailing steps to save it. In the s 56 (Company Law Enforcement Act 2001) report of the liquidator, one of the documents he/she must now enclose with the s 56 report is the director's statement.

(f) Adjournments – a meeting of creditors can be adjourned by the chairman with the consent of the meeting (ie by a majority in number and value of those present in person or by proxy) from time to time to the same place unless otherwise agreed by the meeting (RSC Ord 74, r 65). A quorum is three creditors, in person or by proxy, and if not so present within 15 minutes, the meeting stands adjourned to the following week in the same place and at the same time. Unless a quorum is present a meeting may not act for any purpose apart from the election of a chairman and the adjournment of the meeting (RSC Ord 74, r 66). This rule (in relation to the election of the chairman) would appear to contradict s 266(3) and (4) of CA 1963, which provide the chairman appointed by the directors must 'preside' at the creditors meeting.

(g)   If a creditor claims he has not received notice of the creditors meeting, it will not invalidate the meeting unless the court otherwise allows (RSC, r 64).

(h)   The following creditors cannot vote:

    (i)   A creditor who claims any unliquidated debt or contingent debt or one secured by a bill of exchange or promissory note (RSC Ord 74, r 68).

    (ii)   A secured creditor unless he gives a statement setting out his security, the date given and the value at which he assesses it and he can only then vote on the balance (if any) due after deducting the value of the security (RSC Ord 74, r 69). This is in conflict with RSC Ord 74, r 72, which states the statement above need not be given in a creditors' meeting under s 266 of CA 1963. Either way, secured creditors would be better advised not to vote.

    (iii)   Creditors holding an invalid proxy.

(i)   The chairman of the meeting has the power to admit or reject a proof for the purpose of voting but if he has a doubt he should mark it as objected to but allow the creditor to vote subject to the vote being declared invalid in the event of the objection being sustained (RSC Ord 74, r 71) on appeal to the High Court. This rule was considered in the High Court in *re Titan Transport Logistics Limited (In Voluntary Liquidation)* (High Court, 19 February 2003). The chairman of the meeting had rejected a creditor's claim to vote and the High Court rejected the appeal of the creditor. The grounds of the rejection were that the application should have been made within a two-week period despite the fact that the RSC did not lay down any time limit. The judge indicated that in the event of a contest the application should be made immediately.

(j)   The statement of affairs is the directors' responsibility (CA 1963, s 266(3)(1)). Although, technically, there is no obligation to answer questions in relation to the statement of affairs, it is certainly implied, because:

    (i)   the directors have a duty to 'lay' a full statement before the meeting; and

    (ii)   there is an obligation on the director presiding to keep a record of the meeting (RSC Ord 74, Rule 73), and why be obliged to keep a record unless there are questions and answers to report?

Conversely the director can only be obliged to answer questions relating to the statement of affairs, but typically such questions will relate firstly to the trading history of the company and secondly as to when the directors knew the company was insolvent. As a normal legal principle, the director presiding can refuse to answer questions that might incriminate him.

(k)   As already noted (**paragraph 6.7.4**), once the company in general meeting passes its resolution to wind up and appoint a liquidator, the company is in liquidation and the liquidator has been appointed. If the creditors wish to appoint their own liquidator, s 267(3) of CA 1963 (as inserted by s 47 of the Company Law Enforcement Act 2001) provides that such appointment can be made by resolution of the majority, in value, of the creditors present personally or by proxy, which regularly leads to challenges on a proxy's right (particularly where the chairman holds proxies) to vote. It should be noted that all other resolutions at a creditors' meeting (other than the appointment of a liquidator) should be passed by a majority in value and number of the creditors present in person or by proxy. Some of the principles that have been established by the court are:

(i)   Even though a proxy may not be completed strictly in accordance with the rules, the 'general wishes' of the creditors in admitting such proxies should be taken into account (*Re M & R Electrical Ltd* (High Court, 30 July 1985)), an ex tempore judgment of Barrington J.

(ii) Employees who are owed arrears of wages are entitled to vote, even though they will be able to recover most of their statutory entitlements from the redundancy fund (*In the Matter of Naiad Ltd t/a Metal Product Fastener (In Voluntary Liquidation)* (High Court, 13 February 1995); this case also dealt with statutory notices and tests to remove a liquidator).

(iii) As a general rule, proxies used by directors in respect of loans due to them by the company which tipped the balance in favour of the company's appointed liquidator instead of the creditors' nominees were excluded by the court in an ex tempore judgment of Costello J (*Re Shannon Granary Ltd (In Voluntary Liquidation)* (High Court, 22 November 1990)). However, this was at the time when the creditors had to obtain a majority in number and value and before the Company Law Enforcement Act 2001. Similarly, Costello J, in another ex tempore judgment, *Metro Express Ireland Ltd (In Voluntary Liquidation)*, excluded inter-company loans which tipped the balance in favour of the company's nominated liquidator.

This whole area was considered by Laffoy J in *In the Matter of Balbradagh Developments Limited and the Companies Acts 1963–2007* [2008] IEHC 329.

The facts: A petition had been presented by a creditor (the Petitioner) but had been adjourned for two weeks to allow a creditors' meeting take place and at that meeting a liquidator, other than that proposed by the Petitioner, was nominated by the directors of the company and, on the vote of a majority in value of the creditors, was appointed. The Petitioner proceeded with his petition to wind up as a court winding up and have his liquidator appointed (he did not allege bias against the company's liquidator) on two grounds:

(1)   the directors (and the wife of one of the directors) were creditors and used their votes to secure their nomination as directors; and

(2)   the Petitioner had concerns at matters that needed to be investigated in the winding up.

The learned judge referred to *Metro Express Ireland Limited* and quoted the statement of Vinelott J in *re Falcon RJ Developments Limited* [1987] BCLC 437 as to the court's entitlement to take into account 'general principles of fairness and morality which underlie the details of insolvency law'. The judge also analysed the voting at the creditors' meeting and although the votes of the directors did influence the appointment of the company's nominee as liquidator, the directors were also supported by a number of other 'non-connected' creditors and on that basis she exercised the court's discretion 'in the interests of the generality of the creditors and members of the company' in confirming the appointment of the company's nominee as liquidator. The judge also noted that any allegations of wrongdoing by the directors of the company must be investigated by the liquidator in the light of the section 56 report the liquidator must give to the Director of Corporate Enforcement.

(iv) Where it is proved to the satisfaction of the court that any solicitation was used by the liquidator in procuring his appointment, the liquidator shall not be entitled to any remuneration while acting (RSC Ord 74, r 79 and see also s 301(1) of CA 1963).

(l) The creditors are entitled to appoint to the Committee of Inspection not more than five persons and the company may at the general meeting at which the resolution to wind up is passed, or at a subsequent general meeting, appoint a maximum of three persons to the COI (CA 1963, s 268(1)). Though rarely exercised, s 268(2) gives the creditors the right to refuse to accept the persons appointed by the company.

The members of the COI may not purchase the assets of the company nor may they make a profit from the winding up except with the leave of the court or the sanction of a general meeting of the creditors (*Dowling v Lord Advocate* [1963] SLT 146). The constitution of and the general proceedings relating to a COI in a creditors' voluntary winding up is set out in s 233 of CA 1963 (which relates to court winding up) and also in RSC Ord 74, rr 50–53. It should be noted that the members of the COI are not entitled to be paid but are entitled to recoup their expenses (RSC Ord 74, r 129).

6.10 Issues post-liquidation

Certain sections from ss 269–273 of CA 1963 deal specifically with a creditors' voluntary winding up.

Section 269 of CA 1963 gives three provisos:

(a) A committee of inspection or, if there is no committee, the creditors may fix the remuneration to be paid to the liquidator or liquidators.

(b) If within 28 days of the remuneration being fixed in accordance with (a) above any creditor or contributory, who alleges that the remuneration is excessive, may apply to the court to fix the remuneration.

(c) Section 269(3) provides that at the appointment of the liquidator all the powers of the directors cease except in so far as the committee of inspection or the creditors resolve otherwise – this is different from the compulsory winding up where the powers of the directors automatically cease on the making of a winding-up order.

Section 270 of CA 1963 provides that the creditors may fill the vacancy of the liquidator should a vacancy occur by death, resignation or otherwise.

Section 271 of CA 1963 gives the liquidator power to accept shares as a consideration for the sale of property of the company in liquidation with the sanction either of the court or the committee of inspection (this is a mirror of the right reserved in s 260 of CA 1963 to a liquidator in a members' voluntary winding up).

Section 272 of CA 1963 provides that a liquidator shall summon a general meeting of the company and a meeting of the creditors at the end of the first year of the commencement of the winding up and of each succeeding year or at the first convenient date within three months at the end of each year and the liquidator has to lay before the meeting of the creditors an account of his acts and dealings and the conduct of the winding up in the preceding year.

Section 273 of CA 1963 sets out the procedure for the final meeting and dissolution – the liquidator is obliged to make up an account of the winding up showing how it has been conducted and property disposed of and to call a general meeting of the shareholders and a meeting of the creditors and lay before that meeting the account of his dealings and to give an explanation thereof. The meeting of the shareholders and the creditors must be advertised in two daily newspapers circulating in the district where the registered office of the company is situate and such notice must specify the time, place and the object thereof and be published 28 days at least before the meetings.

The company is formally dissolved three months following the liquidator filing a return (of the final meeting) with the Registrar of Companies. Once the liquidator has discharged all the liabilities of which he was aware and made his final account and the registration in the Companies Registration Office has been effected, the company is deemed to be dissolved three months after the date of such registration. In the case of in *Re Cornish Manures Limited* [1967] 1 WLR 807, the liquidator received a demand for tax the day after the final meeting had been held. A creditor issued a motion outside the two-year limit (the equivalent of s 310 of CA 1963) arguing, because of the tax demand, the company had not been dissolved and seeking a declaration under that section (s 310) that the dissolution was void. The court held it had no jurisdiction to re-open the liquidation and held that the company had in fact been fully wound up as the liquidator had held his final meeting and discharged all the liabilities of which he was aware and filed his necessary accounts.

6.11   Provisions applicable to every voluntary winding up

The CA 1963 provides (under s 274) that ss 275–282 inclusive apply to every voluntary winding up whether a members' or a creditors' and these are set out briefly below.

(a) Section 275 of CA 1963 (as amended) provides the general rule that creditors of an insolvent company are to be paid *pari passu* save for preferential creditors' payments under the Companies Acts. The effect of the *pari passu* principle is that an asset which is owned by a company at the commencement of its winding up and might be the subject of a contract entered into for consideration and for *bona fide* commercial purposes is available to the liquidator to distribute. This princple would not apply to every contract; for example, retention of title clauses and contracts for the sale of goods and clauses in building contracts confirming rights of retention moneys are *not void* because the property in those goods or the retention moneys no longer belong to the company (*Glow Heating Limited v Eastern Health Board* [1988] IR 110).

(b) Further, s 276 of CA 1963 sets out the powers and duties of a liquidator in a voluntary winding up and in essence it confers on the liquidator the same power as a liquidator in a court winding up and with the sanction of the COI or the creditors if there is no committee, or with the sanction of the members (in a members' voluntary winding up) exercising any of the powers given by s 231(1) (d) (e) and (f) of CA 1963 which would be given to a liquidator with the sanction of the court in a court winding up.

(c) Under s 276A unless the liquidator prior to his appointment has signified his written consent to the appointment, his appointment shall be of no effect. There is an obligation also on the chairman of any meeting at which a liquidator is appointed, to notify the liquidator in writing, within seven days of the meeting, of his appointment unless the liquidator or his authorised representative is present at the meeting where the appointment is made (shareholders' meeting, or should the creditors appoint their own liquidator, the creditors' meeting).

(d) Section 277 briefly sets out the power of the court to appoint and remove a liquidator in a voluntary winding up but this is on the basis of cause shown and as already noted (in *re Niaid Limited*) an element of bias must be proved.

(e) Section 279 is a rarely used section which relates to arrangements entered into between a company about to be or in the course of being wound up and its creditors. Such an arrangement shall, subject to a right of appeal to the court, (within three weeks by a creditor or contributory) be binding on the company, in the course of the winding up, if it's sanctioned by a special resolution of the members of the company and shall be binding on the creditors if acceded to by three-fourths in number and value of the creditors. The important point to note is that the requisite majority of the creditors is not just three-fourths of those attending a meeting in person and by proxy and voting, but three-fourths in number and value of all the creditors.

(f) Section 280 gives power to the liquidator, a contributory or a creditor to apply (by notice of motion and grounding affidavit) to the High Court to determine any question arising in the winding up of the company. The court may make any order it thinks just and beneficial in the circumstances and s 280(3) provides that:

> if an order is made by the court anulling the resolution to wind up or staying the proceedings in the winding up it must be forwarded to the Registrar of Companies.

The power of the court to annul a resolution to wind up was considered by Carroll J in the case of *Oakthorpe Holdings (In Voluntary Liquidation) v Registrar of Companies* [1987] IR 632 where the judge stated there was no express power conferred on the court in a voluntary winding up to annul a resolution but the interpretation of s 280(3) of CA 1963, which provides 'an office copy of an order made by virtue of this section annulling the resolution to wind up or ... shall forthwith be forwarded by the company to the registrar of companies for registration', meant the court had the power to annul a winding-up resolution (see also *Favon Investments Co Limited* [1993] 1 IR 87).

(g) Section 281 provides that all costs, charges and expenses that are properly incurred in the winding up including the liquidator's remuneration shall be payable out of the assets of the company in priority to all other claims. We have already seen the postion of pre-liquidation expenses (*Compustore Limited*) and there have been a number of cases determining what are properly 'costs, charges and expenses' and they include such items as:

(i) corporation tax on income arising to the company after the commencement of a voluntary winding up (*Noyek & Sons Limited* [1989] ILRM 155);

(ii) rent accruing on a leasehold premises retained by the liquidation (*CHA Limited (In Liquidation)* [1999] 1 IR 437; *GWI Limited* (High Court, 16 November 1987) and the seminal *Tempany v Royal Liver Trustees* [1984] ILRM 273); or

(iii) proceedings during a liquidation where an action is brought after a resolution to wind up, the costs of the successful litigant against the company rank in priority to all other claims (*Comhlucht Paipear Riomhaireachta Teoranta v Údarás na Gaeltachta* [1990] ILRM 266).

(h) Section 282 is a curious section that is more or less a repeat of s 267 and s 277 of CA 1963 in providing that the winding up of a company, as a voluntary winding up, shall not bar the right of any creditor or contributory to have it wound up by the court but in the case of a contributory (but not a creditor) the court must be satisfied that he would be prejudiced by a voluntary winding up. Normally in order for such an application to be successful it must be shown that there is some wrongdoing by the company which needs to be investigated and not being investigated by the liquidator or an element of bias by the liquidator (*In the Matter of Euro Chick Ireland Limited*).

(i) Finally there is a reference under this heading to ss 282A–C of CA 1963 which were introduced by s 49 of the Company Law Enforcement Act 2001. Section 282A allows the Director of Corporate Enforcement (the Director) to have access and facilities to inspect and take copies of the books and papers of the company as the Director may require with the right for him to apply to the court for that purpose.

(j)   Section 282B gives the court of its own motion (this wording was considered in *CB Readymix Limited (In Liquidation) Cahill v Grimes* [2002] IR 372, on the application of the Director to summon any officer or person known or suspected to have in his possession property of the company to be examined on oath and provides (at subsection (6)) that a person so examined is not entitled to refuse to answer any question on the grounds that his answer might incriminate him and the answer by him may be used in evidence against him in any proceedings except proceedings for an offence (criminal) other than perjury in relation to his answer – this section is largely identical to s 24 of CA 1963.

(k)   Section 282C follows on from an examination under the previous subsection permitting the court on motion to make an order compelling the person examined to pay either a debt to the liquidator or to hand over property, documents and paper.

6.12   Representing a creditor at a meeeting of creditors

If the solicitor is the proxy holder, he should ensure the proxy form is properly completed and is returned to the registered office of the company in time. The solicitor should also know the amount of the debt due and have in his possession a copy of the invoice or statement and be satisfied as to whether his client can claim ROT.

The solicitor will need to make Companies Registration Office searches to establish whether the company has been 'struck off' and to be familiar with the last set of accounts filed. Finally the solicitor should be familiar with the voting rules at a creditors' meeting.

6.13   Representing the company

If a solicitor is representing the company, he will be more particularly advising the director who is presiding at the creditors' meeting.

The solicitor should accordingly:

(a)   have some knowledge of the statement of affairs;

(b)   ensure the liquidator has consented to act;

(c)   check that the notices have been advertised and proxies sent out;

(d)   check the proxies returned to the company;

(e)   ensure that a room has been booked and that copies of the statement of affairs and list of creditors are available at the door; and

(f)   make a Companies Registration Office search to ensure the company has not been struck off.

The liquidator on his appointment must notify the Companies Registration Office within 14 days and in addition to filing notice of his appointment must lodge with the Companies Registration Office a certified copy of the resolution of the creditors appointing him. He must also file a notice in *Iris Oifigiúil* within 14 days of his appointment.

Every invoice, order or business letter issued by the company or the liquidator must include the words 'in voluntary liquidation' after the name of the company (s 303(1) of CA 1963).

The liquidator shall, on his appointment, exercise the powers given to a court liquidator and exercise the powers given under s 231(1)(d), (e) and (b) of CA 1963 with the sanction of the COI or, where there is none, the creditors (CA 1963, s 276). However the liquidator cannot, without the sanction of the court, exercise his powers as liquidator during the period from his appointmnet by the company until the holding of the creditors' meeting (Companies Act 1990, s 131) except for the purposes of:

    (a)   taking control of company assets;

    (b)   disposing of perishable goods or goods whose value is diminishing; or

    (c)   doing or taking all steps necessary to protect the company's assets.

CHAPTER 7

GENERAL CONCEPTS OF RECEIVERSHIPS

Bill Holohan

7.1   Introduction

Although receivership is merely a method of enforcing a security, it is in practice always treated as a form of insolvency procedure. What is a receiver? As his name implies, the receiver is the person who is granted the legal right to receive property belonging to others. Coupled with the right to receive, a person appointed as a 'receiver and manager' of a limited liability company has the power to manage and trade with the company's assets. A person appointed simply as a 'receiver' is appointed without a right to manage, but with the power to sell existing stocks or assets and, in this case, the receiver's relevant powers would be set out in the debenture document.

Although there are different types of receiver in the context of a limited liability company, this chapter is primarily concerned with exploring the rights and duties of the most common type of receiver, that is, one who is appointed by a secured creditor (usually a lending institution), under the contractual powers granted by the company in a debenture/ charge. This method of appointment is the most prevalent in the commercial world, and such a receiver can be termed a 'contractual receiver'. However, where there is no such contractual power afforded in the debenture, the creditor may apply to the court for the appointment of a receiver to the company. The debenture is a contractual development, hence all of the powers of the debentureholder and of the receiver depend on this document, with the exception of a few statutory provisions.

7.1.1   Court-appointed receivers

It is possible for a receiver to be appointed by the court in the following ways:

(a)   pursuant to a specific statutory power, for example a receiver appointed pursuant to s 19 of the Conveyancing Act 1881 (which is the only relevant modern provision) who is appointed over lands with a view to collecting rents and profits. Receivers appointed pursuant to a statutory power can be termed 'statutory receivers'. This class of receiver does not play a very important role under the modern law of receivers;

(b)   in its equitable jurisdiction pursuant to the Supreme Court of Judicature Act (Ireland) 1877; or

(c)   under the Rules of the Superior Courts (RSC).

In the last instance, a charge is not necessary for the receiver's appointment. However, in all other instances outlined above, the appointment of the receiver arises in connection with a charge. Although the court is unlikely to be called upon by a debentureholder who has an express power of appointment to appoint a receiver under its equitable jurisdiction, a certain event which may not have been covered by or which may not be within the scope of the debenture may justify an application being made to the court. For example, in

Angelis v Algemene Bank Nederland (Ireland) Ltd (High Court, 4 June 1974) Kenny J said:

> It is not necessary to cite authority for the proposition that when assets charged by a debenture are in danger of seizure, a debentureholder may immediately appoint a receiver.

In this case certain assets which were comprised in a floating charge had become vulnerable to execution at the hands of the sheriff and the debentureholder had responded by appointing a receiver. Another example whereby the court's power to appoint a receiver under its equitable jurisdiction may need to be invoked occurs where the company had agreed to execute a debenture/charge but had never actually done so. In such instances, the court could appoint a receiver at the request of the intended debentureholder as in the case of *Alexander Hull and Co Ltd v O'Carroll Kent and Co Ltd* [1955] 18 ILTR 70.

No statutory distinction is drawn in Ireland (as opposed to in England pursuant to the UK Insolvency Act 1986, Pt III) between an administrative receiver and a receiver. The law concerns itself with a receiver who is appointed by a secured creditor under a debenture containing a fixed and/or floating charge over all or most of the company's assets.

7.1.2   The governing law

Very little statute law covers receivers. Case law has mainly determined the rights, duties, powers and liabilities of receivers. As to statute law see:

(a)   Pt VII, ss 314–23 of the Companies Act 1963 (CA 1963);

(b)   Pts VI (ss 144–45) and VIII (ss 170–79) of the Companies Act 1990; and

(c)   ss 52, 53, 55 and 58 of the Company Law Enforcement Act 2001.

7.2   How and when receivers are appointed

7.2.1   Introduction

In Ireland, the receiver is a person appointed by the holders of a debenture, which constitutes a charge over the undertaking and assets of a company incorporated under the provisions of the Companies Acts. He will usually, but not always, be an accountant. The restrictions on persons being appointed receiver are the prohibition on a body corporate acting as receiver under s 314 of CA 1963 and the restrictions contained in s 315 of CA 1963 (as amended by s 170 of the Companies Act 1990).

The receiver will usually be appointed because:

(a)   the principal under a debenture is in arrears;

(b)   the interest under a debenture is in arrears; or

(c)   some other event has happened by which, under the terms of the debenture, the security has become enforceable, for example a winding-up order or because the security is in jeopardy.

As his name implies, the receiver is one who receives. He has the legal right to receive property belonging to others. Coupled with the right to receive, the receiver may be given power to carry on the business of a company and in this instance he is known as a 'receiver and manager'.

7.2.2   Date of commencement of appointment

Receipt by the receiver of notification of his appointment is a condition precedent to the coming into effect of the appointment. The appointment commences on the date on which the receiver, having been handed the Deed of Appointment or otherwise informed of it, expressly or impliedly accepts the appointment.

7.3 Powers, duties and functions of a receiver

7.3.1 Introduction

The function of a receiver appointed by a debentureholder is to take possession of the assets subject to the debentureholder's charge. A receiver will usually then realise those assets and discharge the debt owing to the debentureholder. However, a receiver may, depending of course upon the terms of both the security and his appointment, continue to operate the business with either a view to increasing the value of the company's assets or, alternatively, sell the business as a going concern or sell part of the business whilst winding down the unprofitable part.

If a receiver is appointed on foot of a floating charge as distinct from a fixed charge, a receiver must first pay in full those creditors whose claims would be afforded priority in a winding up, that is, the preferential creditors. A receiver and liquidator may act concurrently in respect of the same company but a liquidator is unable to deal with those assets under a receiver's control.

Regardless of whether the receiver is officially an agent of the company, his primary responsibility is to the debentureholder. The Debenture Deed should always be consulted to ensure that the receiver acts within his stated powers. Essentially, the powers, duties and functions of a receiver can include the following:

(a) to exercise care in disposing of company property (*McGowan v Gannon* [1983] ILRM 516; *Holohan v Friends Provident and Century Life Office* [1966] IR 1; *Casey v Irish Intercontinental Bank* [1979] IR 364; *Standard Chartered Bank Ltd v Walker* [1982] 3 All ER 938);

(b) to satisfy notification requirements laid down in the Act;

(c) to take possession of, collect and get in the property charged by the debenture, and take all and any proceedings in the name of the company or otherwise as may be necessary for that purpose;

(d) to carry on or concur in the carrying on of the business where he is appointed receiver and manager;

(e) to raise money on the premises charged in priority to the debenture or otherwise, where he is given that power;

(f) to sell or concur in selling any of the property charged by the debenture and to use the company seal for that purpose;

(g) to make arrangements or compromises which are in the interests of the debentureholder;

(h) to receive as agent of the company if so specified (and the receiver usually is so specified);

(i) to insure/repair;

(j) to employ agents and employees;

(k) to hive down part of the business;

(l) to furnish reports and accounts (s 321 of CA 1963);

(m) to make arrangements or compromises which are in the interests of the debentureholder; and

(n) to apply proceeds of sale in manner fixed by law.

With regard to the receiver's duty to apply the proceeds of sale in the manner fixed by law, s 98 of CA 1963 will require a receiver who is appointed by a debentureholder and realises assets subject to a floating charge, to pay all preferential creditors before applying the proceeds to discharge the debts owed to the debentureholder. If a company is in the course of being wound up, s 98 will not apply. However, the obligation to pay the preferential creditors continues if a liquidator is appointed prior to the receiver complying with the requirements under s 98. In the 1996 High Court case of *Re Manning Furniture Ltd* [1996] 1 ILRM 13 the court held that even though the proceeds of the floating charge were not used to discharge moneys due under the debenture, the receiver was required to pay the preferential creditors out of any assets coming into his hands.

In contrast, where a receiver only realises the assets subject to a fixed charge as opposed to realising or taking into his possession the assets which are the subject of a floating charge, it would seem that he is not obliged to pay the preferential creditors under s 98 of CA 1963 (see *United Bars Ltd v Revenue Commissioners* [1991] 1 IR 396).

7.3.2   Functions and powers of a receiver and manager

In this section, the functions of the receiver as a receiver and manager appointed pursuant to a floating charge are considered in more detail.

Immediately upon his appointment, the receiver should ensure that the statutory provisions as to advertisement and notice to the Registrar of Companies of his appointment under s 317 of CA 1963 are complied with. The debentureholder will usually attend to these formalities.

A number of practical matters should be attended to by the receiver as soon as possible after his appointment. He should arrange insurance cover, notify the company's bank, solicitors, directors and secretary, suppliers, creditors and debtors, agents, employees and persons having dealings with the company of his appointment, and seek payment from debtors. He should ensure that all company stationery and invoices are overprinted with the words 'Receiver/Receiver and Manager appointed' or 'In Receivership'.

The powers of the receiver depend largely on the terms of the debenture under which he has been appointed and are supplemented by various statutory provisions affecting those powers and by implied powers. The debenture contains the express powers of the receiver appointed pursuant to that debenture.

7.3.2.1 *Debenture deed: to take possession*

The first part of this power expresses what is in fact the main duty of the receiver and manager; that is, to take possession of the assets charged by the debenture so that they can be sold in order to pay off the debentureholder and others entitled in priority to the debentureholder (possibly a prior debentureholder or, in the case of a floating charge, the preferential creditors). If anyone prevents the receiver from obtaining possession or interferes with his possession when obtained, proceedings can be taken to obtain possession or prevent interference. As a general rule, the receiver as such is not entitled to bring such proceedings in his own name, but he has the right to sue in the company's name, even in the absence of an express power (*M Wheeler and Co Ltd v Warren* [1928] Ch 840). The receiver should go into possession as quickly as possible after appointment and should seek to find out as much as he can about the business of the company to enable him to plan his strategy for the job which he has undertaken.

7.3.2.2 *Debenture deed: to carry on business*

Unless expressly authorised, a receiver cannot carry on business and for that reason debentures almost invariably confer an express power to carry on the business of the company. Where there is such an express provision, then although the person appointed is termed simply a receiver, he is, in effect, a receiver and manager. Generally, the receiver has the power to carry on the business and he is given an express power to borrow money on the assets charged to the debentureholder and in priority to that security. The power to borrow money can be vital if the receiver is to be able to carry on the business and thus enable outstanding contracts with high added value to be completed and a sale of the business as a going concern to be effected.

In carrying on the business, the receiver must bear in mind his primary responsibility to the debentureholder and must ensure that he can achieve an adequate return on any business that he undertakes and that he does not depreciate the value of the assets over which he is receiver.

7.3.2.3 *Debenture deed: to sell*

This is one of the common standard forms of express powers conferred on a receiver and manager and it is found in various forms; the debenture usually includes the power to convey the legal estate. The need for such a conveyancing power is a consequence of the nature of a floating charge. If a solicitor finds that a debenture does not grant the receiver an express power to convey in the name of or as attorney for the company, he may find it necessary to advise the debentureholder to consider selling the property as mortgagee in possession.

7.3.2.4 *Debenture deed: to compromise*

The final express power usually incorporated in the debenture implies the debentureholder's lack of confidence in the financial stability of the company which has granted the debenture. Because of the financial problems leading to the appointment of a receiver, disputes with third parties are likely to arise and result in litigation. The receiver frequently inherits litigation based on disputes which arose prior to his appointment, and for this reason he is given an express power to make compromises or arrangements in the interest of the debentureholder. An important factor in considering whether or not to compromise an action is the question of costs. In the case of *Bacal Contracting v Modern Engineering* [1980] 2 All ER 655 a successful defendant in an action taken by a company which later went into receivership obtained its costs against the receiver in the action from the date on which the company (being in receivership) went into liquidation. There is no set rule but the court has the discretion to award costs against the receiver as an expense in the receivership, although this would probably only happen in exceptional circumstances.

7.3.3 Implied powers

In addition to the express powers conferred by the debenture, a receiver, as agent of the company, has other implied powers.

7.3.3.1 *To insure and repair*

The receiver should invariably arrange blanket cover from the moment of his appointment over all the assets over which he is appointed, since the cover held by the company will frequently be quite inadequate.

7.3.3.2 *To employ agents or employees*

The power to carry on the business of the company gives the receiver an implied power to employ agents or employees for the purpose of carrying on or selling the business, although most well-drawn debentures avoid argument on the point by incorporating an express power, frequently in the following terms:

> To appoint managers, accountants, servants, workmen and agents for the aforesaid purposes upon such terms as to remuneration or otherwise as the receiver may determine.

7.3.3.3 *To incorporate a subsidiary and sell assets to it*

Many modern floating charges also empower the receiver to incorporate a subsidiary company and to sell the assets of the company to it. The 'hiving down' of a viable part of a business to a subsidiary company enables the purchaser in some cases to avail of taxation and stamp duty advantages. Hiving down will be discussed in **Chapter 8**.

7.3.4   Receiver's power of sale

The exercise of the power of sale by the receiver is the aspect of the receiver's duties most likely to bring the receiver into contact with solicitors other than his own legal adviser. The power of sale of a receiver has been equated to that of a mortgagee exercising his power of sale and in *Re B Johnson and Co (Builders) Ltd* [1955] All ER 775 it was stated that the receiver's power of sale is in effect that of a mortgagee. In other words, the same standards are expected of a receiver exercising his power of sale as are expected of a mortgagee exercising his power of sale. The receiver has a duty to act in good faith and in addition to that duty he also owes a duty of care in the conduct of the sale. That duty was established in *Cuckmore Brick Co Ltd* v *Mutual Finance Ltd* [1971] 2 All ER 633; [1971] Ch 949 and has been approved in a number of subsequent English decisions. It had been accepted in Ireland in the case of *Holohan v Friends' Provident and Century Life Office* [1966] IR 1 as applying to mortgagees in possession exercising a power of sale, and by extension to others such as receivers.

The receiver, whether he carries on the business or not, will eventually need to sell the assets over which he has been appointed, as advantageously as possible. Section 316A of CA 1963 (as inserted by s 172 of the Companies Act 1990) provides that:

> A receiver, in selling property of a company, shall exercise all reasonable care to obtain the best price reasonably obtainable for the property as at the time of sale.

Those assets will typically include real property, stock in trade, goodwill and debtors. The method of sale may be by private treaty, tender or auction but in any event, the receiver should obtain professional advice on the most appropriate method and should obtain professional valuations of all assets being disposed of. The receiver must be cautious about disposing of assets for less than such valuation and he should obtain confirmation from a suitably qualified professional person that the price achieved by him is reasonable in the circumstances.

In the case of a sale of the business as a going concern the receiver's solicitors will draft an agreement for the sale of assets, the parties to which will be:

    (a)   the company as vendor;

    (b)   the receiver as the agent of the company; and

    (c)   the purchaser.

The form of such agreement differs only in minor respects from a sale by the company itself. For example, it will provide for a specific exclusion from liability for misrepresentation on the part of the receiver and will express the fact that he enters into the contract as agent for the company only and without personal liability. Due to the receiver's lack of knowledge, the agreement will specifically exclude all warranties as to title to assets which a purchaser would expect to receive in a normal commercial transaction. The price paid may reflect the absence of such warranties. The value of debtors purchased will also have to be substantially discounted. In some cases, the receiver will appoint the purchaser as his agent for collection of debts if he cannot achieve a reasonable cash offer for them.

The receiver will not normally be concerned with the provisions of the Sale of Goods and Supply of Services legislation, as he does not usually sell to a consumer. Similarly, he will usually escape liability under the Liability for Defective Products Act 1991 because goods sold by a receiver would not ordinarily be intended for private use or consumption. If real property is included in the sale, the agreement will incorporate the Standard Law Society conditions of sale. It is important to delete certain of the General Conditions from those Conditions of Sale and, in particular, the warranty as to planning and the declaration relating to identity of the property as the receiver will have only limited knowledge of these matters. A special condition providing that if required by the purchaser the assurance to the purchaser will be executed by the charge-holder is frequently included in cases where the debentureholder has a fixed charge. All debentureholders, including those who appointed the receiver, would, in any case, be required to execute a discharge of their debentures. However, it is essential that the debenture under which the receiver sells is not released until after the date of the assurance to the purchaser where the receiver conveys as attorney for the company. In the case of subsequent debentures, consideration should be given to a sale by the mortgagee in possession rather than by the receiver, as a sale by the mortgagee will defeat the interests of puisne mortgagees whereas a sale by the receiver is subject to their interest.

7.3.5 Use of the seal

The use of the company seal by the receiver has been considered in the *Cork Shoe Company* case (*Industrial Development Authority v Moran* [1978] IR 159). Kenny J, in the course of his judgment in the Supreme Court in that case, commented as follows:

> I wish to point out that the power given to the receiver by Clause 10 is 'to carry any such sale into effect by deed in the name and on behalf of the company'. When a receiver is selling under such a clause, the more usual and better practice is for him to execute the deed of transfer by writing the name of the company and underneath this to write words that indicate that the name of the company has been written by the receiver as attorney of the company under the power of attorney given by the debenture. In addition, he should execute the deed in his own name. In that way he has the best of both worlds. The writing of the name of the company by the authority of the company given when it executed the debenture brings the case within the words of the debenture itself, and execution by the attorney personally gives the advantage of s 46 of the Conveyancing Act 1881.

It is advisable for a number of reasons, especially for purposes of taxation and stamp duty, that each asset be allocated a proportion of the purchase price in the sale agreement and it is preferable that this be agreed during the negotiations.

7.3.6 Absence of specified powers

The powers of the receiver are derived from the debenture under which the receiver is appointed and in the case of fixed charges from the Conveyancing Acts. The receiver will not have any power to carry on the business of the company if this power has not been given to him by the debenture. If the debenture is defective in this respect, it may instead be necessary for the debentureholder to apply to the court to appoint a liquidator. The receiver will not have any power of sale if such power is not in the debenture, as the Conveyancing Acts do not confer a power of sale on the receiver whose function under these Acts, as his name implies, is to receive the income of the mortgaged property. If the receiver has no power of sale and the debentureholder still wishes to appoint a receiver, where the debentureholder has a legal mortgage, the problem may be overcome if the debentureholder sells the assets as mortgagee and the receiver does the necessary preparatory work leading up to the sale.

7.4   Receiver as agent of company/debentureholder

The receiver is empowered to act as the company's agent but the relationship does not fall neatly within traditional agency rules and obligations. This is due to the fact that the relationship between receiver and company differs greatly from the usual agent/principal relationships in that the receiver may be bound by some of the company's obligations and in other instances may choose to repudiate those obligations (*Ardmore Studios (Ireland) Ltd v Lynch* [1965] IR 1). The difficulty, of course, arises as a result of the fact that the receiver is appointed (usually) by the debentureholder and will, therefore, always pursue the debentureholder's interests in relation to the company. Thus, the company is not in a position to instruct the receiver regarding the carrying out of his duties or on the exercise/ ambit of his powers.

Even in instances whereby the debenture expressly provides that the receiver is the agent of the company, the court may still infer an agency relationship between debentureholder and receiver based on actions of the debentureholder. A prime example of this occurred in the case of *American Express International Banking v Hurley* [1986] BCLC 52. In this case, a bank was the debentureholder. The bank had directed the receiver to sell the assets at an undervalue, and in so doing had created a relationship of principal and agent between the bank and the receiver. Hence, the bank was held by the court to be liable to the guarantor for the company's debts.

7.5   Notification/publication

Receipt by the receiver of notification of his appointment is a condition precedent to the coming into effect of the appointment. Section 107 of CA 1963 states that the debentureholder is primarily responsible for notification of the appointment which must be published within seven days in *Iris Oifigiúil* and one daily newspaper. In addition, the receiver must notify the company within 14 days of his appointment under s 319 of CA 1963. Once the receiver has notified the company, directors are under an obligation to submit a statement of affairs to the receiver within 14 days pursuant to s 320 of CA 1963. Yet in practice, this obligation is rarely complied with on time.

Section 319(A) of CA 1963 (as inserted by s 52(b) of the Company Law Enforcement Act 2001) requires that when the Registrar of Companies becomes aware of the appointment of a receiver, he must inform the Director of Corporate Enforcement of the appointment. The Registrar should 'become aware' by receiving a notice from the person appointing the receiver, as required by s 107 of CA 1963.

Section 319(7) of CA 1963 (as amended by s 52(a) of the 2001 Act) states that where a receiver ceases to act, his final return shall include a statement of his opinion as to whether or not the company is solvent and the Registrar of Companies is obliged to forward a copy of this documentation to the Director of Corporate Enforcement. This opinion will be relevant to the Director in considering whether to exercise his powers in respect of a company which is not liquidated following receivership, due to insufficiency of assets.

It is difficult to understand why the 2001 Act did not impose a requirement for direct notice to the Director, but it is to be presumed that in practice receivers will also notify the Director directly.

7.6   Effect of a receiver's appointment

7.6.1   The company

The receiver can only be appointed over assets which have been charged. The appointment of a receiver does not affect the legal status of a company. However, once the receiver is appointed all invoices, goods orders or business letters issued by or on behalf of the company must, pursuant to s 317(1) of CA 1963, contain a statement stipulating that a receiver has been appointed. If the company, officer, liquidator and/or receiver defaults in satisfying this requirement, they may incur a fine pursuant to s 317(2) of CA 1963.

In the event of a holder of a floating charge appointing a receiver over the entire undertaking and assets of the company, s 320 of CA 1963 requires that the directors and secretary of the company or such other person as may be specified by the receiver, submit to the receiver within 14 days of his appointment a statement as to the affairs of the company.

Furthermore, a receivership is a temporary condition affecting a company which, unlike liquidation, does not necessarily lead to the company's dissolution. After a receiver has been discharged, the directors resume their normal functions in relation to all of the company's affairs, unless a liquidator has been appointed in the meantime.

Unlike a liquidation, a receivership will not bring to an end the life of the company. If at the conclusion of the receivership the receiver has a surplus on hand, he will normally pay or transfer the surplus to the company or to its liquidator if it is then in liquidation. If there are subsequent charges, it is considered that the holders should be notified before any return of assets to the company so that they can take action to safeguard their position and indeed it may be unsafe for the receiver to pay the surplus to the company when he is on notice of a subsequent charge.

In addition, a receiver has the power to manage the company, that is, to continue the management of the business of the company. In practice, most receiverships do result in the dissolution of the company's business.

7.6.2 The directors

Directors' powers regarding the company's assets are suspended upon the receiver's appointment, as at that time the receiver assumes controls over assets which are the subject of the charge. The directors remain in office and are permitted to exercise any power not conferred on the receiver.

In the event that a receiver is appointed regarding a specific asset only, directors' powers will only be suspended regarding that asset and will remain in respect of all other remaining powers and duties. If, however, a receiver is appointed over all of the assets and undertakings of the company, the directors' powers and duties will obviously be significantly hindered, but the directors will still retain the residual decision-making powers.

7.7 The receiver's position when appointed

7.7.1 Receiver's liability

The receiver will be the agent of one of the parties to the debenture according to its terms. Normally, he is stated to be the agent of the company over whose assets he is appointed, as this means that the debentureholder does not come under any personal liability for debts incurred in carrying on the business of the company by the receiver or for torts, negligence or omissions of duty in the course of the performance of the receiver's duties. Under s 316 of CA 1963, the receiver may become personally liable to persons contracting with him except in so far as the contract otherwise provides, but he is entitled to be indemnified out of the company's assets.

7.7.2   Receiver's qualification

Although the Companies Acts (s 314 of CA 1963) do not prescribe any qualifications as a requisite for appointment as a receiver, they do prohibit the following persons from so acting:

(a)   a body corporate;

(b)   an employee or partner of an officer or servant (an officer or servant of the company in this context includes references to an auditor);

(c)   a person who is an officer, auditor or servant of the company, or has been, within 12 months of the commencement of the receivership;

(d)   an undischarged bankrupt (which, by virtue of the Company Law Enforcement Act 2001, is now defined to include a bankrupt under the laws of the state or elsewhere);

(e)   a parent, spouse, brother, sister or child of an officer; or

(f)   anyone disqualified from acting as a receiver of the company's holding or subsidiary company or a subsidiary of its holding company.

Pursuant to s 315(2) of CA 1963, if a receiver becomes disqualified, he must immediately vacate office and notify the company, the Registrar of Companies, the debentureholder or court that he has vacated his office due to the disqualification. If a receiver fails to so vacate office after disqualification, he is continuing a criminal offence, which, pursuant to s 315(5) of CA 1963, is punishable by a fine.

7.7.3   Receiver's remuneration

Those receivers who are appointed by the court will be paid at the court-appointed rate, whilst those receivers who are appointed by virtue of the debenture will have their rate of pay fixed by the terms of the debenture. However, the receiver's remuneration, even if fixed by the terms of the debenture, may be fixed where a liquidator, member or creditor of a company applies to the court pursuant to s 318 of CA 1963 (*Re City Car Sales Ltd (In Receivership and Liquidation*) [1995] 1 ILRM 221).

7.7.4   Resignation

When a receiver is appointed by the court, he may, pursuant to s 322C(2) of CA 1963, only resign if the court grants its consent and subject to the terms laid down by the court. If the receiver fails to so comply with these notice provisions, he may be liable to a fine.

A receiver appointed under a debenture may resign pursuant to s 322C(1) of CA 1963, provided he has given one month's notice to the holders of floating charges over all or part of the company, the company itself or its liquidator, and the holders of all fixed charges over all or part of the company.

Additionally, pursuant to s 322A(1) of CA 1963, the court has power to remove a receiver and appoint another, provided due cause is evinced. In the event that such proceedings take place, notice must be served on both the receiver and the person who appointed him at least seven days prior to the hearing. Both the receiver and the person who appointed him must be afforded a chance to appear and be heard at such proceedings under s 322A(2) of CA 1963.

As mentioned above, s 52(a) of the 2001 Act provides, by way of amendment to s 319(7) of CA 1963, that where a receiver ceases to act, his final return shall include a statement of his opinion as to whether the company is solvent and the Registrar of Companies is obliged to forward a copy of this documentation to the director.

7.8   Council Regulation (EC) No 1346/2000

Council Regulation (EC) No 1346/2000 (the Insolvency Regulation) came into force on 31 May 2002. It does not apply to receiverships. The Insolvency Regulation is covered in detail in **Chapter 13**.

CHAPTER 8

ADVISING PARTIES INVOLVED IN A RECEIVERSHIP

Bill Holohan

8.1 Advising the various parties

This chapter is written as a guide for the solicitor advising parties involved in a receivership. Some checklists are included in the text for ease of reference.

8.1.1 The existence and powers of the company

The first questions that the solicitor needs to ask himself are:

(a) Does the company exist?
(b) Can it borrow/create debentures?
(c) Was it incorporated prior to the creation of the mortgage/debenture?

Your first task as acting solicitor will be to advise on the validity of the receiver's appointment and what his powers are. If there is any flaw in his appointment, he will be unable to enforce any claims to priority over other parties interested in the property and he may incur liabilities as a trespasser. If his appointment is challenged, it is for the receiver to justify it.

Your duties will usually involve the following matters:

(a) checking the company's Memorandum and Articles of Association to see that the company has the power to create the debenture; and
(b) checking that the debenture was duly sealed in accordance with the company's Articles of Association.

8.1.2 The existence and scope of the debenture

(a) Was it created after the company came into existence?
(b) Was it properly created, executed, scaled, stamped, registered etc?
(c) Check in the Companies Registration Office to see that the debenture was duly registered within the period of 21 days prescribed by s 99 of Companies Act 1963 (CA 1963) or that the court, under s 106 of CA 1963, extended the time for registration.
(d) Check in the Companies Registration Office to see that the date of incorporation of the company is earlier than the date of the debenture.
(e) Check the extent of the property captured by the debenture. Obviously, the receiver will not be able to collect the income from or realise assets not included within the scope of the debenture.
(f) Check the powers of the receiver. These are derived from the debenture under which the receiver is appointed and, in the case of fixed charges, the Conveyancing Acts. The receiver will not have any power to carry on the business of the company if this power has not been given to him in the debenture. If the debenture is defective in this respect, it may instead be necessary for the

debentureholder to apply to the court to appoint a liquidator. The receiver will not have any power of sale if such power is not in the debenture, as the Conveyancing Acts do not confer a power of sale on the receiver whose function under these Acts, as his name implies, is to receive the income of the mortgaged property. If the receiver has no power of sale and the debentureholder still wishes to appoint a receiver, the problem may be overcome where the debentureholder has a legal mortgage by the debentureholder selling the assets as mortgagee with the receiver doing the necessary preparatory work leading up to the sale.

(g) Check that the debenture has been properly and adequately stamped.

(h) Check that an event of default has actually occurred which, under the terms of the debenture, enables the debentureholder to appoint a receiver. The most common events are:

  (i) Failure to repay moneys due, or interest, following the sending of a written demand for payment by the debentureholder to the company. The demand must have been made in accordance with the provisions for service of a demand in the debenture. If the demand has to be sent to the company's registered office, see that the demand has been sent to the current registered office at the date of the demand (which will not necessarily be the same address as that given in the debenture). The power to appoint can be validly exercised in such cases only if the demand is made prior to the appointment being communicated to the receiver.

  (ii) If the company passes a resolution to liquidate, a petition is presented, or an order is made to liquidate the company.

  (iii) If execution is levied against the company's property.

  (iv) If the company should cease to carry on its business.

  (v) If the company should be in breach of any condition in the debenture.

  (vi) If a receiver should be appointed over any part of the assets of the company.

  (vii) If the company threatens to or actually ceases to trade.

  (viii) If any other debenture becomes enforceable against the company.

  (ix) If the company is unable to pay its debts.

  (x) If the company's balance sheet discloses that the company's liabilities are in excess of its assets, including its uncalled capital.

  (xi) If the company reduces its capital.

  (xii) If the company, without the debentureholder's consent, creates any mortgage or charge ranking in priority to or *pari passu* with the security created by the debenture.

  (xiii) If circumstances occur which in the judgement of the debentureholder render it necessary or desirable to appoint a receiver. This event might not be as safe a ground for making the appointment as, for instance, non-payment following a demand, as it might be possible for the company to challenge the validity of the appointment by trying to prove to the court that there were no such circumstances in existence or no reasonable grounds for arriving at the judgment made by the debentureholder.

8.2   Advising the potential receiver

8.2.1   Eligibility

Will the nominee agree to act? One cannot assume that the person nominated by the debentureholder as the receiver will agree to act. There may be many reasons why the first nominee of the debentureholder would be unwilling to act: perhaps either because of some connection with the company (business or personal), or because they are one of the directors or one of the shareholders of the company. It is not unknown, in fact, for certain nominees to have held shares in companies in respect of which they were nominated as receiver. In addition, the nominee may be unwilling to act because of prior commitments. Accordingly, one should not automatically assume that the nominee will act. The nominee should be asked in writing whether he would be willing to accept the nomination and the debentureholder should receive confirmation prior to the formal appointment and acceptance.

As to whether the nominee is eligible, see ss 314 and 315 of CA 1963 (as amended). Section 314 provides that certain persons be excluded from eligibility. Section 315 (as amended by s 170 of the Companies Act 1990) provides that none of the following qualify for appointment as receiver of the property of a company:

(a)   a body corporate;

(b)   an undischarged bankrupt (which by virtue of the Company Law Enforcement Act 2001 is now defined to include bankrupts under the law of the state and other jurisdictions);

(c)   a person who is or within 12 months prior to the commencement of the receivership has been an officer or servant of the company;

(d)   a parent, spouse, brother, sister or child of an officer of the company;

(e)   a person who is a partner of or in employment of an officer or servant of the company; and

(f)   a person who is not qualified by virtue of the subsection for appointment as receiver of the property of any other body corporate which is that company's subsidiary or holding company or a subsidiary of that company's holding company or would be so disqualified if the body corporate were a company.

An officer or servant of the company in this context includes reference to an auditor.

8.2.2   Debentures not providing for receivers

If the debenture does not contain provisions enabling the appointment of a receiver, the mortgagee has only the rights of appointment of a receiver under s 19 of the Conveyancing Act 1881 when the mortgage is made by deed and the mortgage money has become due. Apart from express provisions in the mortgage deed, under s 24 of that Act the appointment cannot be made until the mortgagee has become entitled to exercise the statutory power of sale, that is, unless and until notice has been served on the mortgagor or one of several mortgagors requiring payment of the mortgage money default in payment of the money or any part thereof has been made for three months after service or unless and until some interest is in arrears and unpaid for two months after becoming due or there has been a breach of some provision contained in the mortgage deed or in the Act (other than the covenant for payment of the mortgagee money or interest).

If the mortgage is silent as regards appointment of a receiver and his powers, the receiver will have only the very limited powers conferred on him by the Conveyancing Acts. Under s 24 of the 1881 Act, the receiver is given power to demand and recover all the income of the property over which he is appointed receiver, by action, distress, or otherwise, in the name either of the mortgagor or of the mortgagee, to the full extent of the estate or interest which the mortgagor could dispose of, and to give effectual receipts for the same. This section also states that the receiver shall be deemed to be the agent of the mortgagor and that the mortgagor shall be solely responsible for the receiver's acts or defaults unless the mortgage deed otherwise provides. It further provides that the receiver shall, if so directed in writing by the mortgagee, insure and keep insured against loss or damage by fire, out of the money received by him, any buildings, effects or property comprised in the mortgage being of an insurable nature. The Conveyancing Acts do not authorise the appointment of a receiver in the case of a floating charge, nor can a receiver under these Acts be appointed of book debts comprised in a mortgage of a business.

8.2.3   Indemnity

It is obviously a good idea in every case, from the receiver's point of view, to get an indemnity from the debentureholder who is appointing him. The indemnity should cover both the acts of the receiver in carrying out the receivership and any liabilities arising from the debenture under which he is appointed proving to be defective. There will be a special need for an indemnity in certain cases, for example:

(a)   if a debenture is of recent creation, because of the risk of it (being a floating charge) becoming invalid or partly invalid under s 288 of CA 1963 in the event of a winding up within 12 months of its creation, or (being either fixed or floating) because of the risk of it being invalid as a fraudulent preference of its creditors under s 286 in the event of commencement of a winding up within six months of its creation;

(b)   if the company is already in liquidation or very likely to be put into liquidation, because the receiver will lose the protection of being the agent of the company from commencement of the winding up; or

(c)   if it is likely from the nature of the company's business that the receiver will be entering into contracts where it may be difficult to limit the receiver's statutory personal liability for contracts.

Institutional debentureholders will usually be reluctant to give an indemnity and it may only be possible to obtain one where one of these special factors applies.

8.2.4   Receiver's fees/remuneration

Is remuneration for the receiver agreed in advance? The potential receiver should agree with the debentureholder on the rate of remuneration to be paid to the receiver, if necessary by the debentureholder, regardless of whether or not the receiver would be entitled or able to recover remuneration from the company. The appropriate analogy would be an agreement in relation to solicitor and client costs on an hourly basis as distinct from costs one would be entitled to recover on a party and party basis in litigation.

   Section 318 of CA 1963 provides statutory provisions enabling a court to fix the remuneration of a receiver. Section 318(1) of CA 1963 provides that the court may, on an application made to it by the liquidator of a company or by any creditor or member of the company, by order, fix the amount to be paid by way of remuneration to any person who, under the powers contained in any instrument, has been appointed as receiver of the property of the company, notwithstanding that the remuneration of such receiver has been fixed by or under that instrument. Section 318(2) of CA 1963 provides that the power of the court shall, where no previous order has been made in relation thereto:

(a)   extend to fixing the remuneration for any period before the making of the order or the application therefor;

(b)   be exercisable notwithstanding that the receiver has died or ceased to act before the making of the order or the application therefor; and

(c)   where the receiver has been paid or has retained for his remuneration for any period before the making of the order any amount in excess of that fixed by the court for that period, extend to requiring him or his personal representatives to account for the excess or such part thereof as may be specified in the order.

The power conferred under paragraph (c) above shall not be exercised by the court in relation to any period before the making of the application for the order unless, in the opinion of the court, there are special circumstances making it proper for the power to be so exercised. The court may also from time to time, on application by the liquidator, by any creditor or member of the company or by the receiver, vary or amend an order made by the court in relation to remuneration.

8.2.5   Appointment

Has a default occurred? Under the standard form of debenture, certain events are specified as giving the debentureholder the right to appoint a receiver. These have already been mentioned above. Generally speaking, the provisions require that the company has been in breach of one or other of the provisions of the debenture. While a provision is usually incorporated providing that the debentureholder may appoint a receiver if some event occurs or if circumstances occur which in the judgement of the debentureholder render it necessary or desirable to appoint a receiver, it is generally preferable not to rely on such a provision for the appointment of a receiver, as it may be difficult to show that such circumstances or events objectively justify the appointment of a receiver.

If necessary, the court may also appoint a receiver under its equitable jurisdiction. It is unlikely to be called upon by a debentureholder who has an express power of appointment but some event, which may not have been covered by or which may not be within the scope of the debenture, might justify an application being made to the court. For example, in *Angelis v Algemene Bank Nederland (Ireland) Ltd* (High Court, 4 June 1974), Kenny J said:

> It is not necessary to cite authority for the proposition that when assets charged by a debenture are in danger of seizure, a debentureholder may immediately appoint a receiver.

In that case, certain assets which were comprised in a floating charge had become vulnerable to execution at the hands of the sheriff and the debentureholder had responded by appointing a receiver. In addition, for example, if the company agreed to execute a debenture/charge but had never actually done so, then the court could appoint a receiver at the request of the intended debentureholder. This occurred in the case of *Alexander Hull Ltd v O'Carroll Kent Ltd* [1955] 18 ILTR 70.

8.2.6   The form of notice of appointment

There is no specified or prescribed form for the Deed of Appointment of a receiver. However, certain items should be included, and these are:
  (a)   the name of the company which issued the debenture;
  (b)   the name and address of the debentureholder;
  (c)   the date of the relevant debenture under which the appointment is to be made;
  (d)   a recital that an event has occurred which gives rise to the exercise of the power of appointment (it is better not to specify a particular event in the actual Deed of Appointment);
  (e)   the name and address of the receiver;
  (f)   a recital that the receiver has agreed to accept the appointment; and
  (g)   a statement that the receiver is appointed over the assets charged by the debenture or alternatively a statement that the receiver is appointed as receiver over certain specified assets.

If there are any requirements specified in the debenture as to the execution of the Deed of Appointment, then these should be followed. The Deed of Appointment would normally be under seal. If the debenture provides for the Deed of Appointment to be signed by or on behalf of the debentureholder, then it does not need to be under seal. It is important, however, to ensure that the Deed is signed by an appropriate category of person to whom authority is given by the debenture. Preferably the Deed of Appointment should recite the capacity of the person signing the Deed of Appointment on behalf of the debentureholder.

It is not necessary for the Deed of Appointment to list out all of the powers of the receiver, as the Deed of Appointment cannot confer on a receiver a power that does not exist under the provisions of the debenture or under statute.

8.2.7   Acceptance by the receiver

If possible, the Deed of Appointment should also provide at the end of it for the signature by the receiver signifying his acceptance. Receipt by the receiver of the Deed of Appointment and acceptance is a condition precedent to its coming into effect. The appointment will commence on the date on which the receiver, having been handed the Deed of Appointment or otherwise informed of it, expressly or implicitly accepts the appointment.

8.2.8   Prior charge-holders

Any debentureholder wishing to appoint a receiver will have to give consideration to charges which are registered in priority and in particular to the question of whether or not such charges/debentures would allow the earlier charge-holders/debentureholders to appoint a receiver. If possible, the agreement, in writing, of the prior charge-holders to the appointment of a receiver should be obtained.

Notwithstanding the strict legal rights of prior charge-holders, it may also be possible on occasion to secure some form of inter-lender agreement between the charge-holders whereby they agree, in consideration of a later charge-holder agreeing to carry the cost of the receivership for the charge-holders, to rank *pari passu*.

8.2.9   Resources

Both the debentureholder and the potential receiver should ensure that the receiver has sufficient resources available, in terms of manpower etc, to effectively carry out the receivership. The amount of resources required will obviously depend on the nature and the scale of the operations carried on by the company. The potential receiver may be leaving himself open to an action at the hands of the company or the debentureholder if he fails to exercise sufficient skill and expertise through lack of available resources, be it time, manpower or otherwise.

8.3   Advising the receiver when appointed

8.3.1   Deed of appointment

As we have seen above, the Deed of Appointment does not have to be in any specific format. The particulars listed in **8.2.6** above should be included and the requirements set out for valid execution should also be complied with.

8.3.2   Acceptance

Receipt by the receiver of notification of his appointment is a condition precedent to the coming into effect of the appointment. The appointment commences on the date on which the receiver, having been handed the Deed of Appointment or having otherwise been informed of it, expressly or impliedly accepts the appointment.

8.3.3 Publication

Notice of the receivership must be made by:

(a) publishing notice of the appointment in the prescribed form in newspapers/*Iris Oifigiúil* (s 107 of CA 1963);

(b) giving notice to the company and its directors; and

(c) all notepaper, invoices, letters, orders, statements and other documents must contain a statement as to receivership usually complied with by inserting 'In Receivership' in brackets after the name of the company.

Under s 107 of CA 1963, a person who appoints a receiver must within seven days of the appointment:

(a) publish in one daily newspaper circulating in the district where the registered office of the company is situated a notice in the prescribed form; and

(b) deliver to the Registrar of Companies a notice in the prescribed form (Form No 53).

8.3.4 Notification

Under s 319 of CA 1963, where a receiver of the whole or substantially the whole of the property of a company is appointed on behalf of the holders of any debentures secured by a floating charge, the receiver has to send notice to the company of his appointment. Section 319(2A) of CA 1963 (as inserted by s 52(b) of the Company Law Enforcement Act 2001) requires that when the Registrar of Companies becomes aware of the appointment of a receiver, he shall inform the Director of Corporate Enforcement of the appointment. The Registrar should 'become aware' by receiving a notice from the person appointing the receiver, as required by s 107 of CA 1963.

Under s 317 of CA 1963, where a receiver has been appointed over the property of the company, every invoice, order for goods or business letter issued by or on behalf of the company or the receiver or the liquidator of the company, being a document on or in which the name of the company appears, must contain a statement that a receiver has been appointed. There is provision for a fine of €127 for an offence under this section. The section is normally complied with by inserting after the name of the company in brackets the words 'In Receivership'.

8.3.5 Insurance

As part of the general duty of care owed by a receiver to the company, the receiver should ensure that sufficient insurance is in place in respect of the assets of the company. The receiver should also examine the particular terms and conditions of the insurance policies to ensure that he would be regarded as the person entitled to receive the proceeds. It may well be that the receiver would be entitled to take possession of the assets of the company but would not be entitled to take possession of the proceeds of insurance policies in the event that such assets were destroyed by fire etc. In such circumstances, the receiver ought to ensure, so far as possible, that his interest is noted on the policies, or, alternatively, should effect insurance in his name as well as that of the company.

In addition, the receiver should ensure that he has sufficient professional indemnity insurance to ensure indemnity in the event that any actions are brought against the receiver in relation to conduct of the receivership. This would be in addition to the indemnity which the receiver would have obtained from the debentureholder.

8.3.6   Rivals

It is quite possible that more than one receiver could be appointed over the company's assets. It is possible that a number of charges/debentures could exist, providing for receivers to be appointed over different assets of the company. As stated in **8.1.2** above, the appointment of a receiver over any part of the assets of the company is usually recited as one of the grounds on which a receiver may normally be appointed. If there is any conflict in respect of assets, then the first receiver appointed takes possession of the assets. For example, if there were two successive debentures, each of which included, say, the book debts of the company, the first receiver in time appointed would be entitled to collect the book debts, and the subsequent appointment of another receiver would not affect the powers of the first receiver.

Another potential rival to the receiver is a liquidator. Generally speaking, the appointment of a liquidator does not prevent the subsequent appointment of a receiver and the appointment of a receiver does not prevent the appointment of a liquidator. The appointment of a liquidator and its effects on the agency of the receiver vis-à-vis the company are dealt with in greater detail in **8.7** below. Section 319 of CA 1963 provides for certain obligations of disclosure on the part of the receiver. If necessary, these may also be enforced by the liquidator. Furthermore, s 322(1)(b) of CA 1963 states that a liquidator, if appointed, may insist that the receiver account to him, the liquidator, for all receipts and payments and that he pay over the balance, if any, due.

8.3.7   Resignation/removal

Resignation must be on notice to the court, liquidator, company and charge-holders (CA 1963, s 322C, as inserted by s 177 of the Companies Act 1990).

Section 315 of CA 1963 prescribes who is qualified for appointment as receiver of a company. This is dealt with in greater detail above. However, if during the course of a receivership the receiver finds that were he now to be appointed as receiver to the company he would not be eligible, then s 315(2) requires him to vacate the office of receiver and give notice to the company, the Registrar of Companies, the debentureholder or the court, depending on who appointed the receiver, of the fact that he has vacated the position of receiver, by reason of the fact that he would be disqualified if he were now to be appointed.

Section 322C of CA 1963 (as inserted) now provides a procedure whereby the receiver may resign. It has been thought by some, up to the passing of the 1990 Act, that the resignation of a receiver might constitute a breach of contract as between the receiver and the debentureholder under the terms negotiated between them, and on foot of the notice of appointment. However, s 322C (as inserted) specifically provides for a power of resignation and this can now be regarded as overriding any contractual provisions between the parties. The section provides that the receiver may resign, provided he has given one month's notice of his intention to resign to:

(a)   the holders of floating charges over all or any part of the property of the company;
(b)   the company or its liquidator; and
(c)   the holders of any fixed charge over all or any part of the property of the company.

Section 322C(2) (as inserted) provides that, if the receiver is appointed by the court, he may only resign with the authority of the court and on such terms and conditions, if any, as may be imposed by the court.

8.3.8   Restriction/removal

The powers and functions of the receiver may be limited in whole or in part or the receiver may be removed. Under s 322B of CA 1963 (as inserted by s 176 of the Companies Act 1990), the liquidator of a company that has been wound up (other than by means of members' voluntary winding up) and in respect of which a receiver has been appointed, may apply to the court and the court may order that the receiver shall cease to act as such from a specified date or prohibit the appointment of any other receiver or may order that the receiver act only in respect of certain assets specified by the court. Such an order can be made on such terms and conditions as the court thinks fit and the court may subsequently rescind or amend any such order.

Also under s 322A of CA 1963 (as inserted by s 175 of the Companies Act 1990), the court may, on cause shown, remove a receiver and appoint another receiver.

8.4   Director of Corporate Enforcement

8.4.1   Notification

Section 319(2A) of CA 1963 (as inserted by s 52(b) of the Company Law Enforcement Act 2001) is a requirement that when the Registrar of Companies becomes aware of the appointment of a receiver, he shall inform the Director of Corporate Enforcement (the Director) of the appointment. The Registrar should 'become aware' by receiving a notice from the person appointing the receiver, as required by s 107 of CA 1963.

Section 319(7) of CA 1963 (as amended by s 52(a) of the 2001 Act) provides that where a receiver ceases to act, his final return shall include a statement of his opinion as to whether or not the company is solvent and the Registrar of Companies is obliged to forward a copy of this documentation to the Director. This opinion will be relevant to the Director in considering whether to exercise his powers in respect of a company which is not liquidated following receivership, due to insufficiency of assets.

It is difficult to understand why the 2001 Act did not impose a requirement for direct notice to the Director, but it is to be presumed that, in practice, receivers will also notify the Director directly.

8.4.2   Production of books and records

Section 53 of the Company Law Enforcement Act 2001 allows the Director to seek production of the books and records of a receiver. The Director may, 'where he considers it necessary or appropriate', request the production of the receiver's books for examination, being either the books regarding a particular receivership or the books of all receiverships undertaken by that receiver, subject only to a limitation that any request may not relate to a receivership which ended more than six years prior to the request being made. The requirement for the Director to consider it 'necessary or appropriate' does not apply under s 57, which is the corresponding section dealing with liquidators. There is no corresponding section dealing with examiners.

The Director's request to the receiver must specify the reason why the request is being made. Where the request is made, the receiver is obliged to furnish the original books to the Director 'for examination', even though the case may be ongoing. The receiver is also obliged to answer 'any questions concerning the content of the books and the conduct of a particular receivership or receiverships, and give to the Director all assistance in the matter as the receiver is reasonably able to give'.

A question obviously arises as to whether the receiver must actually deliver the books to the Director at his offices (in Parnell Square, Dublin) or whether he can fulfil the requirement as to 'production' by making them available at the offices of the receiver. Where the matter is ongoing, and/or where the Director wishes to put questions to the receiver, the latter may not be an unreasonable position to adopt, particularly as the failure to comply with the request or answer a question is a criminal offence and the benefit of any doubt as to interpretation must be given to the receiver.

8.4.3　Disciplinary findings

Where the disciplinary committee of a prescribed professional body (being a body set up by the Minister under a statutory instrument) makes a finding that a member of a professional body has not maintained appropriate records or has reasonable grounds for suspecting that the member has committed an indictable offence under the Companies Acts in the course of a receivership (or liquidation), the professional body must report the matter to the Director forthwith, giving details of the finding, or, as the case may be, the alleged offence.

8.5　Advising contractors and suppliers

The receiver will examine all outstanding contracts of the company with its suppliers in arriving at his decision whether or not to carry on the business of the company. As the agent of the company, he can enforce an existing contract with the company but cannot be sued by the supplier should he decide not to complete the contract. The supplier would have the right to sue for breach of contract but would rank as an unsecured creditor only in respect of any award made in its favour. In the case of *Airline Airspace Ltd v Handley Page Ltd and Another* [1970] 1 All ER 29, Graham J was of the opinion that a receiver might disregard the contractual obligations of a company over which he was appointed if he could show that in order to fulfil the contractual obligations there would be benefit neither to the company nor to the debentureholder. The receiver, however, does owe a duty to the company not to act recklessly in exposing it to unnecessary claims by his conduct. The court held as follows:

> The receiver, within limit(s) ... is in a better position than the company, qua current contracts ... otherwise almost any unsecured creditor would be able to improve his position and prevent the receiver from carrying out, or at, any rate carrying out as sensibly and as equitably as possible, the purpose for which he was appointed. It would not be inequitable for the receiver to prefer (one contractor) to other secured creditors, and it is in the best interests of all such creditors that he should be able to sell that part of (the company's) business which will constitute a viable unit in the way which will secure the highest price. If, in so doing, he does decline to take over (one) contract, he may, of course, render the (company) liable in damages and may also, to some extent, at any rate, damage their reputation as a trustworthy company which can be expected to honour its contracts. This, however ... he is entitled to do, so long as the realisation of the net assets of the company ... to the best advantage is not impaired.

This case involved a company in receivership which had one valuable asset, namely a design for a plane. The company had a contract with the plaintiffs whereby the plaintiffs were given the exclusive right to sell all aircraft of that design and were to be paid a commission for every aircraft sold. If the design were sold off to the hived down subsidiary, then the plaintiffs would no longer be able to exercise their rights. Accordingly, the plaintiff sought an injunction against the company and it was held that the receiver could not be prevented from carrying out his proposed cause of action on the grounds that a receiver ordinarily cannot be forced to cause the company to perform a pre-receivership contract.

The receiver is, pursuant to the provisions of s 316(2) of CA 1963, deemed to be personally liable on any contract entered into by him unless he specifically excludes personal liability. He is entitled to an indemnity out of the assets of the company coming into his hands.

8.6   Advising creditors

Creditors can be broadly divided into five classes:

(a)   secured creditors;

(b)   special creditors;

(c)   preferential creditors;

(d)   unsecured creditors; and

(e)   judgment creditors.

8.6.1   Secured creditors

Secured creditors are those creditors who have advanced moneys to the company secured over the assets of the company. The debentureholder who appointed the receiver would fall into this category, but the receiver must ensure by carrying out a Companies Office search that there are no other secured creditors with a charge ranking in priority to his own charge. If there are prior charges, the rights of such debentureholders must be recognised by the receiver, even though he has not been appointed by the debentureholder concerned. There may also be a secured creditor with a second fixed charge ranking after the fixed charge for the debentureholder but ahead of his floating charge. Again, the receiver must recognise the rights of such second fixed charge-holder.

8.6.2   Special creditors

Special creditors include hire purchase companies, landlords, public services, general rates and persons holding liens. The hire purchase company's right to repossess its goods means that its claim is in a special position; the receiver must evaluate the equity held by the company under such agreements. In relation to landlords, if there are neither arrears of rent nor breaches of covenant, the landlord is not entitled to terminate a lease upon the appointment of a receiver unless the lease specifically provides that he may do so. Although the receiver is not a party to the lease and not personally liable, he may have to pay rent with arrears and perform necessary obligations if he wishes to avoid forfeiture of the lease. He is not obliged to pay any rent if he considers it advantageous to allow the landlord to forfeit the property: *Hand v Blow* [1901] 2 Ch 721. Although a clause in a lease may provide that the landlord can terminate the lease upon the appointment of a receiver, the latter can usually negotiate with the landlord in order to remain in occupation or dispose of the unexpired term of the lease for the benefit of the debentureholder. If there are arrears of rent, the landlord has the right to distrain on any goods of the company remaining on the premises.

The public services, such as gas, electricity and water supply, are in a special position, as it is usual for the suppliers of such services to threaten to withhold further supplies unless their arrears are paid in full. A receiver is not a new customer with a statutory right to supply if he is acting as agent of the company, although a subsidiary is a new customer and one of the bonuses of hiving down is that, in principle, whatever the reluctance of the utilities may be, the subsidiary is entitled to a supply of gas or electricity. The receiver will usually be asked to give an undertaking to the utility company agreeing to pay arrears (and for the service used by the receiver) upon disposal of the company's assets.

Local authority rates are frequently in arrears when a receiver is appointed. The receiver appointed is a new occupier and therefore not liable to pay arrears of rates except in so far as these are preferential (those which have become due and payable within one year before the date of appointment).

Frequently there will be claims for a lien raised by solicitors and others, and in all cases, the receiver should verify that the lien is valid and examine the conditions of contract incorporating such liens.

8.6.3   Preferential creditors

Section 98 of CA 1963 provides that, on the appointment of a receiver on behalf of the holders of any debenture secured by a floating charge or where a debentureholder enters into possession of property subject to the charge, certain debts are to be paid as preferential. Those are the debts set out in s 285 of CA 1963 (as amended from time to time).

If the receiver is continuing the business of the company, he may require continuing supplies from the company's previous suppliers. In that case, the creditor should ensure that he obtains written confirmation of orders signed by the receiver or an authorised member of his staff so that the receiver is liable personally to pay for any such continuing supplies made after the date of receivership.

8.7   Advising a liquidator appointed to the company

A floating charge created within 12 months prior to the commencement of a winding up is invalid as to any prior advances unless the company was solvent 'immediately' after the creation of the charge (CA 1963, s 288). A company is solvent if it can pay its debts as they fall due (see s 286 of CA 1963 as to fraudulent preference).

8.7.1   Effect of appointment on the receiver

Ordinarily the instrument creating the debenture confers on the holders or their trustees a right to appoint a 'receiver and manager'. A supervening liquidation will not affect their right to appoint. Indeed, that standard form of debenture specifies the presentation of a petition or a resolution for a voluntary liquidation as events which give rise to an immediate liability to repay all outstanding principal and interest and to a right to appoint a receiver and manager. Just as the event of liquidation does not prevent the appointment of a receiver, the appointment of a receiver does not prevent a liquidation.

The commencement of a winding up, in particular the appointment of a liquidator, may deter a potential receiver and manager from accepting a preferred appointment if he has reason to suspect that the charge under which his appointment would be made is in any way vulnerable. The charge may be a fraudulent preference or infringe the statutory provisions restricting the creation of floating charges within a certain period prior to a winding up. It may not have been registered or properly executed or there may be some other flaw.

8.7.2   Effect on receiver's agency

Usually the mortgage debenture provides that a receiver and manager appointed thereunder shall be the agent of the company. A compulsory winding-up order automatically terminates that agency. Likewise, the commencement of a voluntary winding up, by the passing of a resolution to wind up, brings to an end the agency of a receiver and manager. As far as the receiver is concerned, although he retains his right to custody and control over the company's assets, the company whose agent he is no longer has full and free capacity to continue its business in terms of the objects in its memorandum. The company cannot authorise the receiver to do any act which it is unable to do itself, so that it cannot empower the receiver, after the date of the liquidation, to carry on its business so as to create debts provable against the unmortgaged assets of the company; but the receiver can still continue to exercise his powers in the name of the company, although the company is no longer liable for any debts which he may incur in so doing. The agency ends, but not the receivership, and the receiver is still in control. His position is peculiar and made more difficult. He cannot bind the company with fresh obligations. Acting, as he does, as a principal he will be personally liable in respect of contracts, albeit with the right to be indemnified out of the assets of the company. If, despite the termination of his agency, he purports to act in the name of the company, he may be held liable for breach of warranty or authority.

8.7.3   Effect on receiver's powers

While a compulsory winding-up order or the commencement of a voluntary winding up brings to an end the agency of the receiver and manager, some of his powers survive the death of his agency. He may continue to carry on the company's business, although not so as to impose fresh liabilities on the company. He is, of course, entitled to take possession of the assets comprised in the debenture, and so that power remains. He may continue to get in and realise all the company's assets, both real and personal, comprised in the debenture. Again, he retains the power to continue proceedings in the name of the company in order to collect assets of the company comprised in the debenture. The termination of the authority of the receiver to act as agent of the company does not affect his power to hold or dispose of property comprised in the debenture.

Another power, which remains undisturbed by the event of liquidation, is the right of the receiver and manager to retain all documents needed to evidence the title of the debentureholder. If those documents have found their way into the hands of the liquidator, they can be recovered.

8.7.4   Effect on receiver's duties

The receiver is subject to an obligation to deal with preferential creditors in accordance with s 98 of CA 1963.

8.7.5   Floating charges

The priority of charges registered will obviously also be relevant if one is acting not for the receiver but for a party who wishes to challenge the appointment of the receiver or the validity of the debenture under which the receiver is appointed, for example, the company itself or an unsecured creditor of the company or a liquidator of the company. Since the facts may, however, be difficult to check without winding up the company such person may also have to consider liquidating the company and this will definitely be necessary if one wishes to be able to invoke the provisions of s 288 of CA 1963 (as amended), which provides:

> Where a company is being wound up, a floating charge on the undertaking or property of the company created within 12 months before the commencement of the winding up shall, unless it is proved that the company immediately after the creation of the charge was solvent, be invalid, except as to money actually advanced or paid, or the actual price or value of goods or services sold or supplied, to the company at the time of or subsequently to the creation of, and in consideration for, the charge, together with interest on that amount at the rate of 5 per cent per annum.

For the purposes of s 288(1), the value of any goods or services sold or supplied by way of consideration for a floating charge is the amount in money which at the time they were sold or supplied could reasonably have been expected to be obtained for the goods or services, in the ordinary course of business, and on the same terms (apart from the consideration) as those on which they were sold or supplied to the company.

Where a floating charge on the undertaking or property of a company is created in favour of a connected person, s 288(1) shall apply to such a charge as if the period of 12 months mentioned in that subsection were a period of two years.

8.7.6   Connected persons

In s 288 of CA 1963 'a connected person' means a person who, at the time the transaction was made, was:

(a)   a director of the company;

(b)   a shadow director of the company;

(c)   a person connected, within the meaning of s 26(1)(a) of the Companies Act 1990, with a director;

(d)   a related company, within the meaning of s 140 of the Companies Act 1990; or

(e)   any trustee of, or any surety or guarantor for the debt due to, any person described in paragraph (a), (b), (c) or (d).

Section 288 of CA 1963 does not avoid the debt itself so that the debentureholder can still prove in the winding up as an unsecured creditor for a debt incurred before the floating charge was given to secure it, or for interest in excess of five per cent.

When a floating charge is invalidated by the company being wound up, the charge is invalidated for all purposes so that mortgagees and others may assert rights against property subject to the floating charge and thus prevent the liquidator from taking it for the benefit of the unsecured creditors of the company (*Capital Finance Ltd v Stokes* [1968] IR 573).

8.7.7   Time of creation of the charge

It should be noted that the courts have liberally construed the requirement that the loan should be made at the time of or subsequently to the creation of the floating charge so as to uphold it in the company's liquidation. If a loan is made on the understanding that a floating charge will be given as security, the charge is taken as being created at the time the loan is made even though the debenture is not actually executed until some time after the lender advances his money, provided the company's promise to give the floating charge is unconditional (*Re Columbian Fireproofing Ltd* [1910] 2 IR 120; *Re FE Staunton* (No 2) [1929] 1 ER 180).

The section will not apply if the debentureholder can prove that the company was solvent immediately after the creation of the charge. It has been held that a company is not solvent at the time unless it is able to pay its debts as they fall due (*Re Patrick and Lyon Ltd* [1933] Ch 786 1). Therefore, the mere fact that the value of its assets exceeds its total liabilities does not necessarily mean that the company is solvent.

8.7.8   Rule in *Clayton's Case*

Note the application of the rule in *Clayton's Case* [1816] 1 Mer 572 if a company goes into liquidation within 12 months of the creation of a floating charge. All moneys paid into the company's bank account after the floating charge is executed are deemed to have been appropriated to reduce the debt outstanding at the time of execution, and all subsequent drawings amount to new lendings secured by the charge. Therefore, if the amount so paid in equals or exceeds the debt outstanding at the time of execution, the charge will be fully effective (*Re Thos Mortimer Ltd* (1925) [1965] 1 Ch 187 and *Re Yeovil Glove* [1965] Ch 148.

8.7.9   Fraudulent preference

Under the provisions of s 286 of CA 1963, any mortgage, debenture or other act created or done within six months before commencement of its winding up which would in the case of an individual be void as a fraudulent preference in bankruptcy is likewise void in the event of the company being wound up, but there can be great difficulty in successfully invoking this section as it is necessary that the mortgage, debenture or other act was entered into with a view to preferring the mortgagee over other creditors.

However, it may now be easier for a liquidator to prove fraudulent preference than it has been in the past, in view of the decision in *Re FP and CH Matthers Ltd* [1982] 1 All ER 339. Here, the Court of Appeal held that a payment was made with a view to giving a creditor preference over the other creditors within the meaning of s 44 of the Bankruptcy Act 1914 if at the time of making the payment the debtor knew that he could not pay his debts as they arose and intended to pay one of his creditors in full ahead of the others; it was not sufficient for a debtor to genuinely believe that all the creditors would be paid three to six months in the future.

There is no fraudulent preference if the mortgage is not given voluntarily. If the company pays a debt under the threat of legal proceedings, there is no preference, but a company cannot be said to discharge an obligation under the threat of legal proceedings when the obligation is owed to its own directors. Where the directors benefit from a transaction, the court is more willing to infer an improper motive. An improper motive was inferred when directors who had guaranteed the company's bank overdraft repaid it at a time when they knew the company was insolvent and when they had already stopped paying its current trading debts (*Re M Kushler Ltd* [1943] 2 Ch 481) and similarly a mortgage of the company's property which the directors gave to themselves as an indemnity against their liability under their guarantee of the company's overdraft was held to be a fraudulent preference (*Gaslight Improvement v Terrell* [1870] LR 10 EG 168). See **10.4** for further discussion of fraudulent preferences.

The result of a transaction being held to be a fraudulent preference is that the liquidator may recover the money paid or property transferred to the creditor, or have any mortgage or charge given to him set aside. The money or property recovered is distributable among the creditors of the company generally and the holder of a floating charge on the company's undertaking has no prior charge on it.

Note: since the Companies Act 1990, it is open to a liquidator to apply under s 322 of CA 1963 (as amended by s 176 of the Companies Act 1990) to limit or bring to an end a receivership. The liquidator can also seek the co-operation of the lender to have the receiver removed without the necessity for a court application.

8.8   Advising directors

8.8.1   Directors' statement of affairs

The provisions which govern the statement of affairs are ss 319–20 of CA 1963. Section 319 of CA 1963 requires the directors to submit a statement of affairs of the company, in the prescribed form, to the receiver within 14 days after the receipt by the company of notice of appointment of the receiver. Frequently, the directors will turn to their solicitor for advice in relation to completing such a statement and if they fail to complete it, they are liable to a fine. The values attributed to assets of the company should be modestly valued, as the statement would be filed in the Companies Office and would be available to creditors of the company in the event of a liquidation taking place. The directors are entitled to their costs for the preparation of the statement of affairs from the receiver.

The receiver, within two months of receipt of the statement of affairs, has to send a copy of it and of any comments he sees fit to make on it to the Registrar of Companies, to the company, to any trustees for the debentureholders on whose behalf he was appointed, to the debentureholders and to the court if he was appointed by the court.

Section 320 of CA 1963 provides that the statement of affairs must show as at the date of the receiver's appointment particulars of the company's assets, debts and liabilities names and residences of this creditors, and information about their securities. The statement of affairs is to be submitted by, and verified by affidavit of, one or more of the directors and by the secretary or by such other persons named in the section as a receiver may require. The receiver, out of his receipts, has to allow the reasonable costs and expenses incurred in preparing the statement of affairs.

8.8.2   Suspension of powers

Directors have no ongoing say in the business and are not removed. They are in effect in a limbo situation. In considering the effect of a receivership on the powers of directors, it is important to bear in mind the distinction between a receiver on the one hand, and a receiver and manager on the other. A receiver appointed over a specific property of the company has no power of management of the company's business and accordingly the management powers remain with the directors. A receiver and manager appointed under the terms of a floating charge has considerable powers of management but, since a company cannot be managed by two different and conflicting managements, it is the management by the receiver which prevails. However, the appointment of a receiver and manager does not remove all the functions of the directors and they have some continuing powers and duties. For example, their statutory duties in relation to the preparation of annual accounts, the auditing of those accounts and calling of statutory meetings with shareholders, maintaining the Share Register and lodging of returns remain. Indeed, the directors can start proceedings in the name of the company without the receiver's consent, as happened in the case of *Newhart Developments Ltd* v *Co-operative Commercial Bank Ltd* [1978] QB 814 and a similar challenge was mounted in *Irish Oil and Cake Milk Ltd* (High Court, 27 March 1984).

8.8.3   Proceedings

With the consent of the receiver, the directors may defend proceedings brought against the company. The receiver may in many cases have no interest in defending such proceedings as the plaintiff may be an unsecured creditor only and accordingly not of concern to the receiver.

8.9   Advising shareholders/guarantors

There is little or no effect on shareholders and guarantors. Their rights are unchallenged. Frequently the directors and/or the shareholders will have issued personal guarantees to the debentureholder and it is very important to them that the receiver obtain the best possible price for the assets of the company so as to minimise their liability. The receiver's duty is to obtain the best price bearing in mind his liability to guarantors of the company and possibly even to ordinary creditors for negligent mishandling of a sale of the company's property. This liability has been acknowledged in the case of *Standard Chartered Bank Ltd v Walker* [1982] 3 All ER 938. This case underlines the importance of the receiver obtaining professional advice to confirm the reasonableness of the price at which he proposes to sell the company's assets; if the receiver has a particular concern, he is at liberty to apply to the High Court for directions pursuant to s 316 of CA 1963.

8.10   Advising employees

The appointment of a receiver out of court by the debentureholders does not terminate contracts of employment except where the continuation of the employment of some particular employee would be inconsistent with the receivership itself. For example, it has been held that the appointment of a full-time receiver would automatically terminate the contract of a managing director (*Griffiths* v *Secretary of State for Social Services* [1974] QB 468).

If the receiver proposes to sell any part of the company's business, he must abide by the provisions of the European Communities (Protection of Employees' Rights on Transfer of Undertakings) Regulations 2003 (SI 131/2003), which implemented Council Directive No 2001/23/EC of 12 March 2001 on the approximation of the laws of the Member States relating to the safeguarding of employees' rights in the event of transfers of undertakings, businesses or parts of undertakings or businesses (as amended). These require him, *inter alia*, to consult with and inform employees' representatives.

In addition, he is bound to observe the consultation and notification procedures prescribed by the Protection of Employment Act 1977, as amended by the Protection of Employment Order 1996 (SI 370/1996); the Protection of Employment Act 1977 (Notification of Proposed Collective Redundancies) Regulations 1977 (SI 140/1977); and the European Communities (Protection of Employment) Regulations 2000 (SI 488/2000) particularly if collective redundancies are anticipated. A receiver appointed out of court does not incur any personal responsibility for employees since, for example, if the receiver dismisses an employee, he will be deemed as doing so as agent of the company except to the extent that he might have renewed the contract of employment or made a fresh one or has not disclaimed personal responsibility under s 316(2). Section 316(2) provides that a receiver of the property of a company is personally liable on any contract (including an employment contract) entered into by him in the performance of his functions, whether or not the contract is entered into by him in the name of the company or in his own name as receiver or otherwise, unless the contract specifically provides that he is not to be personally liable. The subsection also provides that the receiver is entitled to an indemnity out of the assets of the company in respect of that liability. A receiver who is appointed by the court is substituted as an employer and therefore becomes personally responsible and liable for all the usual consequences of a dismissal of an employee.

If the receiver is appointed under a debenture, this has no effect on the employees, as the receiver is the agent of the company. The recent EAT decision of *McCarthy v Mooreview Developments Ltd* re-affirmed that a receiver must take account of employee rights when making redundancies. If the receiver is court-appointed, employees' contracts are terminated.

8.10.1   Receiver appointed under a debenture

If the receiver is appointed under a debenture, it does not affect the employees, as the receiver is the agent of the company. If the receiver is court-appointed, contracts are terminated. The rights of employees are a matter of great importance both to the employees concerned and to the receiver. The receiver should decide as soon as possible whether he wishes to continue the employees' contracts or dismiss them. Dismissal by a receiver amounts to redundancy, and the employee will seek the necessary forms from the receiver to enable him to obtain payment from the Redundancy Fund operated by the Minister for Labour (see the Protection of Employment (Employers' Insolvency) Acts 1984–2001, which derive from a European Directive of 1980 relating to the protection of employees in the event of the insolvency of their employer). The receiver must be careful, if he continues the employment of the company's employees, that he does not take any action in relation to those contracts which would lead to the contract being deemed a new contract for which the receiver would be personally liable.

The general rule is that the appointment of a receiver who is the agent of the company does not of itself automatically terminate contracts of employment: *Re Foster Parks Ltd Indenture Trusts* [1966] 1 WLR 125. The rule also was applied in *Re Mack Trucks (Britain) Ltd* [1976] 1 All ER 977. This is in contrast to the position on the appointment of a liquidator. However, there are certain exceptions; for example, in the case of a sale or hiving down of the business or if the receiver enters into a new agreement with a particular employee which is inconsistent with the old agreement or where the continuation of the employee's services is inconsistent with the role and functions of the receiver.

8.10.2   Action against the receiver

One potential remedy that any dismissed employee should consider is his remedy for wrongful dismissal. If the dismissal amounts to a repudiation of his contract, there is a civil remedy in damages, although this remedy may be rather academic if the company is insolvent. However, the remedy can be of value if the receiver on his own personal responsibility has retained the employee and then wrongfully dismissed him, as the receiver can then be sued personally.

The question of whether an employee can take action for unfair dismissal, because he has been unfairly selected for redundancy or been dismissed as a result of a transfer of a business or because the company has failed to observe the statutory consultation periods, depends on whether the receiver can demonstrate that the dismissal was for 'economic, technical or organisational reasons entailing changes in the work-force'.

8.10.3   Preferential payments

Remuneration and other awards due to employees when a company goes into receivership have preferential status under s 285 of CA 1963 and the Redundancy Payments Acts; preferential status is, however, limited to a maximum payment of €3,174 per claimant in respect of wages and holiday pay for each employee, plus their redundancy entitlement. Directors' fees, *per se*, are not preferential. Items such as VHI, and union or savings deductions can be preferential in so far as they fall within the €3,174 amount.

The best course for a receiver who wishes some or all of the employees to continue is to go on making payments of wages, salaries etc, under their existing contracts. If he does not need their services, he should inform them that money is not available to continue payment of their remuneration and they should regard their employment contracts as terminated. This will reduce the risk of the receiver becoming personally liable for redundancy payments, unfair dismissal and other claims. If the receiver finds it essential to change any of the contracts of employment in ways that may amount to adopting them, to re-engage employees or to engage new employees, he should always try to do so as agent for the company and on the basis that his personal liability is expressly excluded (*Re Mack Trucks (Britain) Ltd* [1976] 1 All ER 977).

8.10.4   Continuity/transfer of employment

It should be noted that the appointment of the receiver or even his personally entering into fresh contracts of employment with the employees does not of itself constitute a break in the continuity of employment for the purpose of calculating redundancy payments.

A purchaser of the business from the receiver will wish to know that the receiver has made all employees redundant prior to taking over the business to ensure that there is a break in service, so that the purchaser does not inherit lengthy periods of service giving rise to substantial redundancy payment claims in the future. Where the receiver has hived down the business of the company to a subsidiary company there will be a continuity of employment if the subsidiary company has adopted the contracts of employment. Such hive down operations are particularly subject to Council Directive 2001/23/EC of 12 March 2001 and to the European Communities (Protection of Employees' Rights on Transfer of Undertakings) Regulations 2003 (SI 131/2003). The purpose of the regulations is to safeguard employees' rights in the event of a transfer of undertakings, businesses and parts of businesses. This is achieved by providing that on a relevant transfer of a business all the rights and obligations of employment contracts are automatically transferred.

8.11   Sale of the company/assets by a receiver

The power to sell is one of the standard powers conferred on a receiver (and manager). The need for a conveyancing power is a consequence of the nature of a floating charge. The full nature and extent of the power of sale is considered at **7.4.3**.

8.11.1   Hive down

It is possible that some portion of the company's business is viable and if that is the case then the receiver should consider selling off that part of the business by means of what is commonly referred to as a 'hive down'. Part or the entire successful/viable portion of the business would be transferred to a new company, which would be controlled by the receiver. The shares in the new company would then be sold in the expectation that a far better price would be obtained by this means rather than by a straightforward sale of the assets. Essentially the receiver would be selling a business rather than selling assets. It is not unusual to find that the purchasers of the shares in such circumstances would be former employees or executives of the company.

There are certain advantages to be gained by such a course of action. If the assets are transferred into a new company, which is controlled by the receiver and the trading is done by that company, then the receiver could not be held personally liable on any contracts entered into by that company in the course of the business. Those contracts would be binding on the hive down company and not on the receiver. The profitable assets of the company, along with tax losses, could be transferred into the new company, making it a very attractive purchase proposition. The hive down, unless it commences trading, will not have any debts of its own and will not be responsible for the old company's debts and liabilities. A case in point would be that of *Airline Airspace Ltd v Handley Page Ltd* [1970] 1 Ch 193.

If the entire business of the company is hived down, then the employees of the company are treated as having been dismissed. If the hive down of the company's business is of only a part of the business, it depends on the circumstances whether particular employees' contracts have been determined.

8.12   Checklist for assessing the validity of an appointment

The following documentation should be checked when assessing the validity of appointment:

(a)   Memorandum and Articles of Association (powers to borrow/give security?);
(b)   debentures (creates the charge?);
(c)   minutes authorising securities;
(d)   Form C1;
(e)   certificate of registration (issued by Registrar?);
(f)   letter of demand (usual, before appointment of receiver. Valid demand? Precondition to appointment?); and
(g)   the debenture deed.

Check the following:
>   date of deed;
>   stamp duty paid;
>   registration date;
>   nature of specific security;
>   power to appoint receiver;
>   circumstances when exercisable; and
>   nature of receiver's power.

8.13   Checklist of practical points to consider when advising the potential receiver

Some practical points for consideration when advising the potential receiver are:

(a)   scope of the proposed appointment;
(b)   type of business involved and assets owed;
(c)   other secured creditors, and whether there is any agreement between them;
(d)   validity of appointment;
(e)   reservation of title claims;
(f)   hire purchase and/or leasing agreements;
(g)   insurance arrangements;
(h)   stock levels (particularly relevant if business is continuing); and
(i)   number of employees' and whether they can/should be retained.

8.14   Checklist when purchasing from liquidator or receiver

What special documents should be insisted upon when purchasing from a receiver or liquidator of a company? The proper standard of practice from a conveyancing point of view is set out in the following sections.

8.14.1   Liquidator

(a)   Court liquidation:
  (i)   Official copy of winding-up order of High Court.
  (ii)   Ensure that court order contains appointment of liquidator. If not, copy of order of such appointment should be obtained.
  (iii)   Confirmation as to whether application made for order for sale. If so, obtain copy of such order.
(b)   Creditors' liquidation:
  (i)   Copy of ordinary resolution of company as to winding up as filed in the Companies Office.
  (ii)   Copy of resolution appointing liquidator.
  (iii)   Copy of notice of appointment of liquidator with his endorsed acceptance of appointment as filed in the Companies Office.
  (iv)   If directors are to be joined in sale, copy of authority of Committee of Inspection sanctioning the continuance of the powers of the directors (CA 1963, s 269(3)).
(c)   Members' liquidation:
  (i)   Copy of special resolution of company as to winding up as filed in the Companies Office.
  (ii)   Copy of resolution of company appointing liquidator.

(iii) Copy of notices of appointment of liquidator with his endorsed acceptance of appointment as filed in the Companies Office.

(iv) If directors are joining in the sale, obtain copy of liquidator's authority sanctioning the continuance of the powers of directors (s 258(2) of CA 1963).

8.14.2 Receiver

(a) Unregistered land:

(i) Satisfactory documentary evidence that the right to appoint receiver has arisen, for example, that demand has been made but not met.

(ii) Certified copy of appointment of receiver.

(iii) Original mortgage if all property in mortgage being released, or

(iv) Certified copy of mortgage if only partial release. A plain copy is never sufficient.

(v) Original release (and memorial) duly executed by bank and stamped (or cheque to cover it).

(b) Registered land:

(i) Satisfactory documentary evidence that the right to appoint receiver has arisen, for example that demand has been made but not met.

(ii) Certified copy of appointment of receiver.

(iii) Original instrument creating charge is fully discharged.

(iv) Certified copy of instrument creating charge together with undertaking that original charge will be lodged in the Land Registry for the purpose of the dealing.

(v) Original deed of discharge duly executed by bank and stamped.

(vi) Original certificate of charge either to be handed over or lodged in Land Registry depending on whether full or partial release.

(vii) Letter addressed to Land Registry from party which originally lodged dealing in Land Registry that returnable documents should be sent to purchaser's solicitor on completion of dealing.

Other than those set out above, the normal requirements as to documentation and searches apply. It should be noted that where the mortgage or debenture affects lands other than the subject of the purchase, it is unnecessary to require an undertaking for production, safe custody or delivery of copies.

8.14.3 Execution of documents

As to the execution of documents the following rules apply:

(a) Liquidator:

The liquidator takes over the function of the directors and accordingly the execution of a Deed of Assurance by a company in liquidation should be effected by the affixing of the company seal, which should be attested by the signature of the liquidator. The liquidator should also be joined in the Deed and executed as liquidator to confirm the sale.

(b) Receiver:

The receiver acts on behalf of the company and normally with the benefit of a power of attorney contained in the instrument under which he is appointed and signs the Deed of Assurance as attorney for the company.

One should check that the company is in receivership and that the required power to give a power of attorney exists and that such power of attorney was contained in the instrument under which the receiver is appointed. If any of the elements is missing, then the company and its directors must execute in the normal fashion, or the bank must convey as mortgagees.

CHAPTER 9

ALTERNATIVES TO WINDING UP

Doug Smith

In this chapter, references to 'the Act' are references to the Companies (Amendment) Act 1990 (as amended by ss 180 and 181 of the Companies Act 1990 and as amended by the Companies (Amendment) (No 2) Act 1999).

This chapter focuses on the formal statutory alternatives to winding up. However it should be noted that it is possible for an insolvent company to reach an arrangement or agreement with its creditors on a voluntary basis without resorting to the statutory alternatives to winding up. This is often referred to as a voluntary arrangement. Such an arrangement is predominantly a matter of contract law. All creditors affected must agree to the company's proposal. It will usually involve creditors agreeing to accept a lesser sum than they are due and/or the payment of that liability over an extended period. Such arrangements are rarely a viable option and can be extremely difficult to manage to a successful conclusion. Some of the key ingredients in a successful voluntary arrangement are:

(a)   that there are a limited number of creditors involved;

(b)   that the incumbent executives are credible and enjoy good relations with the company's creditors; and

(c)   the availability of sufficient resources to fund an acceptable dividend for the creditors.

A further point to note in this regard is that the Revenue Commissioners do not have power to voluntarily forgo their preferential status. Companies in financial difficulties often have large preferential liabilities and this may impact on the company's ability to fund a voluntary arrangement.

9.1   Examinerships

9.1.1   Who may present a petition

When advising a client who wishes to present a petition for the appointment of an examiner, the first thing which the solicitor must consider is whether or not that party has the requisite capacity to present a petition under the Act. Section 3(1) of the Act provides that a petition for the appointment of an examiner under s 2 of the Act may be presented by:

(a)   the company;

(b)   the directors of the company;

(c)   a creditor, including a contingent or prospective creditor (including an employee), of the company; or

(d)   shareholders holding not less than one-tenth of shares carrying the power to vote at general meetings at the time of presentation of the petition.

The above parties may present a petition together or separately. Section 3(2) contains particular provisions dealing with insurers, banks and building societies which should be referred to if necessary. Section 3(5) provides that where a petition is presented by a contingent or prospective creditor the court will not give the petition a hearing until such time as security for costs is given.

9.1.2   The petition

As soon as a petition for the appointment of an examiner is presented in the Central Office of the High Court, the company is under protection pursuant to the Act. The extent of that protection is discussed below.

Firstly, the nature and form of the petition is dealt with here. Section 3(3) provides that a petition shall nominate a person to be appointed examiner. Section 3(3A) provides that the petition shall be accompanied by the report of an independent accountant. In the absence of an independent accountant's report, an application to court for protection is necessary.

The Act provides that the independent accountant is somebody who is either the auditor of the company or a person who is qualified to be appointed as an examiner of the company. In *Tuskar Resources plc* [2001] IR 668, the question of whether or not the independent accountant can then become the examiner was considered by the court. It had been argued that an independent accountant would not be 'independent' if the purpose of his report was to determine whether he personally should or should not be appointed to the position of examiner. Mr Justice McCracken indicated that:

> In view of the fact that the legislature did not take on itself to prohibit the independent
> accountant from acting as Examiner, I do not think that there is any statutory restriction on
> the court in so appointing him, although I can see there may be cases where it would be
> undesirable to do so.

Thus whilst it is possible that the independent accountant might also be the nominee as examiner, it is preferable that this is not the case. In this regard see the comments of Costello J in *Re Wogan's (Drogheda) Limited* (High Court, 9 February 1993) where the requirement of independence on the part of the examiner was emphasised.

Section 3(3B) of the Act details the fundamental requirements in respect of the contents of the report of the independent accountant. The report of the independent accountant must, at a minimum, contain the following:

(a)   the names and addresses of the officers of the company, including shadow directors;

(b)   the names of any other bodies corporate of which the directors of the company are directors;

(c)   a statement of affairs of the company, which includes, where reasonably possible, the company's assets and liabilities (including contingent and prospective liabilities) as at the latest possible date and the names and addresses of its creditors, the securities held by them and the dates when such securities were given by the company;

(d)   his opinion that any deficiency between the assets and liabilities has been satisfactorily accounted for or, if not, whether there is evidence of a substantial disappearance of property that is not adequately accounted for;

(e)   his opinion as to whether the company, and the whole or any part of its undertaking, would have a reasonable prospect of survival as a going concern and a statement of the conditions necessary to ensure such survival, whether as regards the internal management and controls of the company or otherwise;

(f)   his opinion as to whether the formulation, acceptance and confirmation of proposals for a compromise or scheme of arrangement would offer a reasonable prospect of the survival of the company, and the whole or any part of its undertaking, as a going concern;

(g)   his opinion as to whether an attempt to continue the whole or any part of the undertaking would be likely to be more advantageous to the members and creditors as a whole than a winding up of the company;

(h)   recommendations as to the course he thinks should be taken including, if warranted, draft proposals for a compromise or scheme of arrangement;

(i)   his opinion as to whether further enquiries are warranted with a view to proceedings under ss 297 or 297A of CA 1963;

(j)   details of any funding requirements for the protection period and the source of those funds;

(k)   his recommendations as to which pre-petition liabilities should be paid;

(l)   his opinion as to whether the examiner would be assisted by a direction of the court in relation to the role or membership of any creditors' committee referred to in s 21 of the Act; and

(m)   anything else he considers relevant.

The report of the independent accountant is fundamental to the presentation of the petition. The importance of the report of the independent accountant will be explored further below in the context of the petitioner discharging the onus of proof that the company has a reasonable prospect of survival. Section 3A of the Act provides for interim protection pending the independent accountant's report for a period of ten days, in exceptional circumstances outside the control of the petitioner. Thus, in circumstances where a petition is presented in the absence of an independent accountant's report, the company is not under protection unless the court makes an order to that effect. This section provides that the court may make an order placing the company concerned under protection for such period as it thinks appropriate in order to allow for submission of the independent accountant's report. But this interim protection period shall expire not later than the tenth day after the making of the order unless that day falls on a Saturday, Sunday or Public Holiday, in which case it will expire on the first following day that is not a Saturday, Sunday or Public Holiday. It should be noted that the fact that a receiver stands appointed shall not, in itself, constitute exceptional circumstances outside the control of the petitioner. Section 3A(8) provides that any liabilities incurred by the company during this period of interim protection pending delivery of the independent accountant's report may not be the subject of a certificate under s 10(2) of the Act.

Order 75A, r 4(3) of the Rules of the Superior Courts 1986 (RSC) provides that the petition shall comply with s 3(3) of the Act and shall also, in so far as applicable, comply with Form No 2 in Appendix M of the RSC.

Thus, the petition must state the following:

(a)   name and address of the petitioner;

(b)   capacity of the petitioner;

(c)   date of incorporation of the company in question;

(d)   registered office of the company in question;

(e)   nominal and paid-up share capital of the company in question; and

(f)   objects of the company in question.

In addition, s 2 of the Act provides that the petition must show that:

(a)   the company is or is likely to be unable to pay its debts;

(b)   no resolution subsists for the winding up of the company; and

(c)   no order has been made for the winding up of the company.

9.1.3   Affidavit verifying contents of petition

RSC Ord 75A, r 4(3) provides that the petition must be verified by affidavit. There is no particular form in the RSC for the verifying affidavit, but usually it would restate in more detail the contents of the petition.

9.1.4   Duty to act in good faith

It is imperative that the petition and verifying affidavit contain all matters which are material to the court's consideration of the application. In addition to the general obligation to act with utmost good faith in ex parte applications, s 4A of the Act contains a statutory duty to act in good faith. That section states as follows:

> The court may decline to hear a petition ... or, as the case may be, may decline to continue hearing such a petition if it appears to the court that, in the preparation or presentation of the petition or in the preparation of the report of the independent accountant, the petitioner or independent accountant:
>
> (a)   has failed to disclose any information available to him which is material to the exercise by the court of its powers ... ; or
>
> (b)   has in any other way failed to exercise utmost good faith.

9.1.5   Application for directions and the appointment of an interim examiner

RSC Ord 75A, r 4(4) provides that a petitioner shall, on the same day as the presentation of the petition, make an application to the court for directions. RSC Ord 75A, r 5(1) provides that the court may make such order or orders as it thinks fit and may give such directions as it thinks fit. In particular, RSC Ord 75A, r 5(1) indicates that the court may give directions as to the parties on whom the petition should be served, the mode of service, the time for such service, the date for the hearing of the petition (if different to that appointed by the Registrar) and whether the said petition should be advertised and directions as to the mode of such advertising. RSC Ord 75A, r 5(2) provides that the court may appoint any proposed examiner as interim examiner with the same powers and duties in relation to the company until such time as the hearing of the petition or such other adjourned date. In most cases the petitioner will apply for the appointment of an interim examiner. Generally, the reason for this is that the time period within which the examiner must complete his task (70 days – which may be extended by a further 30 days in certain circumstances) is relatively short and runs from the date of presentation of the petition as opposed to the date of hearing of the petition. Thus, it makes sense for the examiner to begin his task as soon as possible.

9.1.6   The effect of presenting a petition

Section 5(1) of the Act provides that for a period of 70 days from the date of presentation of the petition, which period may be extended by a further 30 days by s 18(3) of the Act, the company shall be deemed to be under protection. In essence, creditors are prevented from taking the type of action that we might normally expect.

Section 5(2) of the Act goes into some considerable detail in setting out the manner in which creditors' remedies are curtailed during the period of protection, as follows:

(a) no proceedings for the winding up of the company may be commenced or resolution for winding up passed in relation to that company and any resolution so passed shall be of no effect (even if a petition for winding up has been presented or a meeting of members convened for the purpose of passing a resolution to wind up and appoint a liquidator to the company);

(b) no receiver may be appointed;

(c) no attachment, sequestration, distress or execution shall be put into force against the property or effects of the company, unless permitted by the examiner;

(d) where any claim against the company is secured by a mortgage, charge, lien or other encumbrance or pledge, on or affecting the whole or any part of the property, effects or income of the company, no action may be taken to realise the whole or any part of that security, except where permitted by the examiner;

(e) no steps may be taken to repossess goods in the company's possession under any hire-purchase agreement except where permitted by the examiner. It should be noted that the definition of a 'hire-purchase agreement' includes a conditional sale agreement, a retention of title agreement and an agreement for the bailment of goods which is capable of subsisting for more than three months;

(f) where any third party (being any person other than the company) is liable to pay all or any part of the debts of the company none of the above-mentioned actions may be taken against that third party and no proceedings of any sort may be commenced against that party in respect of the debts of the company; and

(g) no order pursuant to s 205 can be made by the court.

Previously, the Act provided that no set off between separate bank accounts of the company could be effected except with the consent of the examiner. The Amendment Act of 1999 deletes this provision. Thus, it would seem logical that set off between separate bank accounts of a company is permitted, even though the company may be under protection.

In addition, no other proceedings in relation to the company may be commenced without leave of the court and subject to such terms as the court may wish to impose. Further, the court has discretion to make such order as it thinks proper in relation to any existing proceedings including an order staying such proceedings, upon the application of the examiner.

9.1.7   The effect of presenting a petition on a receiver

Where a receiver has been appointed to the company for a continuous period of at least three days prior to the presentation of the petition, then the court may not hear a petition for the appointment of an examiner (s 3(6) of the Act). Where a receiver has been appointed for a period of less than three days and an examiner is appointed, the court may make such order as it thinks fit including an order as to any or all of the following matters:

(a) that the receiver should cease to act from a date specified by the court;

(b) that the receiver shall, from a date specified by the court, act only in respect of certain assets specified by the court;

(c)   directing the receiver to deliver all books, papers and other records, which relate to the property or undertaking of the company (or any part thereof) and are in his possession or control, to the examiner within a period to be specified by the court; or

(d)   directing the receiver to give the examiner full particulars of all his dealings with the property or undertaking of the company.

Section 98 of CA 1963 provides that a receiver appointed on foot of a floating charge must discharge preferential payments as would be required in a winding up. Section 6A of the Act provides that the court may make an order restraining a receiver from making payments to preferential creditors in circumstances where an examiner has been appointed, or has not but in the opinion of the court may yet be appointed, and where the making of such an order is likely to facilitate the survival of the company. Such an order may only be made where the preferential creditors are given an opportunity to be heard.

It should be noted that the Act is silent in relation to whether the three-day period mentioned above includes non-working days, and as insolvency assignments have a habit of arriving at 5 pm on a Thursday evening it should be presumed that non-working days are included in the calculation of this three-day period.

9.1.8   Effect of the appointment of an examiner where a provisional liquidator stands appointed

Where a provisional liquidator stands appointed and the court makes an order appointing an examiner, the court may make similar orders to those which it may make where a receiver stands appointed for a period of less than three days. However, in addition, the court may order that the provisional liquidator be appointed as examiner.

9.1.9   Appointment

Section 2(2) of the Act (as amended by s 5 of the Companies (Amendment) (No 2) Act 1999) significantly changes the test which the court must apply in determining whether or not to appoint an examiner pursuant to s 2 of the Act. The amended section provides as follows:

> The court shall not make an order under this section unless it is satisfied that there is a reasonable prospect of the survival of the company and the whole or any part of its undertaking as a going concern.

Previously, the court had considerably more discretion in arriving at its decision as to whether or not to appoint an examiner. McCracken J, in his decisions in relation to *Circle Network (Europe) Ltd* (15 February 2001) and *Tuskar Resources plc* [2001] IR 668, considered at length the effect of the above amendment on the court's discretion in this regard. Consequently, the petition must show evidence that there is a reasonable prospect of survival.

The Supreme Court in *In the matter of Vantive Holdings* [2009] IESC 68 considered what was necessary in order to satisfy the court that there is a reasonable prospect of survival. In that decision Murray CJ stated that:

> In order to be satisfied that a company has a reasonable prospect of survival as a going concern the court must have before it sufficient evidence or material which will permit it to arrive at such a conclusion on the basis of an objective appraisal of that evidence or material. Mere assertions on behalf a petitioner that a company has a reasonable prospect of survival as a going concern cannot be given significant weight unless it is supported by

an objective appraisal of the circumstances of the company concerned and an objective rationale as to the manner in which the company can be reasonably expected to overcome the insolvency in which it finds itself and survive as a going concern.

If the court is satisfied that there is a reasonable prospect of survival, then the court has discretion to appoint the examiner. In *Re Gallium Limited* [2009] 2 ILRM 11 Fennelly J stated that:

> The entire purpose of examinership is to make it possible to rescue companies in difficulty. The protection period is there to facilitate examination of the prospects of rescue. However, that protection may prejudice the interests of some creditors. The court will weigh the existence and degree of any such prejudice in the balance. It will have regard to the report of the independent accountant.

In *Re Traffic Group Limited* [2008] 2 ILRM 1 Clarke J stated that:

> it is clear that the principal focus of the legislation is to enable, in an appropriate case, an enterprise to continue an existence for the benefit of the economy as a whole and, of equal, or indeed greater, importance to enable as many as possible of the jobs which may be at stake in such enterprise to be maintained for the benefit of the community in which relevant employment is located. It is important both for the court and, indeed, for examiners, to keep in mind that such is the focus of the legislation. It is not designed to help shareholders whose investment has proved to be unsuccessful. It is to seek to save the enterprise and jobs.

Thus the court first has to consider whether or not the petitioner has discharged the onus of proof that the company in question has a reasonable prospect of survival. Assuming the court is so satisfied then certain discretionary factors may be taken into account by the court in determining whether an examiner should be appointed. Where the court appoints an examiner, s 4 also gives the court jurisdiction to appoint the examiner to be the examiner of a related company. In these circumstances, the related company is also deemed to be under the protection of the court. For a consideration of the courts' jurisdiction to appoint an examiner to a related company, see the decision of the High Court in *Tuskar Resources plc* [2001] IR 668.

9.1.10 Notification of appointment

Section 12 of the Act sets out notification obligations in this regard, which are as follows:

(a) notice of the petition must be delivered by the petitioner to the Registrar of Companies within three days of its presentation;

(b) notice of appointment as examiner must be published by him in two daily newspapers within three days after appointment;

(c) notice of appointment as examiner must be published by him in *Iris Oifigiúil* within 21 days after appointment;

(d) within three days after his appointment, the Examiner shall deliver a copy of the court order appointing him to the Registrar of Companies; and

(e) where a company is under the protection of the court, every invoice, order for goods or business letter issued by or on behalf of the company shall include the words 'In Examination (under the Companies (Amendment) Act 1990)' immediately after the name of the company.

Failure to comply with these provisions is an offence and a person guilty of such an offence shall be liable to fines not exceeding the euro equivalent of £1,000 on summary conviction and the euro equivalent of £10,000 on conviction on indictment.

9.1.11   Examiner's powers

Section 7 of the Act enumerates some of the Examiner's powers as follows:

(a) the Examiner has the same rights and powers which an auditor has in relation to the supplying of information and co-operation;

(b) the Examiner has the power to convene, set the agenda for, and preside at meetings of the board of directors and general meetings and to propose motions or resolutions;

(c) the Examiner is entitled to reasonable notice of, to attend and be heard at all meetings of the board of directors and all general meetings;

(d) the Examiner has power to take whatever steps are necessary to halt, prevent or rectify the effects of any act, omission, course of conduct, decision or contract which in his opinion is or is likely to be to the detriment of the company or any interested party;

(e) the Examiner has power to seek directions regarding any question arising in the examinership; and

(f) the court may give the Examiner the power to ascertain and agree claims against the company. This provision is rarely applied. Generally speaking, unagreed claims will be dealt with through a dispute resolution mechanism contained in the Examiner's proposals.

Section 8 of the Act bestows considerable powers on an Examiner in relation to the production of documents and evidence by officers and agents of the company or a related company. These powers also extend to persons who are not officers or agents of the company. The Examiner may examine on oath, either by word of mouth or by written interrogatories any of the above. If any of the above persons refuse to produce such documents and evidence, refuse to attend before the Examiner, or refuse to answer questions put by the Examiner in relation to the affairs of the company, the Examiner may certify that refusal and the court may then enquire into the matter and make any order or direction it thinks fit.

Section 10 of the Act provides that the Examiner may certify liabilities of the company incurred during the protection period. The Examiner must be extremely careful in issuing certificates under this section. The Examiner's decision in this regard may be reviewed by the court: see *Re Don Bluth Entertainment Limited* [1994] 3 IR 141 and *Re Clare Textiles Limited* [1993] 2 IR 213. In *Re Eden Park Construction Limited* [1994] 3 IR 126 and in *Re Don Bluth Entertainment Limited* [1994] 3 IR 141 it was decided that an Examiner cannot certify liabilities pursuant to this section in arrears nor can they be certified *en bloc* prior to being incurred. Liabilities so certified shall be treated as expenses properly incurred under s 29(1) of the Act. Section 29(3A) of the Act provides that under any compromise or scheme of arrangement or in any receivership or winding up, such expenses shall be paid in full and shall be paid before any other claim (including a claim secured by a floating charge), but after any claim secured by a mortgage, charge, lien or other encumbrance of a fixed nature or a pledge.

Section 11 of the Act gives the Examiner power to deal with charged property. An Examiner may apply to court for permission to dispose of property which is the subject of fixed or floating charges or retention of title, hire purchase or lease finance agreements. Before the court will make such an order it will have to be satisfied that such a disposal would be likely to facilitate the survival of the whole or any part of the company as a going concern. Where the assets are subject to a charge which, as created, was a floating charge, the holder of that security shall have the same priority in respect of any property of the company directly or indirectly representing the property that was disposed of as the secured creditor would have had in respect of the property that was the subject of the security. Alternatively if the assets in question are the subject of a fixed charge or a hire purchase agreement (as defined), then the disposal will be conditional upon either the net proceeds or the net amount which would be realised on a sale of the property or goods in the open market by a willing vendor, being applied towards discharging the sums secured by the security or payable under the hire purchase agreement.

9.1.12 Directors' powers

The powers of directors survive both the presentation of a petition for the appointment of an examiner and the appointment of an examiner. As such, the directors remain responsible for the day-to-day management of the company. This is in stark contrast to a liquidation where the directors' powers cease on the appointment of a liquidator. The principal task of the examiner is to formulate a compromise or scheme of arrangement. However, in certain circumstances it may be undesirable to permit the incumbent directors to maintain their powers. Section 9 of the Act provides that the examiner may apply to the court and if it is just and equitable to do so, the court may make an order that some or all of the functions or powers of the directors be transferred to the examiner. Section 9(2) of the Act provides that the court is to have regard to the following matters in making such an order:

(a) that the affairs of the company are being conducted, or are likely to be conducted, in a manner which is calculated or likely to prejudice the interests of the company or of its employees or of its creditors as a whole;

(b) that it is expedient, for the purpose of preserving the assets of the company or of safeguarding the interests of the company or its employees or its creditors as a whole, that the carrying on of the business of the company by, or the exercise of the powers of, its directors and management should be curtailed or regulated in any particular respect;

(c) that the company, or its directors, have resolved that such an order should be sought; and

(d) any other matter in relation to the company the court thinks relevant.

In *Fate Park Limited* [2009] IEHC 375 Finlay Geoghegan J found that:

> Whilst s 9(1) enables the Court to make orders transferring powers of the directors to an examiner the power to do so is not a general power. It must be exercised having regard to the matters referred to in sub-section (2). They primarily relate to the manner in which the directors have been, or are conducting, the affairs of the company, or any perceived necessity in the interests of the company, its employees or creditors, that the exercise of those powers be curtailed or regulated or, indeed, where the directors resolve to support the examiner seeking an order for the transfer of certain of their powers.

9.1.13 Members

The powers of the members of a company under protection remain largely intact. Significantly, however, as mentioned previously, if the members pass a resolution to wind up the company, it will have no effect. In addition, members cannot obtain an order pursuant to s 205.

9.1.14 Contracts (pre-protection)

Section 7(5A) of the Act provides that an Examiner may not repudiate a contract entered into by the company prior to the period during which the company is under protection. Section 7(5C) of the Act provides an exception to this rule in that an Examiner may avoid certain provisions of an agreement entered into by the company, in particular negative pledge clauses, if the Examiner is of the opinion that the provision would be likely to prejudice the survival of the company or the whole or any part of its undertaking as a going concern. If the Examiner is to evoke this provision, he must serve a Notice on the other party or parties to the agreement informing them of that opinion.

However s 20 of the Act provides that:

> where proposals for a compromise or Scheme of Arrangement are to be formulated in relation to a company, the company may, subject to the approval of the court, confirm or repudiate any contract under which some element of performance other than payment remains to be rendered both by the company and the other contracting party or parties ...

An example of the court exercising this jurisdiction can be seen in its decision in *Chartbusters Limited* (High Court, 9 April 2009) where the court permitted the company to repudiate its obligations on foot of a number of leases of real property. Section 20 also provides that any person who suffers loss or damage as a result of the repudiation shall be treated as an unsecured creditor for the amount of such loss or damage. The court has jurisdiction under this section to make an order determining the amount of any such loss or damage so as to give certainty in relation to the claim in the context of the examinership.

9.1.15 Contracts (during protection)

Section 13(6) of the Act provides that an Examiner shall be personally liable on any contract entered into by him, in his own name or the name of the company, in the performance of his functions, unless the contract provides otherwise. But an Examiner shall be entitled to a full indemnity out of the assets of the company in respect of such liability.

9.1.16 Restriction on payment of pre-petition debts

The payment of pre-petition debts is restricted by s 5A of the Act, which provides that no payment may be made by a company, during the period it is under the protection of the court, by way of satisfaction or discharge of the whole or part of the liability incurred by the company before the date of the presentation of the petition. There are two circumstances where payments in respect of pre-petition debts may be made: firstly, where the report of the independent accountant recommends that the whole or part of that liability should be discharged or satisfied, and secondly, where an application is made by the examiner or any interested party for an order authorising the payment or discharge of the liability. In this regard, the court must be satisfied that failing to discharge or satisfy the debt would considerably reduce the prospects of the company, or the whole or any part of its undertaking, surviving as a going concern.

9.1.17 Meetings of creditors and members

Section 18 of the Act provides that the Examiner must formulate proposals for a compromise or scheme of arrangement as soon as is practicable after his appointment, and in any event within the time frame set out below. Section 22 of the Act sets out what the proposals should contain. Once he has formulated his proposals, the Examiner must convene and preside at such meetings of the members and creditors as he thinks proper and report back to the court on those proposals within 35 days of his appointment.

Together with the Act, RSC Ord 75A, r 18 sets out the manner in which these meetings are to be convened and run.

The number of meetings will depend on the different classes of members and creditors that are involved. For example, creditors may be broken down into secured and unsecured, contingent, preferential and so on. Members may also be divided into different classes according to the company's Articles of Association.

The meetings must be convened by notice in writing to each member of each class of members and creditors, giving not less than three days' notice. The proposals, together with a statement explaining the effect of the compromise or scheme of arrangement on the interested parties and forms of proxy (both special and general), should also be sent with the notice.

At the meetings, the Examiner puts forward his proposals for the consideration of those present either in person or by proxy. The Examiner will answer questions put to him in relation to the scheme of arrangement and the examinership. Modifications to the scheme may be proposed, but will only be incorporated into the scheme with the consent of the examiner.

The Examiner's proposals are then put to a vote. The proposals are deemed to be carried at a particular meeting if a majority in number holding a majority in value vote in favour of the proposals. Votes may be cast in person, by proxy or by a person authorised pursuant to s 139 of the Companies Act 1963 (CA 1963).

To be valid, a quorum must be present at each meeting. In the case of a members' meeting, at least two members must be present; in the case of a creditors' meeting, at least three creditors must be present.

The Examiner acts as chairman of the meetings and must arrange for minutes of the meetings to be kept. The chairman, as in creditors' meetings, may deal with the validity of proxies and votes.

The court is precluded from approving the examiner's proposals unless at least one class of creditors whose interests would be impaired by the implementation of the proposals voted in favour of the proposals.

Section 23(4A) provides that an abstention shall not be construed as a vote against the proposals.

9.1.18 Guarantees

When acting for a creditor whose liability is secured by a guarantee, beware. Where that creditor wishes to enforce the guarantee, onerous notice provisions apply. In summary, the creditor must serve notice on the guarantor offering to transfer the creditor's rights to the guarantor to vote at the creditors' meetings on the proposals for a compromise or scheme of arrangement. Section 25A of the Act deals with this area. The notice provisions are as follows:

(a) where 14 days' notice is given of the creditors' meeting, the notice must be served on the guarantor at least 14 days before the meeting;

(b) where less than 14 days' notice is given of the creditors' meeting, the notice must be served by the creditor on the guarantor within 48 hours of having received his notice; and

(c) the transfer notice must be in writing and must contain an offer to transfer to the guarantor the creditor's rights to vote in respect of proposals for a compromise or scheme of arrangement.

Clearly, failing to comply with the above notice provisions has very serious consequences for a creditor. When advising a creditor in relation to an examinership, one of the first questions which must be asked is whether or not the liability is secured by a guarantee. If the liability is so secured, then these provisions must be explained. If a compromise or scheme of arrangement is not entered into or does not take effect, a creditor may enforce a guarantee with leave of the court even if the creditor has failed to comply with these notice provisions.

9.1.19   Leases and hiring agreements

Section 25B of the Act provides that in relation to a lease in respect of land neither a compromise or scheme of arrangement nor modifications made by the court:

(a)   can provide for a reduction in rent or other periodical payment or any extinguishment of the right of the lessor to such payments; or

(b)   can provide for the non-exercise by the lessor of the right to recover possession, effect a forfeiture, otherwise enter on the land or to recover rent or other periodical payments or other relief for failure to comply with an obligation or covenant.

The above provisions also apply in relation to leases or hiring agreements in respect of property other than land where in the opinion of the court the property is of substantial value. Where a scheme purports to include such provisions, they are deemed unfairly prejudicial pursuant to s 24(4)(c)(ii) of the Act and as such the court cannot confirm the proposal. The section does not define 'substantial value'. However, it does provide that in considering whether or not property is of substantial value the court shall have regard to the length of the unexpired term of the lease or hiring agreement. It will be interesting to see what other factors the court will consider in determining whether property is of substantial value.

9.1.20   Report to the court and confirmation of proposals

Section 18 of the Act provides that the Examiner is obliged to report to the court on the outcome of the meetings of members and creditors. Section 19 of the Act sets out what this report shall contain. The Examiner is obliged to report to the court within 35 days of his appointment or such further period as the court may allow, but s 5(1) of the Act provides that the company is under protection for a period of 70 days from the date of presentation of the petition. The court may extend this 70-day period by a further 30 days. Thus the Examiner has 100 days, from the date of presentation of the petition, to report to the court pursuant to s 18 of the Act. In practice, the Examiner will not be in a position to report to the court within the 35-day period stipulated and this will necessitate applications to the court for extensions subject to the maximum of 100 days mentioned above.

The Examiner is obliged to deliver a copy of his section 18 report to the company on the same day as he delivers it to the court. He is also obliged to supply a copy of the report to any interested party following written application but s 18(7) and (8) provide that the court may direct that parts of the report may be omitted.

Where the Examiner is unable to formulate proposals, he may apply to the court for directions and the court may make such orders as it deems fit, including an order for the winding up of the company.

Pursuant to s 24, following delivery of the Examiner's report the court must set it down for consideration by the court. The company, the Examiner, and any creditor or member whose claim or interest would be impaired if the proposal were implemented, are entitled to attend and be heard. Section 22(5) provides that a creditor's claim against the company is impaired if he receives less in payment of his claim than the full amount at the date of presentation of the petition. For a consideration of s 22(5), see *Jetmara Teoranta* [1992] 1 IR 147 and *Antigen Holdings Ltd* [2001] 4 IR 600. Section 22(6) sets out the grounds upon which the interest of a member of a company would be regarded as being impaired.

Section 24(4) provides that the court may not confirm the proposals:

(a) unless at least one class of creditors whose interests or claims would be impaired by implementation has accepted the proposals;

(b) if their sole purpose is the avoidance of tax due; or

(c) unless the court is satisfied that the proposals are fair and equitable in relation to any class of members or creditors that has not accepted the proposals and whose interests would be impaired by them and that the proposals are not unfairly prejudicial to the interests of any interested party. For a consideration of what the court might regard as unfair and prejudicial, see *Antigen Holdings Ltd and Jetmara Teoranta* (cited above) and see *Holidair* (High Court, 6 May 1995). In *Antigen Holdings Limited* McCracken J stated:

> I should add generally when considering whether creditors have been unduly prejudiced, the position must be considered in light of the particular circumstances on each case. What may be unfair in one case may be fair in another.

Thus what is 'unfairly prejudicial' will be decided by the courts on a case by case basis. A general rule of thumb that is applied by the courts in considering whether or not the treatment of creditors is unfairly prejudicial is to draw a comparison between what creditors are to receive pursuant to the examiner's proposals versus what creditors would notionally receive in the winding up or receivership of the company. However this is only a rule of thumb. In the case of *Traffic Group Limited* [2007] IEHC 45 Mr Justice Clarke confirmed examiner's proposals in circumstances where there was evidence that the preferential creditor would probably have received more in a winding up. In that case Mr. Justice Clarke found that:

> there remains, therefore, only a possibility that, on winding up, there might have been more funds available to meet the entitlement of the Revenue as preferential creditor. It is clear … that a court can approve of a scheme … even where a creditor may be likely to do worse under the scheme than the same creditor might on a winding up.

The decision of the High Court in *Birchport Limited* (High Court, 2 December 2008) to confirm proposals which provided for the reduction in the value of a secured creditor's security interest caused great concern and anxiety amongst the secured creditor community. In fact in that case the reduction was consensual. The question being posed in the wake of the *Birchport* decision was whether an examiner could write down a secured creditor's claim. It is submitted that there is nothing contained in the Act which expressly precludes an examiner from writing down the claim of a secured creditor. However any such write down or interference with the rights of secured creditors will be subject to the limitations governing the contents of an examiner's proposals set out above. It is likely that a secured creditor will be in a stronger position to argue that proposals are unfairly prejudicial when compared with other creditors. Perhaps a more relevant practical consideration in relation to this question is the fact that the company will almost certainly require bank funding in the future. Often this bank funding will come from the incumbent bank. This practical consideration is likely to have a significant bearing on the ability of an examiner to write down a secured creditor's claim.

Section 25 provides that at the s 24 hearing a creditor or member whose interest or claim would be impaired by the proposals may object to their confirmation on any of the following grounds:

(a) where there was some material irregularity at or in relation to the members' or creditors' meetings;

(b) acceptance of the proposals was obtained by improper means;

(c)   improper purpose; or

(d)   unfair prejudice.

Where a party has voted in favour of the proposals, the grounds for objection are narrower. In these circumstances objections can only be made where:

(a)   acceptance was obtained by improper means; or

(b)   after voting to accept the proposals, the objector became aware that the proposal had been put forward for an improper purpose.

Having heard objections, s 24(3) provides that the court may confirm the proposals (with or without modification) assuming there is no other reason why it would not. When confirming the proposals, the court may make such orders for their implementation as it deems fit. The court must fix a date when the proposals come into effect but this date cannot be more than 21 days after the date of confirmation. Following their confirmation by the court, the proposals become binding on the company, its members and its creditors.

Section 26 provides that the protection afforded to the company ceases when the compromise or scheme comes into effect or at any earlier date as the court may direct. The examiner's appointment comes to an end when protection ceases.

Where the court does not confirm the proposals, it may make any order it deems fit including an order winding up the company.

9.1.21   Examiner's remuneration, costs and expenses and their priority

Section 29 provides that the remuneration, costs and expenses of the examiner will be sanctioned by the court. RSC Ord 75A, r 22 provides that an application for remuneration, costs and expenses shall be made ex parte, grounded on an affidavit of the examiner setting out a full account of the work carried out by him and a full account of the costs and expenses incurred by him and shall vouch same, and of the basis for the proposed remuneration which he is seeking to be paid. The affidavit must also specify the use made by the examiner of the company's staff and facilities as required under s 29(4). The court may also direct that the application be on notice. The court will, at the very least, scrutinise and in certain instances disallow remuneration, costs and expenses claimed by an examiner. This can be seen in *Re Wogan's (Drogheda) Ltd (No 3)* (High Court, 9 February 1993) and in *Re Clare Textiles Ltd* (High Court, 7 May 1992).

If the examinership is unsuccessful, the question of where the examiner's remuneration, costs and expenses rank will come into sharp focus. Section 29(3) provides that the remuneration, costs and expenses of the examiner which have been sanctioned by the court shall be paid before any other claim, secured or unsecured. Liabilities which have been certified by the examiner are treated as expenses properly incurred by him and will rank before any other claim, including one secured by a floating charge, but will rank after a claim secured by a mortgage, charge, lien or other encumbrance of a fixed nature or a pledge. The definition of 'a claim' includes the costs, charges and expenses of winding up, including the remuneration of the liquidator.

9.1.22   Revocation

The court has jurisdiction on the application of the company or any interested party made within 180 days after the confirmation of the proposals to revoke the confirmation where the confirmation was procured by a fraud. In making such an order the court must have particular regard to the protection of the rights of parties who have acquired interests or property in good faith and for value in reliance on the confirmation of the proposals. RSC Ord 75A, r 21(1) and (2) set out the procedure associated with such an application.

9.2 Schemes of arrangement and compromises: ss 201–204 and 279 of CA 1963

Prior to the implementation of the examinership legislation in 1990, CA 1963 provided a mechanism whereby a company could propose a compromise or arrangement between itself and its members and creditors with the assistance of the court. This mechanism is very rarely used. It is clear from s 201 of CA 1963 that these provisions apply where a company is in liquidation or where it is liable to be wound up. It also applies to a reorganisation of the share capital of a company.

In order to start this process, it is necessary to apply to court for directions regarding the meetings of members and creditors or classes of both envisaged by s 201 of CA 1963. It is not necessary to show that the company has a reasonable prospect of survival before the court will make orders pursuant to these provisions. Where such an application is made, the court has wide discretion to stay or restrain proceedings against the company, on such terms and for such period as it thinks fit. This contrasts with the automatic protection afforded to a company under the Act where such protection is afforded to that company on proper presentation of a petition in the Central Office under the Act. Lynch, Marshall and O'Ferrall, *Corporate Insolvency and Rescue* (1996) suggest that a receiver may still be appointed notwithstanding an application pursuant to s 201 and that the court's discretion would not extend to preventing the appointment of a receiver by a charge-holder as it is not regarded as a process of the court. Conversely, an application could be made pursuant to s 201 even where a receiver stands appointed.

9.2.1 Approval of compromise or arrangement

Section 201(3) of CA 1963 provides that in order for the compromise or arrangement to be approved, it must be approved by a majority in number and three-fourths in value of the creditors or class of creditors or members or class of members present and voting in person or by proxy. Thus, the threshold for approval is far higher than in an examinership. In addition, in order to be binding on the creditors and members or classes of members or creditors, it must be sanctioned by the court. It seems that the court has very broad discretion to either approve or reject a compromise or scheme.

9.2.2 Selecting classes of members and creditors and the position of the Revenue Commissioners

One of the only cases dealing with the provisions under CA 1963 is *Pye (Ireland)* (High Court, 12 November 1984; Supreme Court, 11 March 1985). This case was mainly concerned with the manner in which the classes of members and creditors should be selected.

9.2.3 Revenue Commissioners' ability to compromise

A further issue which arose in the *Pye (Ireland)* case is whether or not the Revenue had power to compromise a preferential debt and it would appear that they do not. However, the Act specifically empowers the Revenue to compromise under the examinership regime.

9.2.4 Examinership compared

Section 201 of CA 1963 is rarely, if ever, used. Perhaps the principal reason for favouring the examinership route is the immediate and extensive protection which is afforded once a petition for appointment is presented. It would also appear that a receiver may still be appointed even though an application has been made pursuant to s 201. But s 201 is still an option where a receiver has been appointed, whereas the appointment of an examiner is not an option where a receiver stands appointed for three days. The threshold for approval is considerably higher under s 201. Even where the statutory majority required under s 201 is achieved, the court has very broad discretion to reject the arrangement, unlike the situation in examinership. The position of Revenue debts also creates a problem. In the case of s 201, there is no third party responsible for putting together the rescue package. Generally speaking, creditors do not have faith in existing management and are more comfortable with the presence of an examiner who is charged with the responsibility of putting together the proposals. In addition, the examinership provisions are more extensive and certain. While the examinership regime has a number of advantages over s 201, in rare cases the s 201 procedure may be the more appropriate one.

9.2.5   Section 279

Section 279(1) of CA 1963 provides that:

> Any arrangement entered into between a company about to be, or in the course of being, wound up and its creditors shall, subject to the right of appeal under this section, be binding on the company if sanctioned by a special resolution and on the creditors if acceded to by three-fourths in number and value of the creditors.

Unlike s 201, this provision only applies where a company is about to be wound up or is in the course of being wound up. The court is not involved under this section unless there is an appeal by a dissatisfied creditor or contributory as provided for. It should be noted that this section does not afford the company any protection from its creditors.

CHAPTER 10

DUTIES AND LIABILITIES OF DIRECTORS OF INSOLVENT COMPANIES

Julie Murphy-O'Connor

10.1   Introduction

There is no obligation under Irish law on a company or its directors to take any steps to wind up the company or to put it into examinership when a company is insolvent. Indeed, neither insolvency nor trading while insolvent in themselves give rise to criminal or civil liability for directors. It is only when the company is put into examinership or liquidation that consequences may flow for directors. Where a formal insolvency procedure has begun, the solvency of the company, not only at the time of the beginning of the insolvency procedure, but at any time prior to the beginning of the insolvency procedure, together with the actions of the directors during that period, will be determined as part of the examiner's or liquidator's investigation into the directors' actions and whether the directors acted honestly and responsibly in the course of their duties.

The rest of this chapter deals more specifically with the various issues by virtue of which personal liability can be imposed on directors of insolvent companies, and the possible restriction and disqualification of directors.

10.2   Fraudulent and reckless trading

Section 297A(I) of the Companies Act 1963 as amended (CA 1963) provides that:

If in the course of winding up of a company (subject to s 251 of the Companies Act 1990 which, in certain circumstances, allows this section to be availed of where the company is not in liquidation, but where the principal reason for its not being in liquidation is the insufficiency of its assets) or in the course of proceedings under the Companies (Amendment) Act 1990 (examinership proceedings), it appears that:

    (a)   any person was, while an officer of the company, knowingly a party to the carrying on of any business of the company in a reckless manner; or

    (b)   any person was knowingly a party to the carrying on of any business of the company with intent to defraud creditors of the company, or creditors of any other person or for any fraudulent purpose

the court, on the application of the receiver, examiner, liquidator or any creditor or contributory of the company, may, if it thinks it proper to do so, declare that such persons should be personally responsible, without any limitation of liability, for all or any part of the debts or other liabilities of the company ...

10.2.1   Fraudulent trading

Part (b) of the above section describes fraudulent trading. Fraudulent trading is also a criminal offence (CA 1963, s 297). Fraudulent trading, even in its civil form, involves conduct on the part of directors which is more blameworthy than reckless trading, as indeed the terms themselves would suggest.

The test for fraudulent trading is doubly subjective, requiring:

(a)   the intent to defraud; and
(b)   knowing participation.

This test of intent to defraud requires actual knowledge that there was no reasonable chance that the creditors of the company would be paid. It is necessary therefore to prove a subjective intention to defraud. The phrases 'intent to defraud' and 'fraudulent purpose' are phrases which, it has been held, 'connote actual dishonesty involving, according to current notions of fair trading among commercial men, real moral blame' (*Re Patrick & Lyon Limited* [1933] Ch 786). Somewhat similarly, it has been held that fraudulent trading involves conduct which goes 'well beyond the bounds of what ordinary people engaged in business would regard as honest' (*Re EB Tractors Limited* (High Court of Justice in Northern Ireland, Murray J, 21 March 1986).

Essentially, if the directors of a company continue to carry on business or to incur debts at a time when they know that there is no prospect of the creditors ever receiving payment (*Re William C Leitch Bros Limited* [1932] 2 Ch 71), or indeed if the directors incur credit on behalf of a company knowing that there is no good reason to think that the funds will be available to pay the debt when it becomes due or shortly thereafter (*R v Grantham* [1984] 3 All ER 166), such conduct on their part constitutes fraudulent trading.

Fraudulent trading will, almost by definition, always amount to reckless trading also, save that liability for fraudulent trading is not confined to the officers of the company and could be perpetrated by parties who have not carried on or even assisted in the carrying on of the company's business, but have nevertheless in some way participated in the fraudulent acts. In addition, the intent to defraud for the purpose of fraudulent trading may not be in relation to the company but may relate to the creditors of some other person or may relate to any other person.

The most helpful Irish case in relation to fraudulent trading is *Re Hunting Lodges Limited* [1985] ILRM 75. This concerned a company which was massively indebted to the Revenue Commissioners. It sold its principal asset, a public house, concealing a substantial part of the purchase price which was paid 'under the counter' to one of the directors. Four directors were made personally liable for the company's debts to differing extents. This case is also authority for the proposition that a single act may be regarded as the 'carrying on of any business of the company', and accordingly be deemed to be fraudulent trading. It is clear, however, that a person will not be deemed to be 'knowingly a party' to fraudulent trading simply because he was aware of fraudulent conduct on the part of other persons, active participation being necessary to attract liability (*Re Kelly's Carpet Drome Limited* (No 2) (High Court, 13 July 1984)).

Liability for fraudulent trading may be compensatory or punitive. In *Re Hunting Lodges Limited*, for example, different levels of liability were imposed on each respondent. Two respondents were made liable for the amount of misappropriated moneys which the liquidator was unable to recover, another respondent was made liable to the extent of monetary advances made to her over a four-year period, and the last respondent was made liable for all of the debts of the company. It is clear from the judgment that Carroll J did not consider it necessary to establish a causal link between loss suffered by creditors and the liability imposed on the directors.

10.2.2   Reckless trading

Paragraph (a) of s 297A(1) of CA 1963 describes reckless trading. Before personal liability can be imposed upon an officer it must be shown that he has been knowingly a party to the carrying on of business in a reckless manner.

In the leading Irish decision on reckless trading, *Re Hefferon Kearns Ltd* [1993] 3 IR 191, Lynch J reviewed the meaning of the word 'reckless'. In doing so he agreed with the definition adopted by Kingsmill Moore J in *Donovan v Landys Ltd* [1963] IR 441, which said that the only test is an objective one: 'Would a reasonable man knowing all the facts and circumstances which the doer of the act knew or ought to have known describe the act as reckless in the ordinary meaning of that word ... the ordinary meaning of that word is a high degree of carelessness'.

However, Lynch J went on to hold that this could not be juxtaposed onto reckless trading within the meaning of that section.

> The inclusion of the word 'knowingly' ... must have been intended ... to have some effect on the nature of the reckless conduct required to come within the sub-section. I think that its inclusion requires that the director is party to carrying on the business in a manner which he knows very well involves an obvious and serious risk of loss or damage to others and yet ignores that risk because he does not really care whether such others suffer loss or damage or because his selfish desire to keep his own company alive overrides any concern which he ought to have for others.

Even if a person is not, in fact found to have been knowingly a party to the carrying on of business in a reckless manner, he can be deemed in law to have been reckless in either of the two circumstances in s 297A(2), which provides as follows:

> Without prejudice to the generality of sub-section (1)(a), an officer of a company shall be deemed to have been knowingly a party to the carrying on of any business of the company in a reckless manner if –
>
> (a)   he was a party to the carrying on of such business and, having regard to the general knowledge, skill and experience that may reasonably be expected of a person in his position, he ought to have known that his actions or those of the company would cause loss to the creditors of the company, or any of them, or
>
> (b)   he was a party to the contracting of a debt by the company and did not honestly believe on reasonable grounds that the company would be able to pay the debt when it fell due for payment as well as all its other debts (taking into account the contingent and prospective liabilities).

Interpreting this provision involving 'deemed recklessness', Lynch J considered that the essential question in respect of (a) was whether a person ought to have known that his actions or those of the company would cause loss to the creditors of the company or any of them. This is an objective test. The second and alternative test under (b) was where a person did not honestly believe on reasonable grounds that the company would be able to pay its debts, as they fell due. This is also an objective test.

Section 297A(6) of CA 1963, however, provides that:

> Where it appears to the court that any person in respect of whom a declaration has been sought under sub-section (1)(a), has acted honestly and responsibly in relation to the conduct of the affairs of the company or any matter or matters on the ground of which such declaration is sought to be made, the court may, having regard to all the circumstances of the case, relieve him either wholly or in part, from personal liability in such terms as it may think fit.

In *Re Hefferon Kearns Limited (No 2)* the directors managed to persuade the court that they had acted honestly and responsibly. The case is not particularly helpful for number of reasons, the principal one of which is that Murphy J, in a preliminary hearing, decided that s 33 of the Companies (Amendment) Act 1990 (the precursor to s 297A of CA 1963, as amended) did not have retrospective effect and therefore limited the period to which the subsequent court could look in deciding whether reckless trading occurred to a period of approximately six weeks. In addition, the loss incurred by creditors during that period was minimal, which the court expressly took into account. Lynch J found that reckless trading pursuant to s 297A(1)(b) had occurred for a period of approximately two weeks, but took into account a number of 'prudent and responsible' steps which the directors took in their concern for the creditors of the company. He noted that:

(a) one of the defendants had personally borrowed money in order to improve the company's cash-flow;

(b) the decision to carry on trading had been taken in the belief (supported by the subsequent examiner's report) that to do so would improve the creditors' position;

(c) the decision to carry on trading was taken on the basis that the company would not incur further credit (although as it happened the overall indebtedness was increased, taking into account the fact that some creditors were paid);

(d) two of the defendants had jointly guaranteed the company's debts with a bank and had been willing to surrender their shares in other companies for the benefit of the company; and

(e) all of the defendants had co-operated fully with the examiner.

Lynch J also took into account the fact that the directors tried to keep creditors informed of the position. In doing so he may have taken cognisance of s 297A(4), which requires the court to have regard to whether a creditor referred to in s 297A(1)(b) was, at the time that the debt was incurred, aware of the financial state of affairs of the company and, notwithstanding such awareness, consented to the incurring of the debt.

It is unclear whether the courts will insist on a causal link between loss caused to creditors and the actions of directors in the context of reckless trading proceedings as opposed to fraudulent trading proceedings. There is a suggestion however in *Re Hefferon Kearns Limited (No 2)* that the courts will try to establish a link before imposing personal liability. Where the applicant is a creditor, however, arising from s 297A(3), the creditor in question must have suffered loss as a consequence of the impugned behaviour. It is noteworthy also that where fraudulent or reckless trading proceedings are brought by a creditor, the court may order payment directly to the creditor in question as opposed to requiring that the proceeds of such an award be held as part of the assets available for the general body of creditors (see *Re Cyona Distributors Limited* [1967] 1 Ch 889).

Finally, as regards reckless trading, it is reasonable to assume that, based on case law relating to fraudulent trading, awareness of reckless conduct on the part of other officers is not sufficient and that active participation only will attract liability and that a single transaction is sufficient to constitute reckless trading. (Clearly where s 297A(2)(b) applies, the incurring of a single debt is sufficient.)

10.3   Failure to keep proper books of acount

Section 204 of the Companies Act 1990 (CA 1990) provides as follows:

(1) Subject to sub-section 2 if:

(a) a company that is being wound up and that is unable to pay all of its debts has contravened section 202, and

(b) the court considers that such contravention has contributed to the company's inability to pay its debts or has resulted in substantial uncertainty as to the assets and liabilities of the company or has substantially impeded the orderly winding up thereof,

the court, on the application of the liquidator or any creditor or contributory of the company, may, if it thinks it proper to do so, declare that any one or more of the officers and former officers of the company who is or are in default shall be personally liable, without any limitation of liability, for all, or such part as may be specified by the court, of the debts and other liabilities of the company.

(2) On the hearing of an application under this sub-section, the person bringing the application may himself give evidence or call witnesses.

Section 202 of CA 1990 prescribes the books of account required to be kept by a company.

Of the three alternatives contained in s 204(1)(b), the third, that the contravention 'has substantially impeded the orderly winding up thereof' would appear to be the easiest to establish.

This provision was employed by a liquidator in the case of *Mehigan v Duignan* [1997] 1 IR 340, which is more commonly known as the *Mantruck* case. In this case, Shanley J found that proper books of account had not been kept. He found that the contravention had not in itself resulted in any loss to the company, but had substantially impeded the orderly winding up of the company or resulted in substantial uncertainty as to its assets and liabilities.

While it would also appear, by analogy with s 297A of the 1963 Act, that liability may be compensatory or punitive, Shanley J opined that the court, in the exercise of its discretion as to whether to impose liability for all of the liabilities of the company, must have regard to the extent to which the contravention resulted in financial loss and if so, whether or not such losses were reasonably foreseeable by the officer as a consequence of the contravention. On the facts of the case, he found that the losses sustained by the company resulting from the contraventions of the provisions in relation to the keeping of proper books of account were reasonably foreseeable by the respondent and made an order imposing personal liability for the additional costs incurred in the liquidation arising from the contravention.

10.4 Fraudulent preferences

A fraudulent preference is a payment or disposal of the property of a company, which at the time is unable to pay its debts as they fall due, in favour of any creditor, within six months of the commencement of a winding up, with a view to giving the creditor a preference over the other creditors (CA 1963, s 286). Such payment is invalid and is recoverable by a liquidator.

Where the payment or disposal of the asset was made in favour of a connected person, the period of six months is replaced with a period of two years, and there is a presumption that an intent to prefer existed (CA 1963, s 286(3)). A 'connected person' is defined in s 286(5) of CA 1963 to include a director, a shadow director, a person connected to a director pursuant to s 26(1)(a) of CA 1990, a related company within the meaning of s 140 of CA 1990 and any trustee or surety or guarantor for a debt due to any such person.

Six conditions have to be satisfied before a security document can be invalidated as a fraudulent preference. Thus a transaction will only be a fraudulent preference if:

(a) a conveyance, mortgage, delivery of goods, payment, execution or other act relating to property was made or done by or against the company;

(b) at the time such act was made or done, the company was unable to pay its debts as they became due;

(c) such act was done or made in favour of a creditor of the company or of any person on trust for such a creditor;

(d) such act was done or made with a view to giving such creditor, or any surety or guarantor for the debt due to such creditor, a preference over other creditors of the company;

(e) the company went into liquidation within six months (or of the act was made or done in favour of a connected person within two years) of the making or doing of such act; and

(f) the company at the commencement of the liquidation was unable to pay its debts (taking into account its contingent and prospective liabilities).

From the foregoing it can be seen that the crucial condition is (d). Case law in this area has found that for a transaction to be a fraudulent preference, it must have been the 'dominant intention' to prefer the creditor in question. The intention is found by examining the motives of the person, or body of persons, within the company responsible for the transaction (usually the directors).

In other words, in order to prove that a transaction is a preference, it is not sufficient to show that the effect of the transaction was to give a preference; rather the phrase 'with a view to giving ... a preference' has been interpreted as meaning that the transaction must have been entered into with a dominant intention to prefer. (See *Corran Construction Co Ltd v Bank of Ireland Finance* [1976–7] ILRM 175; *Station Motors Ltd v Allied Irish Bank Ltd* [1985] IR 756; *Kelleher v Continental Meats Ltd* (High Court, 9 May 1978); *Re Northside Motor Co Ltd* (High Court, 25 July 1985)).

A *bona fide* belief that the company will be able to pay its debts at some future date does not negative an intention to prefer in circumstances where, at the time of payment, the company was well aware of its own insolvency (*Re FP & CH Matthews Ltd* [1982] 2 WLR 495).

If the bank puts sufficient pressure on the company to pay the debts so as to overbear the will of the company's controllers, the transaction will not be regarded as being a fraudulent preference (see *Corran Construction Co Ltd v Bank of Ireland Finance Co; Re Boyd* (1885) 15 LR Ir 521; *Taylor (Assignees of) v Thompson* (1869–70); *Taylor (Assignees of) v Killeleagh Flax Spinning Co* (1869–70) IRCL 120). The logic behind this reasoning is well summarised by Porter MR in the case of *Re Daly & Co Ltd* (1887–88) 19 LR Ir 83, who stated as follows:

> Where pressure exists so as to overbear the volition of the debtor a payment is not made with a view to prefer the creditor extending it, but because the debtor cannot help it. The view to prefer is absent; or at least is not the real view, or motive or reason, actuating the debtor ...

The result of these cases is that the more oppressive the creditor, the less likely that the payment will be regarded a fraudulent preference. It is only where a company has given a charge to a previously unsecured creditor when it was not under pressure to do so that an intention to prefer will more than likely be inferred.

It has traditionally been held in the case of *Re Sarflax Ltd* [1979] Ch 592 that a fraudulent preference does not in itself amount to fraudulent trading (nor, it is reasonable to assume, reckless trading). The rationale for this proposition is that a fraudulent preference, far from causing loss to creditors, in fact constitutes a payment to a creditor and merely upsets the application of the *pari passu* rule in the administration of the assets of the company in liquidation.

This decision is, however, tempered by the later judgment of the Court of Appeal in *West Mercia Safetywear Ltd v Dodd* [1988] BCLC 250, where it was held to amount to a breach of fiduciary duty for a director of an insolvent company to prefer connected creditors over unconnected creditors.

Furthermore, in determining whether a director has been reckless, s 297A(2) of the 1963 Act indicates that one must have regard not only to the actual knowledge, skill and experience of the director, but also to the knowledge, skill and experience which may reasonably be expected of a person in his position. Attributing that level of knowledge etc to him, one must ask whether 'he ought to have known that his actions or those of the company would cause loss to the creditors of the company, *or any of them*' (emphasis added). These italicized words indicate that acting in a manner which one knows or ought to know will cause loss to a single creditor, may amount to recklessness. Accordingly, it can no longer be safely assumed that the decision in *Re Sarflax Ltd* continues to represent good law (without modification) in this jurisdiction.

10.5 Duty of directors to act in the interests of creditors

Case law in Ireland has indicated that the directors of an insolvent company have a duty to act in the interests of its creditors. The leading case is *In Re Frederick Inns Limited* [1991] ILRM 582. In that case four companies in a group went into liquidation. Shortly before their liquidation one of the companies made payments to the Revenue Commissioners out of the proceeds of sale of a pub belonging to it. The Revenue knew of the sale of the pub and had threatened to liquidate the company unless certain tax arrears were satisfied. By agreement the payments made by the company were applied not only in satisfaction of tax due from the company itself but also tax payable by other members of the group. The liquidator challenged the validity of the payments in so far as they related to the liabilities of the other group members.

The court upheld the liquidator's challenge, first, on the ground that the payments were *ultra vires* (which is not relevant to the present discussion) and secondly on the ground that the payments were misapplications of the company's assets made in disregard of the rights and interests of general creditors and that accordingly the Revenue held the payments as constructive trustee for the company and the creditors generally. In the course of his judgment in the Supreme Court, Blayney J said:

> Where, as here, a company's situation was such that any creditor could have caused it to be wound up on the ground of insolvency, I consider that it can equally well be said that the company has ceased to be the beneficial owner of its assets with the result that the directors would have had no power to use the company's assets to discharge the liabilities of other companies. Once the company clearly had to be wound up and its assets applied pro tanto in discharge of its liabilities, the directors had a duty to the creditors to preserve the assets to enable this to be done, or at least not to dissipate them.

The position is also well explained by Street CJ in *Kinsela v Russell Kinsela Pty Ltd* (1986) NSWLR 722 (at 730) where his lordship stated:

> In a solvent company the proprietary interests of the shareholders entitle them as a general body to be regarded as the company when questions of the duty of directors arise. If, as a general body, they authorise or ratify a particular action of the directors, there can be no challenge to the validity of what the directors have done. But where a company is insolvent the interests of the creditors intrude. They become prospectively entitled, through the mechanism of liquidation, to displace the power of the shareholders and directors to deal with the company's assets. It is in a practical sense their assets and not the shareholders' assets that, through the medium of the company, are under the management of the directors pending either liquidation, return to solvency, or the imposition of some alternative administration.

The duty of the directors of an insolvent company to act in the best interests of the creditors generally, is a duty not only owed to the company itself but also to the creditors individually: *Jones v Gunn* [1997] 2 ILRM 245.

10.6 Misfeasance

Section 298 of CA 1963, as amended by s 142 of the Companies Act 1990, specifically deals with the recovery of money misapplied by directors and others. It provides that in the course of a winding up, where a promoter, past or present officer of the company, a liquidator, receiver or examiner:

> has misapplied or retained or become liable or accountable for any money or property of the company, or has been guilty of any misfeasance or other breach of duty or trust in relation to the company

the court may compel restoration of the funds or any part thereof or compel contribution from that person 'by way of compensation'.

It was said by Costello J in *Re Mont Clare Hotels Ltd (In Liquidation) Ray Jackson v Pauline Mortell and Others* (High Court, 2 December 1986) that:

> It is not every error of judgment that amounts to misfeasance in law and it is not every act of negligence that amounts to misfeasance in law. It seems to me that something more than mere carelessness is required, some act that, perhaps, may amount to gross negligence in failing to carry out a duty owed by a director to his company.

> It must be remembered that this section is merely a procedural measure and does not impose any additional duties on officers, nor confer any additional remedies on creditors. It just enables existing duties of officers to be enforced.

In *Re Irish Provident Assurance Company Ltd* [1913] IR 352, Cherry LJ said of the old section similar to s 298, that:

> it applies only to cases where a cause of action would, independently of the section, exist at the suit of the company ...

and went on to say:

> ... it has been settled, and I think rightly settled, that that section creates no new offence, and that it gives no new rights, but only provides a summary and efficient remedy in respect of rights which, apart from that section, might have been vindicated in law or in equity.

Section 298 can only be used in the course of a winding up where the company has been caused to suffer a pecuniary loss as a result of the breach of duty in question.

10.7   Restriction and disqualification

Directors of Irish registered insolvent companies or foreign insolvent companies which establish a place of business in Ireland may be subject to a restriction order, whether the director is resident or non-resident (*Fennell v Frost & Ors* [2003] IEHC 15). The provisions apply to those who are directors, *de facto* directors and shadow directors of the company upon the date of commencement of the winding up or receivership (CA 1990, s 154) or within the previous 12 months.

Section 150 of CA 1990 provides that the court has a mandatory duty to impose a restriction order on a director of an insolvent company unless the court is satisfied that the director falls within one of the three specified exemptions set out below:

(i)   that the person concerned has acted honestly and responsibly in relation to the conduct of the affairs of the company and that there is no other reason why it would be just and equitable that he should be subject to the restrictions imposed by this section;

(ii)   subject to paragraph (i), that the person concerned was a director of the company solely by reason of his nomination as such by a financial institution in connection with the giving of credit facilities to the company by such institution, provided that the institution in question has not obtained from any director of the company a personal or individual guarantee of repayment to it of the loans or other forms of credit advanced to the company; or

(iii)   subject to paragraph (i), that the person concerned was a director of the company solely by reason of his nomination as such by a venture capital company in connection with the purchase of, or subscription for, shares by it in the first-mentioned company.

A restricted director cannot, for a period of five years, be appointed or act in any way, whether directly or indirectly, as a director or secretary or be concerned or take part in the promotion or formation of any company unless that company is capitalised in the case of a public limited company, at least €317,434.52 (IR£250,000) and in the case of any other company, at least €63,486 (IR£50,000). A company with a restricted director is also subject to additional limitations as regards that company providing financial assistance in connection with the purchase of shares; or that company making loans, quasi loans and entering into transactions in favour of directors and persons connected with directors.

The provisions in relation to disqualification are contained in s 160 of CA 1990. Disqualification is a total prohibition on acting as auditor, director or other officer, receiver, liquidator or examiner or being in any way, whether directly or indirectly, concerned or taking part in the promotion, formation or management of any company. A disqualification order may be made in a number of circumstances, generally involving conduct of a more serious nature than that required in order for a restriction order to be made. Such an order may be made if a person has been convicted on indictment of any indictable offence in relation to a company or involving fraud or dishonesty. In a number of circumstances, including where a declaration has been made pursuant to s 297A of CA 1963 (for fraudulent or reckless trading), a disqualification order may be made by the court of its own motion or as the result of an application.

Where any person acts in contravention of these provisions, he is guilty of an offence. Furthermore, a company can recover any remuneration paid to that person and where the company concerned commences to be wound up while that person is acting in such manner or within 12 months of him so acting and is unable to pay its debts, such a person may be declared personally liable, without any limitation of liability, for all or any part of the debts or other liabilities of the company incurred in the period during which he was acting in such manner.

If a director acts in accordance with the directions or instructions or a disqualified person, knowing that such person was disqualified, that director may also be subject to a disqualification order and may also be personally liable for the debts of the company incurred in the period during which he so acted.

Chapter 11 deals in greater detail with the restriction and disqualification of directors, and the procedures involved in, the factors giving rise to, and the consequences of such orders.

10.8   Advising directors of insolvent companies

Trading while insolvent is fraught with difficulty. The safest course of action for directors when a company has become insolvent is to take steps to put the company into creditors' voluntary liquidation (CA 1963, s 251 and ss 266–268) or petition to the High Court for the appointment of an examiner. The reckless trading provisions do not apply during a period when a company is under the protection of the court (CA 1963, s 297A(8)).

If for whatever reason the directors do not want to put the company into either liquidation or examinership, or want time to consider the matter, the only absolutely safe course of conduct to adopt is to neither take further credit nor reduce the assets of the company. It is not safe to keep the level of creditors static because, pursuant to s 297A(2)(b) of CA 1963, for example, liability may be incurred in relation to the contracting of a single debt.

If, therefore, the directors wish to continue to trade while insolvent, in order to ensure that no further credit is incurred, suppliers, including utilities, need to be paid in advance. Even this course of action can only be justified if the continuation of trading is likely to protect, if not increase, the assets which will ultimately be available to creditors in the event that liquidation ensues.

If the directors decide to continue to trade while insolvent, there is clearly a serious risk of personal liability if the company ultimately goes into liquidation. There are a number of steps that they can take to improve their chances of being able to rely on the 'honestly and responsibly' defence, including:

(a)   convening frequent board meetings;

(b)   obtaining financial advice, preferably from an accountant with insolvency experience;

(c)   preparing a budget/business plan;

(d)   keeping creditors informed of the financial state of affairs in relation to the company at all times;

(e)   obtaining legal advice in relation to the insolvency law implications of what they are doing; and

(f)   ensuring that there can be no suspicion of fraudulent preference by, for example, opening a new bank account with a new bank so that all receipts can be lodged to that account and not to the company's own account in reduction of an overdraft or other facilities, particularly where the overdraft or other facilities are personally guaranteed by the directors.

As soon as a director is aware that there is no reasonable prospect of avoiding insolvent liquidation, or fears that that is the case, he must raise the problem with the rest of the board with a view to their taking independent professional advice. Further credit should almost certainly not be incurred pending such advice and directors must take every step to minimise the potential loss to creditors. If a pessimistic director fails to persuade his colleagues despite his best efforts, it may be sufficient for him to resign in protest and he would be well advised to seek independent personal advice to ensure that there are no other steps for the protection of creditors available to him. The onus on the rest of the board will then be greater.

CHAPTER 11

RESTRICTION AND DISQUALIFICATION OF DIRECTORS

Julie Murphy-O'Connor

11.1 Restriction

A director of an insolvent company, or a person who was a director within 12 months prior to the commencement of the winding up of a company, must be restricted by the High Court unless he satisfies the court that he acted honestly and responsibly in relation to the conduct of the affairs of the company and that there is no other reason why it would be just and equitable that he should be subject to restriction. A restriction is a prohibition on acting in any way as a director or secretary or being concerned in or taking part in the promotion or formation of a company, for a period of five years, unless the company has a paid up share capital, in the case of a public company, of €317,435 (IR£250,000) and in the case of a private company, €63,487 (IR£50,000).

The original provisions in relation to restriction orders are contained in Part VII of Chapter 1 of the Companies Act 1990 (CA 1990). The chapter applies only where, at the time of the commencement of the winding up of the company, it is proved to the High Court or at any time during the course of the winding up the liquidator certifies or it is otherwise proved to the High Court, that the company is unable to pay its debts (CA 1990, s 149(1)). The chapter applies to any person who was a director, a *de facto* director or a shadow director within the period of 12 months prior to the commencement of the winding up (CA 1990, s 149(2), (5) and see also *Lyn Rowan Enterprises Ltd* [2002] IEHC 90 for a consideration of the differences between a *de jure* director, a *de facto* director and a shadow director).

Section 150 of CA 1990 provides that the court has a mandatory duty to impose a restriction order on a director of an insolvent company unless the court is satisfied that the director falls within one of the three specified exemptions set out below:

(i) that the person concerned has acted honestly and responsibly in relation to the conduct of the affairs of the company and that there is no other reason why it would be just and equitable that he should be subject to the restrictions imposed by this section, or

(ii) subject to paragraph (i), that the person concerned was a director of the company solely by reason of his nomination as such by a financial institution in connection with the giving of credit facilities to the company by such institution, provided that the institution in question has not obtained from any director of the company a personal or individual guarantee of repayment to it of the loans or other forms of credit advanced to the company, or

(iii) subject to paragraph (i), that the person concerned was a director of the company solely by reason of his nomination as such by a venture capital company in connection with the purchase of, or subscription for, shares by it in the first-mentioned company.

11.2   Application

11.2.1   To whom do the provisions apply?

The provisions of s 150 apply:

  (a)   to an Irish or to a foreign company which establishes a place of business within the state;
  (b)   which is unable to pay its debts; and
  (c)   which goes into liquidation or receivership (CA 1990, s 154).

A person who may be restricted must have been a director, a *de facto* director or a shadow director of such a company upon the date of commencement of the winding up/ receivership, or within the previous twelve months. Non-resident directors are also subject to the restriction provisions (*Fennell v Frost & Ors* [2003] IEHC 15).

The company must be in liquidation for Part VII Chapter 1 of the 1990 Act to apply, save in circumstances where s 251 of the 1990 Act applies (2001 Act, s 54). Section 251 of the 1990 Act provides for the application of certain specified insolvency provisions in relation to a company which has not been wound up where the reason that the company has not been wound up is insufficiency of assets.

11.2.2   Who can make the application?

The Company Law Enforcement Act 2001 specifies the parties who can make an application for a restriction order (s 41(1)(c)) as follows:

  (a)   the Director of Corporate Enforcement;
  (b)   a liquidator; or
  (c)   a receiver.

A liquidator of an insolvent company (whether in court liquidation or voluntary liquidation) is obliged to submit within six months of his appointment a report to the Office of the Director of Corporate Enforcement (ODCE) pursuant to s 56 of the Company Law Enforcement Act 2001. In the report the liquidator must advise the ODCE whether in his opinion each of the directors of the company acted honestly and responsibly in the conduct of the company's affairs and there is no other reason why it would be just and equitable to restrict the directors.

The liquidator must not earlier than three months nor later than five months after the date of his report institute an application pursuant to s 150 of CA 1990 if the Director of Corporate Enforcement does not relieve him of this obligation.

A restriction application is issued by way of notice of motion grounded on an affidavit sworn by the liquidator. The practice direction of the President of the High Court in relation to voluntary liquidations requires a liquidator to put before the court those matters which he considers the court should take into account in determining whether the director has acted honestly and responsibly and also any matter which he considers might be relevant to a determination as to whether there is any other reason why it would be just and equitable that the director should be subject to a restriction order. This practice is also followed in court liquidations.

11.3   Defending a restriction application

In considering restriction applications the court is minded not to view the events surrounding the collapse of a company unduly harshly with the benefit of hindsight. Whether a director acted honestly and responsibly should 'be judged by an objective standard' (In *Re Squash (Ireland) Limited* [2001] 3 IR 35).

In order to avoid a restriction order, the burden of proof is on director to establish to the satisfaction of the court that:

(a)   he has acted honestly in relation to the affairs of the company;
(b)   he acted responsibly in relation to the affairs of the company; and
(c)   there is no other reason why it would be just and equitable that he should subject to a restriction order.

11.3.1   Acting dishonestly

A liquidator is obliged to set out in his application whether he believes that the directors acted both honestly and responsibly. In the majority of cases the liquidator states on the basis of the information and documentation furnished to him, that he has not unearthed any evidence which would lead him to believe that the directors acted dishonestly. In the case of *Re Outdoor Advertising Services Limited* [1997] IEHC 201 the court held that the burden of proving honesty was not discharged by the directors and found that they had not acted honestly as they had consciously and deliberately sought to benefit themselves at the expense of the company's creditors.

In the case of *Re USIT World plc* [2005] IEHC 285 the court suggested that dishonesty 'goes to the core of a person's integrity' and that 'dishonesty implies something akin to improper dealing with money or other assets belonging to the company, or some form of fraudulent trading'. The court also noted that while 'dishonesty will always amount to irresponsibility the converse is not true'.

11.3.2   Acting irresponsibly

In *Re Squash Ireland Limited* [2001] 3 IR 35, McGuinness J considered the principles applicable to the question of a director's responsibility and went on to adopt the test set out by Shanley J in *La Moselle Clothing Ltd v Soualhi* [1998] 2 ILRM 345, who stated that the court should have regard to the following five criteria:

(a)   the extent to which a director has complied with the obligations imposed by the Companies Acts;
(b)   the extent to which the director's conduct could be regarded as so incompetent as to amount to irresponsibility;
(c)   the extent of the director's responsibility for the insolvency of the company;
(d)   the extent of the director's responsibility for the net deficiency in the assets of the company disclosed at the date of the winding up or thereafter; and
(e)   the extent to which the director, in his conduct of the affairs of the company, has displayed a lack of commercial probity or want of proper standards.

There is of course some overlap in the above-mentioned criteria. McGuinness J held that the proper basis to approach a restriction application was to examine the entire tenure of the person's directorship in an objective manner and felt that while 'commercial errors may have occurred, misjudgements may have been made, to categorise such conduct as irresponsible ... one must go further than this'. In the *La Moselle Clothing* case, the fact that the court found that the director had traded at a time when he knew that the company was insolvent led to him being restricted. In the case of *Re Colm O'Neill Engineering Services Limited* [2004] IEHC 83 the court indicated that when considering a director's actions in the context of responsibility, such actions or inactions should be looked at on the basis of a going concern and prior to the commencement of a winding up.

As Murphy J stated in *Business Communications Ltd v Baxter & Parsons* (High Court, 21 July 1995) the restriction provision 'effectively imposes a burden on the directors to establish that the insolvency occurred in circumstances in which no blame attaches to them as a result of either dishonesty or irresponsibility'. In *Re USIT World plc* [2005] IEHC 285,

Peart J quoted the above passage and proceeded to similarly emphasise the correlation between the insolvency of the company and the conduct of the particular director, stating:

> ... the burden on a director seeking to satisfy the Court as to his/her behaviour in relation to conduct in the affairs of the company for the purposes of escaping from an order under [s 150], includes if necessary, establishing that where there are matters about which they can be rightly the subject of criticism, there is in reality no causal link between those culpable matters and the insolvency.

The following factors would influence the courts that directors had acted irresponsibly:

(i)   fraudulent and reckless trading/trading while insolvent;

(ii)   fraudulent preference of one creditor over other creditors;

(iii)   increase in the company's indebtedness in the period prior to liquidation and failure to keep creditors informed;

(iv)   lack of co-operation with the liquidator during the course of the liquidation (*La Moselle Clothing* [1998] 2 ILRM 345);

(v)   failure to file a statement of affairs (*In re Dunleckney Limited* [1999] IEHC 109) or material difference between the directors' estimate statement of affairs and the actual financial position;

(vi)   degree of insolvency;

(vii)   breaches of company law;

(viii) failure to correctly state and/or maintain company returns in the Irish Companies Registration Office and Revenue returns (*Duignan v Carway* [2002] IEHC 109, and *La Moselle Clothing*);

(ix)   failure to maintain proper books and records (*La Moselle Clothing, Re Gasco Ltd (In Liquidation)* [2001] IEHC 20);

(x)   delay in placing the company into liquidation (*Re Camoate Construction Ltd (In Liquidation)* [2005] IEHC 346); and

(xi)   direct causal link between the company's insolvency and the director's actions.

11.3.3   Just and equitable

In considering whether a director has acted responsibly and whether there are any other reasons why it would be just and equitable to restrict a director, the courts have been encouraged not to impose restriction orders in circumstances where:

(a)   the directors sought and followed professional advice when the company was approaching financial difficulties;

(b)   the directors kept creditors informed of the company's financial difficulties;

(c)   there was no significant increase in liabilities in the period prior to liquidation;

(d)   the directors had personally contributed funds to reduce the company's liabilities;

(e)   there was no causal link between the director's actions and the insolvency of the company; and

(f)   the actions taken by one director to place the company into liquidation vis-à-vis other directors.

11.4   Obligations of a non-executive director

The obligations of a non-executive director have been considered in a number of restriction applications. In *Re RMF (Ireland) Ltd Kavanagh v Riedler & Ors* [2004] IEHC 334, Finlay Geoghegan J considered that it was appropriate to distinguish between executive and non-executive directors. However, she made the point that every person who agrees to become a director of a company, whether executive or non-executive or for the purpose of bringing a particular skill to the board of directors, must discharge the general duty of a director which has been summarised by Jonathan Parker J in *Re Barings plc (No 5); Secretary of State for Trade & Industry v Baker & Ors* [1999] 1 BCLC 433 and approved of in *Re Vehicle Imports Ltd* [2000] IEHC 90 as follows: 'Each individual director owes duties to the company to inform himself about its affairs and to join with his co-directors in supervising and controlling them'.

In considering whether a non-executive director has acted responsibly for the purposes of s 150 of CA 1990, she said the courts should recognise that, in general, a non-executive director is entitled both to rely upon information provided by his fellow directors and to rely upon the executive directors carrying out what might be normal executive or management functions. However, there may be factual circumstances which will put a non-executive director on notice that he should not continue to rely either upon information provided or upon executive duties being properly performed and require further action from him or her.

In *Re Tralee Beef & Lamb*, Finlay Geoghegan J again considered the position of non-executive directors, in the context of directors' common law duties of skill and care.

Although the judgment given is lengthy and goes into a significant amount of detail in relation to the directors' backgrounds and roles in relation to the company, the most significant aspect of the decision is the formulation by Finlay Geoghegan J of criteria which the judge considered to represent the minimum duty of care and skill that is required of a non-executive director. They are:

(a) A duty to inform oneself of the affairs of the company to facilitate the discharge of duties as a director. It is not the duty of a non-executive director to produce the relevant information pertaining to the company. However, a non-executive director must take whatever steps are necessary to glean whatever information may be of relevance in relation to the affairs of a trading company whether financial information or otherwise.

(b) The non-executive director must take steps to join with his or her co-directors in supervising and controlling the affairs of the company. This is not to say that there is an obligation on a non-executive director to personally control the company. However, Finlay Geoghegan J held that a non-executive director is under an obligation to participate with his fellow directors in collectively controlling and supervising the affairs of the company at least in the manner stated by the Court of Appeal of New South Wales in the case of *Daniels v Anderson* [1995] 16 ACSR 607 'to take reasonable steps to place [himself] in a position to guide and monitor the management of the company'.

(c) The duty to supervise the discharge of delegated functions to the executive directors and other subordinate offices. It was accepted, however, that the duty to supervise delegated functions does not have universal application and must be considered on a case-by-case basis taking into account the director's particular skills and agreed role on the board.

It is clear from Finlay Geoghegan J's decision in the *Tralee Beef and Lamb* case that the fact that a director has been nominated to join the board by a shareholder in the company to represent its interests does not in any way reduce the duty of care and skill owed by such a non-executive director in discharging the obligations imposed on him under the Companies Acts and by common law. Indeed, Finlay Geoghegan J specifically referred to the fact that she accepted, in considering one of the director's actions, the court should also take into account the fact of his nomination by a shareholder for the purpose of safeguarding its interests. Clearly, a director in a position such as the nominee in this case is not absolved of the duty to: (1) inform himself/herself about the affairs of the company and (2) join with his/her co-directors in supervising and controlling the company's affairs.

However, this was appealed to the Supreme Court (1 February 2008), where Hardiman J overturned the decision of the High Court in so far as it related to the director who had been nominated to the board by the investors. In coming to his conclusion, Hardiman J highlighted his dissatisfaction with a number of issues including the following:

(i)   No reasons are required to be given by the ODCE for refusing the relief sought, and no application had been made to the ODCE in this regard. The High Court inferred from the decision not to provide relief that the ODCE did not agree with the liquidator's conclusion that Mr Coyle had acted honestly and responsibly. Hardiman J was not prepared to infer this.

(ii) He considered it inappropriate that the evidence of another respondent director of the company had been treated as part of the case against Mr Coyle.

(iii) He criticised the blanket reversal of the onus of proof contained in s 150(2)(a) of CA 1990, which provides that 'a restriction order must be made against the respondent unless …'. He felt this was inconsistent with 'fundamental fairness and constitutional justice'. He noted that while being restricted under s 150 was largely symbolic and of little practical effect (requiring only that any new company of which the restricted person is a director be modestly capitalised), being restricted under s 150 was 'gravely damaging' to a person's reputation.

(iv) He took into account that Mr Coyle's position was somewhat similar to those positions outlined in ss 150(2)(b) and (c) of CA 1990 (ie which deal with certain situations where a person is a director of a company, solely by reason of his nomination by a financial institution or by a venture capital company).

It was held in the judgments in *Hunting Lodges* [1985] ILRM 75 and *Re Costello Doors Limited* (High Court, 21 July 1995) that anyone who agree to become a director of a company is not absolved from discharging the duties imposed on directors by the Companies Acts and common law because he or she is a friend, relative or spouse of the proprietor. Having said that, regard should be had to Finlay Geoghegan J's consideration of the duties owed by the directors in *Tralee Beef and Lamb,* which she said must be considered by the court taking into account their particular skills and agreed role on the board. In that case, Finlay Geoghegan J held that the wife, a non-executive director and the wife of the only executive director of the company, had not satisfied the court that she had acted responsibly in relation to the conduct of the affairs of the company because of her failure to take any step to consult with her fellow non-executive directors in circumstances where she was aware of the significant financial difficulties in the company.

This decision seems to be in line with the decision of Murphy J in *Re Vehicle Imports Limited* [2000] IEHC 90 in which the wife of the principal director had taken the initiative of opposing the increased borrowing of the company. The court held that this was, in the circumstances, a responsible position for the wife to take.

11.5   Legal costs

There was no reference to 'costs' in the original s 150 legislation as enacted. Before 2001 the practice had been to make an award of costs in favour of the liquidator even where a director was not restricted on the basis that otherwise the creditors would be out of pocket by having to fund an action which the liquidator was legally obliged to take.

Section 150(4B) of CA 1990, however, was inserted by s 51 of the Company Law Enforcement Act 2001, and provides that the court, on hearing an application 'may order that the directors against whom the declaration is made shall bear the costs of the application and any costs incurred by the applicant in investigating the matter'.

It has, pursuant to this section, been held that a director should only bear the applicant's costs in the event that a restriction order is made against him (*Re GMT Engineering Ltd, Luby v McMahon & Egan* [2003] 4 IR 133).

Where a liquidator's application fails due to some failure on his part, the court has been known to impose an order for costs against the liquidator as applicant as opposed to the company in liquidation. Examples of such failure are the failure to discharge the onus of showing as a probability that the respondent was a director within 12 months of the winding up (*Visual Impact and Displays Limited (In Liquidation)* [2003] 4 IR 451), and in circumstances where the liquidator did not demonstrate any reason for not seeking to be relieved of his obligation to bring a restriction application against a director and did not the director an opportunity of putting his side of the case before the s 56 report was (*Re Digital Channel Partners Ltd, Kavanagh v Cummins & Ors* [2004] 2 ILRM 35).

In *Re Usit World* plc [2005] IEHC 285, Peart J referred to the *GMT Engineering* and the *Visual Impact and Displays* cases with approval. He concluded that in spite of the manner in which s 150(4B) of CA 1990 is couched, there remains in the court a discretion in the matter of an application by a successful respondent against whom no declaration of restriction is made, and in that case he awarded the respondents who sought them their costs despite submissions that the privilege of limited liability brought with it the burden of dealing with an application for restriction, that the making of an order for costs would impose a further burden on the creditors, or that there were many genuine and serious concerns raised by the liquidator in his affidavits grounding the application.

Of note in this case was the observation of Peart J that in his s 56 report, the liquidator indicated that he was continuing his investigations into the actions of the directors, and answered in the negative to the question whether or not he was asking the ODCE to relieve him from the requirement to apply for a restriction order against any of the directors. The ODCE wrote a letter five months later stating that the liquidator was not relieved of his obligation to apply for such restriction order, without waiting for any further report from the liquidator. The judgment is certainly a strong warning to the ODCE not to decide on whether a s 150 application should be made until the liquidator's investigations have completed. 2005 and 2006 saw increases in the number of decisions granting 'relief at this time' by the ODCE in order to give liquidators a further opportunity to complete their enquiries, however, the number of decisions declined in 2007 and stabilised in 2008 (interim reviews of ODCE activity available on www.odce.ie).

11.6   Costs of investigation

Section 11 of the Investment Funds, Companies and Miscellaneous Provisions Act 2006 amends s 150 of CA 1990, and states that the court has authority to order that such directors bear all of the costs and expenses incurred by the applicant 'or such portion of them as the court specifies'. In addition, s 11(1) specifically provides that such 'costs and expenses' include the cost of collecting evidence the subject matter of the application and so much of the remuneration and expenses of the applicant as are attributable to the applicant's investigation and collection of such evidence.

These amendments are clearly intended to address what the legislature perceived as a lacuna in s 150(4B) of CA 1990 thrown up by the cases of *Mitek Holdings Limited & Ors v Companies Act* [2005] IEHC 160 and *Tipperary Fresh Foods Limited (In Liquidation) v Companies Act* [2005] IEHC 153. In both cases, Finlay Geoghegan J applied a literal interpretation to s 150(4B) of CA 1990 and held that the phrase 'costs of the application' meant the liquidator's legal costs of the restriction application and did not extend to the liquidator's remuneration in relation to time spent working on the application, and that, by analogy, the phrase 'costs incurred by the applicant in investigating the matter' could not be construed to include the liquidator's own remuneration in respect of time spent by him in investigating the matter.

The amendments in s 11 of the Investment Funds, Companies and Miscellaneous Provisions Act 2006 should have a real impact on the level of costs required to be paid by directors against whom restriction (and disqualification) orders are made.

11.7   Relief from restriction

Section 152 of CA 1990 provides that a person who has been restricted under s 150 of CA 1990 may, within 12 months of the making of the order, apply to the High Court for relief, in whole or in part, against the restrictions. The court may, if it deems it just and equitable, grant such relief on whatever terms and conditions it sees fit. In the case of *Xnet Information Systems Limited (In Voluntary Liquidation)* [2004] IEHC 82, such application for relief was considered by the court. The liquidator in that case did not object to the application for relief. The Director of Corporate Enforcement opposed the application. The court said that the following matters should be considered in relation to an application to have a declaration of restriction either wholly or partially lifted:

(a)   the overriding principle in all such applications is that the applicant should not be granted relief in whole or in part unless the court is satisfied that the public will not be harmed either by the total removal of the restriction or by its partial removal in conjunction with appropriate conditions;

(b)   the applicant must demonstrate some 'need' or 'interest' which requires the removal of the restriction in whole or in part;

(c)   the applicant must satisfy the court that the capitalisation threshold having regard to his own impecuniosity is an insurmountable obstacle to him; and

(d)   it must also have regard to the deterrent nature of the restriction order, the protection of the public from dishonest and irresponsible directors, the conduct of the applicant since the winding up and the hardship suffered by an applicant.

The court granted partial relief and directed that the restriction order remain in place but that any new company to which the applicant is appointed as a director is required to have a reduced capitalisation requirement of €7,500 paid up share capital. The applicant must also notify the ODCE of the name of the company of which he becomes a director/secretary or takes up any position the subject matter of the declaration of restriction and the court granted the Director of Corporate Enforcement liberty to apply to the court to vary the conditions attached to the granting of relief and/or to revoke the relief in total should circumstances so warrant.

11.8   Consequences of a restriction order

11.8.1   Consequences for restricted companies

A company in which a restricted director becomes involved (a 'restricted company') must be capitalised as follows:

(a)   the nominal value of the allotted share capital of the company shall:
  (i)   in the case of a public limited company, be at least €317,434.52 (IR£250,000),
  (ii)   in the case of any other company, be at least €63,486 (IR£50,000),

(b)   each allotted share to an aggregate amount not less than the amount referred to in sub-paragraph (i) or (ii) or paragraph (a), as the case may be, shall be fully paid up, including the whole of any premium thereon; and

(c)   each such allotted share and the whole of any premium thereon shall be paid for in cash.

A restricted company cannot avail of:

(a)   the exception to the prohibition in the Companies Acts, on a company providing financial assistance in connection with the purchase of shares; or

(b)   the exception to the prohibition on a company making loans, quasi-loans and entering into credit transactions etc in favour of directors and persons connected with the directors.

If a restricted company allots a share which is not fully paid up, the share shall (with certain exceptions) be treated as if its nominal value together with the whole of any premium had been received, but the allottee shall be liable to pay the company in cash the full account that should have been received plus interest, less the consideration actually paid.

However, the High Court can, if it deems it just and equitable to do so, grant relief to a restricted company. The courts' ability to grant relief is, however, confined to cases where the company has not been put on notice by the restricted director that he has been restricted.

11.8.2   Consequences for restricted directors

A restricted director, before he accepts appointment as an officer of a company, must within 14 days of his appointment for so acting, notify the company that he is a restricted person. A restricted director may not accept an appointment or act in any other manner, whether directly or indirectly as a director or secretary or take part in the promotion or formation of any company unless that company satisfies certain minimum capital requirements (outlined above).

If a restricted director acts in breach of his restriction order and the company which he then became concerned with commences an insolvent winding up, either while he is involved or within 12 months of his so being involved, the court may declare on the application of the liquidator or any creditor that such a person shall be personally liable for all or part of the liabilities of the company incurred in the period during which he was acting in such a manner or capacity (subject to his right to apply for just and equitable relief). The restricted company can also recover any consideration paid to the restricted director for services rendered.

There are also criminal sanctions which can be imposed if a restricted director acts in breach of a restriction order. If the restricted director is found guilty of an offence, he is liable to a fine in certain circumstances not exceeding €10,000 and/or a term of imprisonment not exceeding five years and an automatic disqualification order.

11.8.3   Consequences for directors/officers of the restricted company

There are both civil and criminal sanctions for directors or officers of a restricted company, where the restricted company has been notified of a director's restriction and the restricted company carries on business without fulfilling the minimum capital requirements within a reasonable period thereafter. If the restricted company enters into insolvent liquidation, the court may on the application of the liquidator or any creditor or contributory of the company declare that any person who is an officer/director of the company while the company so carried on business and who knew or ought to have known that the restricted company had been notified of the director's restriction be personally responsible for all or any part of the debts or other liabilities of the restricted company. It is open to the directors of the restricted company in such circumstances to apply to the court for relief, having regard to the circumstances of the case.

It is a criminal offence for officers and directors to act in accordance with the directions or instructions of a restricted director, knowing that such a person was restricted. If a director is found guilty in this regard, an automatic disqualification order is made against that person.

11.9 Disqualification

The provisions in relation to disqualification are contained in s 160 of CA 1990. Disqualification is a total prohibition on acting as auditor, director or other officer, receiver, liquidator or examiner or being in any way, whether directly or indirectly, concerned or taking part in the promotion, formation or management of any company.

A disqualification order may be made in a number of circumstances, generally involving conduct of a more serious nature than that required in order for a restriction order to be made. Disqualification is intended for conduct which is 'manifestly more blameworthy than merely failing to exercise an appropriate degree of responsibility in relation to an insolvent company' (Murphy J in *Business Communications Ltd v Baxter & Parsons*). Section 160(2) of CA 1990 lists a number of circumstances in which a court can make a disqualification order.

11.10 Costs

The Company Law Enforcement Act 2001 also provides that the court may make a restriction order if it considers that a disqualification order is not justified and the court may award the costs against a disqualified or restricted person, including the costs of investigating the matter: s 160(9A)–(9B) of CA 1990 (as inserted by s 42(f) of the 2001 Act).

Section 11(2) of the Investment Funds, Companies and Miscellaneous Provisions Act 2006 amends s 160(9B) of CA 1990 by providing that the court has the authority to order that directors who are disqualified or restricted as a result of a s 160 application bear all of the costs and expenses of the applicant or such portion as the court specifies. The definition of 'costs and expenses' includes the cost of collecting evidence and the remuneration and expenses of the applicant attributable to the applicant's investigation and collection of evidence.

11.11 Automatic disqualification

Disqualification is primarily a discretionary sanction, but is automatic in the following circumstances:

(a) where a person is convicted on indictment of any indictable offence in relation to a company or involving fraud or dishonesty (CA 1990, s 160(1));

(b) where a person fails to notify the Registrar of Companies on appointment as a director that he/she has been disqualified in another state or makes a false or misleading statement in this regard (CA 1990, s 160(1A), as inserted by s 42 of the 2001 Act);

(c) where a person is convicted of acting while restricted except in the circumstances permitted by statute (CA 1990, s 161). Any person guilty of acting as a director while restricted, in addition to being automatically disqualified, is also guilty of a criminal offence (for which the maximum penalty is €1,904 and/or 12 months' imprisonment on summary conviction or €12,697 and/or five years' imprisonment on conviction on indictment);

(d)   where a person is convicted of acting while disqualified. Any person guilty of acting while disqualified will automatically have their period of disqualification extended for a further ten years, or such further period as the court may order. Moreover, they are also guilty of a criminal offence, for which the penalties specified in above apply; or

(e)   where a person is convicted of acting as officer, auditor, liquidator or examiner of, or directly or indirectly takes part or is concerned in the promotion, formation or management of any company while being an undischarged bankrupt (s 169).

For many years, very few deemed disqualifications were recorded. However, in 2005 the ODCE set to the task of assembling the relevant information on persons deemed to be disqualified in the previous five years. More than 2,700 are now on the register of disqualified persons. In 2007, 40 directors whose insolvent companies had been struck off by the Companies Registration Office for failing to file returns (and effectively abandoned) were disqualified for periods ranging from 1–5 years, and in 2008, 32 directors were disqualified for this reason.

11.12 Disqualification at the discretion of the court

The court may make a disqualification order for such period as it sees fit where the court is satisfied that any of the grounds set out in s 160(2) of CA 1990 have been made out. In summary, those grounds are:

(a)   Fraud or fraudulent or reckless trading:

Where a person while a promoter, officer, auditor, receiver, liquidator or examiner of the company has been guilty of any fraud in relation to the company, its members or creditors (s 160(1)(a)). A disqualification order may also be made in respect of a person, the subject matter of a declaration under s 297A of CA 1963 (fraudulent and reckless trading) (s 160(2)(c)).

(b)   Breach of duty:

Where a person has been guilty of breach of duty while a promoter, officer, auditor, receiver, liquidator or examiner of the company of any breach of his duty as such promoter, officer, auditor, receiver, liquidator or examiner (s 160(2)(a) and (b)). There is no definition of the term 'breach of duty', in this context. Presumably, it includes a director's fiduciary duties and his duties of care and skill as well as statutory duties.

(c)   Unfitness:

Where the conduct of any person as promoter, officer, auditor, receiver, liquidator or examiner of a company makes him unfit to be concerned in the management of a company (s 160(2)(d)). A disqualification order can also be made on the basis of unfitness in consequence of a report of inspectors appointed by the court or the Minister for Enterprise, Trade and Employment (s160(2)(e)). (*Re National Irish Bank, The Director of Corporate Enforcement v D'Arcy* [2005] IEHC 333.)

(d)   Persistent default:

Where a person has been persistently in default in relation to filing requirements. This may be proved to the court in the ordinary way, but a person is conclusively deemed to have been persistently in default if, in the five years ending on the date of the application, he has been adjudged guilty of three or more filing defaults (whether or not on the same occasion). Guilt for this purpose is proved by a conviction or by an order of court requiring the default to be remedied (s 160(3)).

(e) Failure to keep proper books of account:

Where a person has been convicted of two or more offences under s 202 of CA 1990, which requires the keeping of proper books of account (s 160(2)(g) as inserted by s 42 of the 2001 Act).

(f) Director of company dissolved for failure to make returns:

Where a person is a director of a company which has been dissolved for failing to make returns (s 160(2)(h)), unless the director shows that the company had no outstanding liabilities (s 160(3A)).

(g) Foreign disqualifications:

The court must be satisfied that, if the conduct causing the foreign disqualification had occurred in the state, a disqualification order would have been appropriate. (Section 160(2)(i), as inserted by s 42 of the 2001 Act.)

11.13 Applicants

The range of applicants is very wide. It includes the receiver, liquidator, examiner or creditor of a company of which the respondent has been, is acting, or is proposed to act as officer, auditor, receiver, liquidator, examiner or to be concerned to take part in the promotion, formation or management of that company.

Section 160(6A) of CA 1990 (inserted by the Company Law Enforcement Act 2001) allows the Director of Corporate Enforcement to make an application for a disqualification order. In contrast to applications under s 150 of CA 1990, the onus of proof under s 160 is on the applicant.

11.14 Time limits

There are no periods specified within which the application must be made.

11.15 Period of disqualificaion

The period of disqualification is at the discretion of the court. In the UK, the court has a discretion of between a minimum of two years and a maximum of 15 years. In *Re Cladrose* [1990] BCLC 204 and in *Re Sevenoaks Stationers (Retail) Limited* [1991] Ch 164, the English Court of Appeal suggested guidelines as to the periods of disqualification to be imposed. The top bracket of periods of ten and more years is reserved for particularly serious cases. The bracket of two to five years should be applied where the case was relatively not serious. The intermediate bracket should apply for serious cases which do not merit the top bracket.

The High Court made use of these suggested scales in the *CB Readymix* case. In *Re Clawhammer Limited* [2005] IEHC 85, Finlay Geoghegan J said that:

> the court must have regard to the fact that the Orieachtas intended such order as a more serious sanction than a declaration of restriction ... In the absence of a respondent putting before the court any relevant evidence, it is difficult to conclude that a disqualification order for any period less than five years will be a more onerous sanction for the respondent than a declaration of restriction which must be for five years.

In *Re National Irish Bank, The Director of Corporate Enforcement v D'Arcy* [2005] IEHC 333, Kelly J considered that the rationale of this judgment was that if the respondent puts no evidence before the court as to the appropriate disqualification period, the minimum period ought to be five years. He concluded that having regard to the findings of the inspectors contained in the report, the appropriate period of disqualification should be 12 years. He then reduced this by two years because of a number of mitigating factors. He took into account that the respondent had consented to the application, had resigned as a director of two other companies before these proceedings were instituted and had indicated that he was prepared to undertake in writing not to act as a director, promoter, officer or involve himself in any way in the formation or management of both those companies or any company whatsoever.

In *Re Betarose Limited, Forrest v Harrington* (Ex Tempore, High Court, 12 January 2006), Dunne J held that the proper way to approach the question of the length of disqualification was to approach it in the same manner as one would when sentencing an accused in a criminal case. She felt bound to look at the gravity of the offence, consider the appropriate period, and then see if there were any mitigating factors. On that basis she was unwilling to accept that in the absence of evidence from the respondent the minimum disqualification period should be five years. Section 160 of CA 1990 in contrast to s 150 made no reference to a mandatory period so to start at a minimum of five years was unjustified. She held in that case that the appropriate period should be three years, which she reduced by six months because of certain mitigating circumstances. This was also the first case in which the respondent was both restricted under s 150 and disqualified under s 160 of CA 1990.

11.16 Enforcement of restriction and disqualification orders

11.16.1 Criminal sanctions

A person who acts in a manner or capacity which is prohibited under a restriction declaration or disqualification order commits an offence (CA 1990, s 161(1)).

If any person while a director or other officer of the company acts in accordance with the directions or instructions of a disqualified person or a restricted person acting in a manner prohibited, that person is also guilty of an offence and is thenceforth deemed to be disqualified (CA 1990, s 164(1)).

11.16.2 Civil consequences

(a) Recovery of consideration:
Any consideration given to a restricted or disqualified person for any act done or service performed while he was acting in a manner or capacity prohibited can be recovered by the company as a simple contract debt (CA 1990, s 163(2)).

(b) Personal liability for debts:
Where:
(i) a restricted or disqualified person acts in a prohibited manner or capacity in relation to a company; and
(ii) that company is wound up unable to pay its debts while he is so acting (or within twelve months thereafter),
the court may declare him personally liable for all of the debts or other liabilities of the company incurred during the period he was so acting (CA 1990, s 163(3)).

(c) Personal liability of other officers:
Where a company receives notification from a restricted person of the restriction, but carries on business without fulfilling the capital requirements within a reasonable period and is subsequently wound up unable to pay its debts, any officer of the company, while the company has so carried on business, who knew or ought to have known of the notification, may be personally responsible for the debts or liabilities of the company (CA 1990, s 164(4)).

(d) Personal liability for acting under the instructions of a restricted or disqualified person:

A person who is convicted of an offence of acting in accordance with the directions or instructions of a disqualified or restricted person may also be responsible for the debts of the company incurred during the period he was so acting (CA 1990, s 165(1)).

(e) Public register:

The Registrar of Companies is required to keep a register of restricted persons and disqualification orders (CA 1990, s 168(1)). The Registrar is required to remove the entry at the expiry of the period of disqualification or restriction (CA 1990, s 168(2)).

CHAPTER 12

PERSONAL INSOLVENCY: BANKRUPTCY

Barry O'Neill

12.1 Introduction

12.1.1 Definition of bankruptcy

The classic definition of bankruptcy is considered to be the quotation from an English case in 1874 (*Re Reiman* 20 Fed Cas 490):

> Bankruptcy is a law for the benefit and the relief of creditors and their debtors, in cases in which the latter are unable or unwilling to pay their debts.

Bankruptcy law applies only to debtors who are individuals. The main objects of bankruptcy legislation are:

(a) to secure equality of distribution and to prevent any one creditor obtaining an unfair advantage over the others;

(b) to protect bankrupts from vindictive creditors by freeing them from the balance of their debts where they are unable to pay them in full, and to help rehabilitate them;

(c) to protect creditors, not alone from debtors who prior to bankruptcy prefer one or more creditors to others but from the acts of fraudulent bankrupts; and

(d) to punish fraudulent debtors.

The method of achieving these objectives is the transfer of all assets to a trustee/assignee for the purpose of realisation and then the distribution of the proceeds of sale rateably among the creditors. Because the concept of limited liability is a much newer concept, there are quite a number of rules relating to liquidations which have their foundation in bankruptcy law.

12.1.2 History of law in relation to bankruptcy

Brehon law, which originated in the judgments of pagan Brehons, was recognised through most of Ireland until approximately 1600. It appears to have been the universal remedy by which rights were vindicated and wrongs redressed and constituted an important part of the law in Ireland for about 1,500 years. There are clear references to debtors and creditors, and the rights and obligations of both, in Brehon law.

The first Irish bankruptcy statute was in 1772 and was called an Act 'to prevent frauds committed by bankrupts'. Between 1772 and 1857 there were approximately ten Irish statutes dealing with bankruptcy.

In 1857, the first of two important statutes dealing with bankruptcy was enacted. The Irish Bankrupt and Insolvent Act 1857 was enacted 'to consolidate and amend the laws related to bankruptcy and insolvency in Ireland'. By this Act, a bankruptcy court was established and the powers and procedures relating to that court were set out. In 1872, the Bankruptcy (Ireland) Amendment Act became law. As its name implies, this Act amended the existing law, primarily by giving the court additional powers.

The Banktruptcy Act 1988 (BA 1988) consolidates and modernises statute law relating to bankruptcy. It came into operation on 1 January 1989.

A number of recent Acts have also contained bankruptcy provisions. These are primarily the Solicitors Acts and the Auctioneers and House Agents Acts.

12.1.3 'Acts' of bankruptcy

An act of bankruptcy is an act or default, voluntary or involuntary, committed by a debtor, which is either evidence of an intent to deprive creditors of their rights through fraudulent assignment or is an implication of insolvency. An act of bankruptcy must be committed, and be proven to have been committed, before the High Court will entertain any application to adjudicate a debtor bankrupt. Therefore, the proposed bankrupt must have committed one or more of the following 'acts' of bankruptcy:

(a)   if, in the state or elsewhere, the debtor makes a conveyance or assignment of all or substantially all his property to a trustee(s) for the benefit of his creditors generally (BA 1988, s 7(1)(a));

(b)   if, in the state or elsewhere, the debtor makes a fraudulent conveyance, gift, delivery, or transfer of his property or any part of it (BA 1988, s 7(1)(b)). In a case in 1852, a fraudulent transfer of property was defined as follows:

   (i)   where the transfer has an immediate object to defeat creditors;

   (ii)   where it is made with an objective of preventing equal distribution of the bankrupt's effects under his bankruptcy, which he knows must occur; or

   (iii) where the transfer of property must necessarily in its results be known to the bankrupt to lead to the delay and disappointment of all his creditors except the particular individual to whom the transfer is made.

(c)   if in the state or elsewhere, the debtor makes a conveyance or transfer of his property or any part of it, or creates a charge on it which would be deemed a fraudulent preference in a bankruptcy;

(d)   if, with intent to defeat or delay his creditors:

   (i)   the debtor leaves the state,

   (ii)   being outside the state, remains outside the state,

   (iii) departs from his dwelling house,

   (iv)   otherwise absents himself, or

   (v)   evades his creditors (BA 1988, s 7(1)(d));

(e)   if the debtor files a Declaration of Insolvency in the High Court (BA 1988, s 7(1)(e));

(f)   if execution against him has been levied by the seizure of his goods under an order of any court or if a return of no goods has been made by the sheriff or county registrar whether by endorsement on the order or otherwise (BA 1988, s 7(1));

(g)   if the creditor presenting the petition has served upon the debtor in the prescribed manner a bankruptcy summons, and he does not within 14 days after service of the summons pay the sum referred to in the summons or secure or compound for it to the satisfaction of the creditor (BA 1988, s 7(1)(g));

(h)   where an order is made by the court directing that the deposit maintained in the High Court by an auctioneer shall not be released during a period, or where an order is made by the High Court directing that no banking company shall make any payment out of a bank account in the name of the auctioneer (Auctioneers and House Agents Act 1967); or

(i)   where a creditor obtains a judgment, order or decree against the holder of a banking licence and where the judgment relates to the payment of money due by the creditor in his capacity as a banker (s 28(1) of Central Bank Act 1971).

It is important to note that in certain circumstances, the court can adjudicate bankrupt a debtor who tries but fails to carry through an arrangement with his creditors (BA 1988, s 105).

The most common source of bankruptcy is where the debtor fails to pay his creditors having received a bankruptcy summons.

12.2   Bankruptcy proceedings

12.2.1   The creditor's position

As usual, full instructions should be obtained by the solicitor from the creditor to ensure that bankruptcy proceedings can be used against the debtor. The debt should be for a liquidated (or determined) sum. The creditor should be completely happy that the debtor cannot dispute the debt involved. The best way of avoiding any dispute regarding the debt is for the creditor to have already obtained a court judgment and to use the judgment as the basis for the bankruptcy proceedings. Ultimately, if the debtor is adjudicated bankrupt, and appeals (or 'shows cause') against the bankruptcy order, it will be difficult to persuade the court that the debt is not due if another court has ordered that it is due.

Instructions should be given as to the name, description and address of the person who will swear any affidavits in the case on behalf of the creditor. Details of the procedure involved should be given to the creditor along with a note of the costs. The solicitor's expenses alone will involve stamp duty on many court documents and advertisements in national newspapers. In the petition, the creditor undertakes to advertise and bear the expense of advertising. The petitioner must also indemnify the Official Assignee as to his costs, fees and expenses.

The solicitor should also discuss with his client the benefits of instituting the bankruptcy proceedings. If the creditor is only interested in collecting money which is due to him, then it is critical to ascertain whether or not the debtor has any money to pay the debt. Admittedly, some clients will say that the threat of bankruptcy will ensure that the debtor will get the money one way or another but such optimistic clients should be warned that, in practice, sometimes the bankruptcy proceedings do not result in any payment of the debt and the costs of instituting the proceedings might be lost.

Great care should be taken where the client/creditor claims to have security for the repayment of his debt. Any creditor who holds security of any nature should be warned that ultimately he might be asked to value his security, and adjudicate the debtor bankrupt for an unsecured amount. In certain circumstances, a secured creditor could lose his security if he proceeds with the adjudication.

When a debtor has committed an act of bankruptcy, then the client has three months from the date of the committing of the act of bankruptcy to file the petition to adjudicate the debtor bankrupt (BA 1988, s 11(1)(c)).

The following are basic checklists for solicitors taking instructions from a client who wishes to commence bankruptcy proceedings.

Full details of the debtor:

(a)   name;

(b)   address;

(c)   description; and

(d)   occupation.

Full details of the debt:

(a) must be a liquidated sum;

(b) ideally, a judgment should have been obtained;

(c) explain procedure to the client;

(d) time limits for the various stages;

(e) stamp duty involved;

(f) possible developments along the way;

(g) discuss question of costs with creditors;

(h) query whether bankruptcy proceedings are suitable to collect the debt;

(i) query whether client/creditor will accept a compromise payment;

(j) query whether client has any security for the debt;

(k) if client is a limited company, obtain name, address, description etc of the person representing the company who will swear affidavits etc;

(l) discuss with client the effects of the bankruptcy on the debtor if the bankruptcy ultimately goes ahead; and

(m) discuss interest upon judgment.

A judgment mortgage is not valid as against the property of a bankrupt until three months or more pass before the date of adjudication of the debtor as a bankrupt. This provision is contained in s 51 of BA 1988 and, incidentally, it has been incorporated at s 284(2) of CA 1963 in relation to the winding up of insolvent companies. Note that the reference in s 284(2) of CA 1963 to the 'filing of the petition' now reads as a reference to the date of adjudication (BA 1988, s 51(2)).

An important point is that the petitioning creditor gains no priority in relation to the payment of his debt if he makes the debtor bankrupt. However, the costs of the petitioner are paid next after the costs, fees and expenses of the Official Assignee (BA 1988, s 12). In general, the preferential claims in a bankruptcy are similar to those in a liquidation or a receivership (BA 1988, s 81).

12.2.2   The procedure

BA 1988 came into operation on 1 January 1989. The Act is complemented by the Rules of the Superior Courts (No 3) 1989 (SI 79/1989).

12.2.2.1   *The bankruptcy summons*

The first step is sending a form of demand called 'Particulars of Demand and Notice Requiring Payment prior to the issue of a Bankruptcy Summons'. This form is sent to the debtor by ordinary post, although a posting voucher must be issued by An Post for production at a later stage. An affidavit of posting may be requested. This notice is to be found in Rules of the Superior Courts (RSC) Form No 4. The debtor has four clear days during which he can respond to the Particulars of Demand. If there is no response, then the creditor is entitled to proceed.

The next step is taken by having a bankruptcy summons issued and served on the debtor. The summons is issued by the court. A bankruptcy summons will be issued by the High Court when the debt is €1,900 or more, the debt is a liquidated sum and the relevant notice (served under the RSC) has been served. The form of bankruptcy summons is found in RSC Form No 1. Prior to the court application to issue the bankruptcy summons, you must first attend at the Examiner's Office with the following papers:

(a) two copies of the Particulars of Demand (the posting voucher should be attached to one copy of the particulars); and

(b) affidavit for bankruptcy summons sworn by the creditor (RSC Form No 5). This includes a statement that no form of execution has issued in respect of the debt and remains to be proceeded upon.

When the summons is issued, it must be served on the debtor. Service of a bankruptcy summons must be effected personally on the debtor. The court can make an order providing for substituted service in circumstances where the court thinks fit.

The summons must be served within 28 days after it has been issued and a copy of the affidavit for bankruptcy summons must also be served. Within three days after the service, the summons server must endorse on the summons the day and the date of the service. If the summons is not served within the 28-day period, then it is possible to apply to the court for an order seeking an extension of time. You will have to justify to the court why you are looking for the extension of time.

The time limit for payment under a bankruptcy summons is 14 days from the date of service. After the summons has been served, the debtor can apply to the court to have the summons dismissed. If the debtor is of the opinion that he does not owe the amount demanded, then he should instruct his solicitor to issue a notice of application to dismiss the bankruptcy summons (RSC Form No 7). This form is accompanied by an affidavit in which the debtor states that he is not indebted to the creditor (RSC Form No 6). This affidavit must be filed within 14 days after service of the summons. A date is fixed by the Examiner when the debtor's application will come before the court for determination.

12.2.2.2 *The bankruptcy petition*

If the debtor has not paid the debt within the time limit, then he will have committed an act of bankruptcy. The creditor is entitled to present a petition if:

(a) the debt is €1,900 or more;

(b) the debt is a liquidated sum; and

(c) an act of bankruptcy has been committed within three months before the presentation of the petition, and the debtor

   (i) is domiciled in the state or within a year before the date of the petition;

   (ii) has ordinarily resided in the state;

   (iii) has had a dwelling house or place of business within the state;

   (iv) has carried on a business in the state personally/by an agent/by a manager; or

   (v) has been a member of a partnership which has carried on business in the state by means of a partner, agent or manager (BA 1988, s 11).

The petition asks the court to adjudicate the debtor bankrupt.

If the creditor decides to go ahead with the petition, then the following papers must be filed with the Examiner's Office:

(a) Petition (RSC Form No 11). This document must be signed by the petitioner. Where the petitioner is a company, it must be sealed by the company and signed by two directors or by one director and the secretary. The sealing and signature must themselves be witnessed. The petition must be signed first. It must include notice of the date for the hearing of the petition. On the back of the petition there is an affidavit verifying the details in the petition (also RSC Form No 11).

(b) Affidavit of proof of debt (RSC Form No 12). This must be signed in the normal way giving details of the debt due to the creditor. It is important to note that it must be signed in three places. The Examiner's Office will then allocate a date for the hearing of the petition. Then, a copy of the petition is served on the debtor personally at least seven days before the hearing. An affidavit of service must be filed at least two days before the hearing of the petition.

The original order of adjudication (RSC Form No 15) is filed on the Examiner's File once it has been signed by the bankruptcy judge. The duplicate order of adjudication is given to the 'bankruptcy inspector' who is usually the first person to inform the bankrupt of his bankruptcy. The order of adjudication is served on the bankrupt by the bankruptcy inspector. The duplicate order carries a note on the back which informs the bankrupt that he has three days from the service of the duplicate order to appeal against the validity of the bankruptcy. The court has power to extend this time to a maximum of 14 days. The bankruptcy inspector is entitled to seize the goods of the bankrupt because by act of law at the time of the adjudication of the bankrupt all the bankrupt's assets become vested in the Official Assignee.

12.2.2.3 *Appealing the bankruptcy*

As mentioned, the bankrupt has three days or any extended time as the court thinks fit (not exceeding 14 days) from the service of the duplicate order of adjudication to appeal against the validity of the order (BA 1988, s 16 B).

If no appeal is made, then the following documents must be produced to the Examiner's office:

(a) Advertisement: this is a notice in which the date for the statutory sitting before the court is fixed. The solicitor for the petitioner is obliged to publish the notice in *Iris Oifigiúil* and in newspapers at the direction of the court (RSC Form No 19).

(b) Summons to bankrupt to attend public sittings (in duplicate): this summons is served on the bankrupt when the date for the statutory sitting has been fixed and if the bankrupt does not attend the sitting he is in contempt of court (RSC Form 14).

In the case of an appeal by the bankrupt to have the bankruptcy upset, the application is started by issuing a notice (RSC Form No 16). The bankrupt must file this notice within three days from the date of service of the copy order of adjudication. The court may extend this period to a maximum of 14 days.

The Examiner sets a date for the first hearing of the application before the court. This is known as an application to 'show cause'. On that date the bankrupt should indicate clearly to the court his reasons for trying to upset the bankruptcy and ultimately the court will decide whether the bankrupt's application is valid or not.

When hearing the bankrupt's application to show cause:

(a) the court shall annul the bankruptcy if the bankrupt satisfies the court that the provisions of s 11 of BA 1988 have not been complied with (see section **12.2.2.2** above); or

(b) in any other case, the court may:
  (i) dismiss the application; or
  (ii) adjourn it on certain conditions (BA 1988, s 16).

Very often the debtor cannot dispute any of the provisions of s 11 but he appeals to the court's equitable jurisdiction which allows the bankruptcy judge to make orders on the grounds of equity.

It is important to realise that while the bankrupt is appealing against his bankruptcy, he is still a bankrupt and the bankruptcy continues subject to any orders which the court might make by way of relief to the bankrupt. In particular, the court will probably restrain publication of the existence of the bankruptcy. However, the bankrupt is normally liable to the disabilities of bankruptcy such as not being able to trade or operate a bank account. Ultimately, if the court accepts the application of the bankrupt, the bankruptcy will be annulled. If the bankrupt's application fails, then the bankruptcy proceeds in the usual way.

12.3   The debtor's position

Before anyone is adjudicated bankrupt, there is no doubt that he will have received many warnings. In fact, in a number of cases, the creditor will have obtained a judgment in one of the courts against the debtor and the debtor would have received independent warnings about the judgment.

As soon as the bankruptcy proceedings are threatened, the debtor should immediately approach the creditor who is threatening bankruptcy. This should be done because it is possible to remove the threat of bankruptcy by satisfying this creditor at this stage in the proceedings but, if the debtor is adjudicated bankrupt, then he must deal with all his creditors and the court will insist that all creditors have been satisfied before allowing the bankruptcy to be annulled.

If the money is available, then the debtor should pay the debt straight away, but in normal situations, it is advisable that a statement of affairs of the debtor be produced so that this can be handed to the creditor to disclose the true financial position of the debtor and to persuade the creditor to accept a realistic settlement.

This is also a good time to point out to the creditor that the return to him in financial terms in a bankruptcy is likely to be unsatisfactory. The realisation process can be slow, and because the petitioning creditor will gain no priority over the other creditors, the creditor may receive nothing at the end of the day. By settling immediately, the creditor is avoiding the very heavy costs involved in pursuing the adjudication.

Obviously the debtor should examine the amount claimed by the creditor and if there is any dispute about the figures, then this dispute should be communicated immediately to the creditor. If there is clear evidence of a dispute and this has been pointed out in writing to the creditor, it would be very unwise of the creditor to proceed further without first resolving the dispute. If a disputed debt is used as the basis for bankruptcy proceedings, the court will not look favourably on the creditor and will probably dismiss the bankruptcy summons and may award the costs against the creditor (BA 1988, s 8).

If the bankruptcy does take place, the debtor has the right to appeal, which has already been mentioned. If none of the statutory reasons for appealing are available and therefore the debtor is relying on the equitable jurisdiction of the court, then it is essential that a detailed statement of affairs be produced from which the court will see clearly that the bankrupt has assets. It is also extremely helpful to give the court a programme of realisation of the assets with suggested values and timescales involved. If the court sees that the debtor may be able to discharge his debts in full within a reasonably short time, then it is likely that the court will give the debtor the time required. Usually, the debtor's tax affairs will be in arrears. Because of this, the greatest delays arise when negotiations start with the relevant Inspector of Taxes to agree up-to-date figures. If the appeal against the adjudication fails, then the court will allow the bankruptcy to proceed in the normal way, with publicity taking place (traditionally in two national newspapers and one local newspaper). The bankrupt must co-operate with the Official Assignee/Trustee in every respect.

After 12 years, bankruptcy may be discharged.

12.3.1   Debtor's own petition

Where a debtor considers himself to be insolvent, and where he can prove that his estate will readily realise at least €1,900, he can petition the court for an order declaring him bankrupt (BA 1988, s 15).

The debtor will also have to pay expenses such as stamp duty and advertising fees.

12.4   Arrangements with creditors outside/prior to bankruptcy

12.4.1   Methods

There are two methods by which a debtor can make formal arrangements with his creditors:

(a)   a private arrangement under the control of the court; or

(b)   a private arrangement outside the court.

A private arrangement under the control of the court is governed by ss 87–109 of BA 1988. To start an arrangement under the control of the court, the debtor presents a petition supported by affidavit to the court setting out the reasons for his inability to pay his debts and requesting protection from actions/processes (including bankruptcy proceedings). An order for protection may be granted even if there is an execution order in the hands of the sheriff (BA 1988, s 89).

When the protection order has been granted:

(a)   the court will direct the debtor to hold a preliminary meeting of his creditors. The debtor must present a statement of his assets and liabilities to this meeting and keep a minute of the proceedings;

(b)   the court will give a date for the private sitting of the court, which will take place after the preliminary meeting;

(c)   the debtor must lodge with the Official Assignee a memorandum containing:

   (i)   the date of the protection order,

   (ii)   his name and address,

   (iii) the amount of his liabilities,

   (iv)   the amount of assets; and

(d)   a duplicate of the memorandum must be filed in the Central Office.

The debtor must file in the Official Assignee's office at least two days before the private sitting of the court:

(a)   his statement of affairs incorporating his offer to creditors;

(b)   a copy of the statement of assets and liabilities presented to the creditors at the preliminary meeting; and

(c)   the minutes of the preliminary meeting.

The creditors vote at the sitting of the court. If three-fifths in number and value vote in favour of the proposal, it is deemed accepted. The court must approve the 'accepted' offer. When approved by the court, the offer is binding on all creditors. A creditor for less than €130 is not entitled to vote. The debtor must attend the sitting of the court.

A debtor who makes an offer to his creditors runs a high risk, because the court may adjudicate him bankrupt if:

(a)   he does not file the relevant documents;

(b)   his offer is not accepted;

(c)   his proposal is annulled;

(d) his affidavit (filed with petition) is wilfully untrue, in that assets and liabilities have not been fully disclosed;

(e) it appears that he does not wish to make a 'bona fide arrangement with his creditors';

(f) his proposal is not reasonable;

(g) he does not attend the private sitting before the court;

(h) he fails to obey any order of the court; or

(i) he is 'party to any corrupt agreement with his creditors to secure the acceptance of his proposal'.

Such arrangements are rare, due to the level of costs and risks as above. Note the similarity of this (old) concept to that of examinership (for companies).

12.4.2 Arrangements outside court

In these cases, there is no involvement by the bankruptcy jurisdiction of the High Court. An arrangement made in this way is a matter of contract between the debtor and his creditors.

Normally, the debtor enters into a written agreement with all his creditors, the effect of which is as follows:

(a) the deed transfers the debtor's property (or most of it) to a trustee;

(b) the trustee agrees to dispose of all the property transferred to him and to hold the property/proceeds in trust for the purpose of paying:

    (i) all costs and expenses of and incidental to the deed,

    (ii) preferential liabilities, as per bankruptcy rules,

    (iii) an agreed dividend to creditors,

    (iv) the surplus, if any, to be repaid to the debtor;

(c) the trustee is given power to:

    (i) remunerate himself or any person employed by him and to pay the debtor any allowance he may think fit for services rendered,

    (ii) require a creditor to furnish particulars of the debt claimed,

    (iii) realise the assets in the method considered most appropriate;

(d) the debtor contracts with the trustee and with each creditor that:

    (i) he will give all information concerning his estate and give all assistance to the trustee,

    (ii) he will not object in any way to the sale of any property;

(e) the debtor appoints the trustee to be his attorney so that deeds can be signed on behalf of the debtor; and

(f) the creditors agree to release the debtor from all debts, claims and actions etc (but this is usually done on the basis that it is without prejudice to any rights which the creditor may have against a guarantor).

The transfer of the property to the trustee is an act of bankruptcy and may lead to the debtor being adjudicated bankrupt at any time within three months after the signing of the trust deed. However, if a creditor agrees to join in the arrangement, then that creditor is debarred from relying on the deed as an act of bankruptcy. The major difficulty of an arrangement of this type is that it requires the consent of all creditors. Any debtor trying to conclude an arrangement with his creditors requires detailed information about his financial affairs and the assistance of an accountant is essential.

12.5   After bankruptcy

12.5.1   Disabilities of a bankrupt

When a debtor is declared bankrupt, he immediately suffers some automatic disabilities:

- (a)   all assets (except some minor items: BA 1988, s 45) vest automatically in the Official Assignee (BA 1988, s 44(1));
- (b)   the debtor is not entitled to operate a bank account;
- (c)   under s 183 of CA 1963, an undischarged bankrupt is prohibited from:
    - (i)   acting as a director of any company;
    - (ii)   directly or indirectly taking part in the management of any company; and
    - (iii)   being directly or indirectly concerned in the management of any company.

    The section goes on to say that for the purpose of the section, the word 'company' includes an unregistered company and a company incorporated outside the state which has an established place of business with the state, and s 183A of CA 1963 gives the Director of Corporate Enforcement powers relating to bankrupts.
- (d)   if an Official Liquidator is adjudicated bankrupt, his office is deemed to be vacated and he shall be deemed to have been removed as of the date of his adjudication (RSC Ord 74, r 42);
- (e)   an undischarged bankrupt cannot act as the receiver of a company (s 315 of CA 1963);
- (f)   a bankrupt cannot be a trustee;
- (g)   a bankrupt cannot be a member of the Dáil or Seanad (Electoral Act 1923);
- (h)   a bankrupt cannot be elected a county councillor; and
- (i)   a bankrupt cannot be a member of a local authority.

12.5.2   Bankruptcy offences

In each of the following cases a bankrupt or an arranging debtor is deemed guilty of 'an offence' (BA 1988, s 123):

- (a)   if he does not disclose to the court all his property;
- (b)   if he does not deliver up to the Official Assignee/trustee all property which is in his possession or under his control;
- (c)   if he did not deliver to the Official Assignee/trustee all books and papers relating to his estate;
- (d)   if he conceals any part of his property to the value of €650 or upwards or conceals any debt due to or from him;
- (e)   if he fraudulently removes any part of his property to the value of €650 upwards;
- (f)   if he fails to file or deliver a statement of affairs or makes any material omission in any statement relating to his affairs;
- (g)   if he knowingly fails to inform the Official Assignee/trustee that a false debt had been proved;
- (h)   if he prevents the production of any book or papers affecting or relating to his estate;
- (i)   if he conceals, destroys, mutilates, falsifies any book or paper affecting or relating to his estate;

(j)   if he makes or is privy to the making of any false entry in any book or paper affecting or relating to his estate;

(k)   if he fraudulently parts with, alters or makes any omission in any document affecting or relating to his estate;

(l)   if he attempts to account for any part of his property by fictitious losses or expenses;

(m)   if he obtains by false representation or fraud any property on credit;

(n)   if he obtains, under the false pretence of carrying on business, or if a trader dealing in the ordinary ways of his trade, any property on credit;

(o)   if he pawns, pledges or disposes of any property which he has obtained on credit other than in the ordinary course of trade; or

(p)   if he is guilty of any false representation or fraud for the purpose of obtaining the consent of his creditors or any of them to an agreement with reference to his affairs or his bankruptcy.

Where a person is guilty of an offence, he is liable:

(a)   on summary conviction, to a fine not exceeding €650 or at the discretion of the court, to imprisonment for a term not exceeding 12 months or to both; or

(b)   on conviction on indictment, to a fine not exceeding €2,500 or, at the discretion of the court, to imprisonment for a term not exceeding five years, or to both.

12.6   Winding up by a trustee

A bankrupt's estate may be wound up by either the Official Assignee or by a trustee (normally an accountant/insolvency practitioner).

If, at the statutory meeting before the court, three-fifths in number and value of the creditors present in court vote to have the estate of the bankrupt wound up by a trustee and a committee of inspection, then the trustee takes over from the Official Assignee and proceeds to wind up the affairs of the bankrupt similar to the way in which a liquidator winds up a company. The trustee has all the powers of the Official Assignee. The trustee is appointed by the court and is subject to the control of the court.

12.7   Composition after bankruptcy

At any time after the commencement of his bankruptcy, the bankrupt can apply to the court for an order staying the realisation of his estate to enable him to make an 'offer of composition' to his creditors (BA 1988, s 38). If the court accedes to this application, the bankrupt calls a meeting of his creditors to put the offer to them.

12.7.1   Creditors' meeting

The creditors' meeting takes place before the court (BA 1988, s 39). The creditors must receive notice by post at least ten days before the meeting. The notice must specify the precise offer and must be inserted in *Iris Oifigiúil* at least 10 days before the meeting.

If three-fifths in number and value of the creditors who vote accept the offer, it is deemed to be accepted. The court must approve the offer. When the creditors have accepted it and the court has approved it, the offer is binding on all the creditors. A creditor for less than €130 cannot vote.

A composition may be payable:

(a)   in cash;

(b)   by instalments (security must be given); or

(c)   partly in cash and partly by instalments (again security must be given where the payments are to be by instalments).

12.8   Receivers and managers

Under s 73 of BA 1988 the court can appoint a receiver or a manager of the property or business of a debtor or any part of it.

The RSC provide that:

(a)   after adjudication (as a bankrupt) or after the granting of an order for protection, the court may appoint a receiver or manager of the whole or part of the property of the bankrupt or arranging debtor; and

(b)   a receiver must submit his accounts to the Official Assignee.

Appointments of receivers and managers in this way are very rare. When they take place, they are normally on the application of a mortgagee. The reasons given for the application to appoint a receiver and manager are primarily that it is in the interests of the creditors that the business of the bankrupt or the arranging debtor should be carried on for some time so as to effect a sale of the business as a going concern. In practice, the few cases which have arisen have involved hotels.

12.9   Estates of persons dying insolvent

The introduction of the Bankruptcy Act 1988 brought about changes relating to the estate of a person dying insolvent. Such estates may be wound up by the Official Assignee. A petition for the administration of the estate in this way may be presented to the court by:

(a)   any creditor whose debt would have been sufficient to support a bankruptcy petition against the deceased if he had been alive; or

(b)   the personal representative of the deceased.

On the hearing of the petition, the court may, unless it appears that there is a reasonable probability that the estate will be sufficient for the payment of the deceased's debts, make an order for the administration of the estate by the Official Assignee or, upon cause shown, dismiss the petition with or without costs (BA 1988, s 117).

```
                          ┌─────────────────┐
                          │   Particulars   │
                          └─────────────────┘
                                   │
  Payment ◄──────────────────────┤
                                   │
                          ┌─────────────────┐
                          │ Bankruptcy Summons │
                          └─────────────────┘
                                   │                    ┌──────────────────┐
                                   │                    │  Application to  │
  Payment ◄────────────────────────────────────────────│  Dismiss Summons │
                                   │                    └──────────────────┘
                                   │                       │           │
                                   ▼                       ▼           ▼
                          ┌─────────────┐  ┌────────┐  ┌──────┐   ┌──────────┐
                          │   Petition  │◄─│ Fails  │  │      │   │ Succeeds │
                          └─────────────┘  └────────┘             └──────────┘
                                   │
  Payment ◄──────────────────────┤
                                   │
                          ┌─────────────┐           ┌──────────────────┐
                          │ Return Date │──────────►│ Petition Dismissed│
                          └─────────────┘           └──────────────────┘
                                   │
                          ┌─────────────┐
                          │ Petition Valid │
                          └─────────────┘
                                   │
  ┌────────────┐                   │                  ┌──────────────┐
  │ Show Cause │◄──────────────────────────────────── │ Composition  │
  └────────────┘                                       └──────────────┘
     │       │                                            │         │
     ▼       ▼                                            ▼         ▼
┌─────────┐ ┌───────┐              ┌───────┐         ┌─────────┐
│Succeeds │ │ Fails │──────►  ◄────│ Fails │         │Succeeds │
└─────────┘ └───────┘              └───────┘         └─────────┘
                          ┌───────────────────┐
                          │ 12 Years Discharge │
                          └───────────────────┘
```

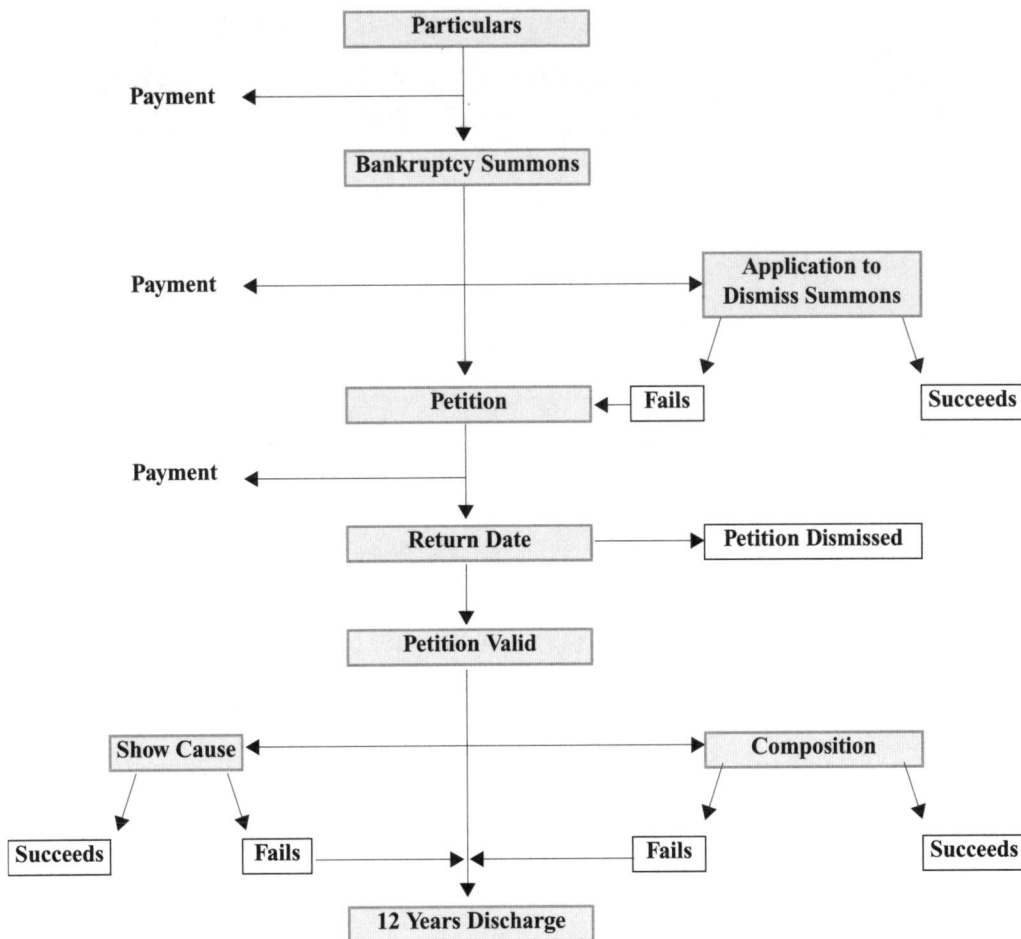

12.10 EU Insolvency Regulation

The EU Insolvency Regulation, Council Regulation (EC) No 1346/2000, came into force on 31 May 2002. It applies to bankruptcy and the administration in bankruptcy of persons dying insolvent.

The Regulation may have a significant impact on cases involving assets and/or enterprises located in different countries which are members of the European Union.

CHAPTER 13

INTERNATIONAL AND CROSS-BORDER INSOLVENCY

Michael Quinn

13.1 Introduction

With the development of the global economy, most cases of any scale give rise to issues as to the cross-border effect of insolvency proceedings. This chapter will briefly outline the issues that arise in such cases. The following topics will be discussed:

(a) the extra-territorial effect of Irish insolvency proceedings;

(b) the effect in Ireland of foreign insolvency proceedings; and

(c) international efforts to streamline the conduct of insolvencies having cross-border effect.

Many of the problems encountered under these headings are resolved by Council Regulation (EU) No 1346/2000 on Insolvency Proceedings (the 'Regulation'), but for issues concerning states outside the EU, the Regulation does not afford the solution.

13.2 Extra-territorial effect of Irish insolvency appointments and orders

The appointment of a liquidator will purport, on its face, to apply to *all* the assets and affairs of a company. This would suggest that an Irish liquidator should be competent to take possession of and realise all the assets of the company, wherever situate. In practice this depends on whether the relevant authorities or third parties in other jurisdictions are willing to recognise the fact that the company is in liquidation and the status and powers of the liquidator. It cannot be assumed, merely because the liquidator, has been properly appointed under Irish company law, that his appointment will be recognised worldwide.

In many cases a liquidator will succeed in realising foreign assets without difficulty. For example, he may simply be able to send his own representatives abroad or appoint local representatives to take possession of moveable goods so that they are returned to the company's possession in Ireland or brought under the liquidator's control and ultimately sold by him for the benefit of creditors. Foreign debtors may recognise his demand for payment and discharge their obligations by making full payment. More commonly, however, a liquidator finds that third parties in other jurisdictions disregard or ignore his appointment. If they are creditors, they may invoke 'self-help' remedies, even if such remedies would be unlawful as against a liquidator, for example seizure of goods in part-payment of a debt, a practice which would only be permissible against a liquidator if the creditor had a valid retention of title clause.

Even if, as a practical matter, third parties can be persuaded to recognise the status of a liquidator, it will frequently be the case that governmental authorities or statutory authorities charged with maintaining public registers of interests in assets, such as immoveable property or intellectual property, may not be empowered to recognise an appointment unless in their own jurisdiction a court order has been made recognising the appointment or giving it local effect.

The extent of recognition varies in different jurisdictions. It is not within the scope of this book to state the laws of all other jurisdictions on this subject. It is, however, useful to summarise the two principal forms of procedures found in other jurisdictions where local courts are asked to assist, which are orders in aid and local winding-up proceedings.

13.2.1   Orders in aid

An order in aid is an order of a local court giving effect in the relevant jurisdiction to the appointment and powers of foreign liquidator, administrator, assignee or trustee. Such an order will generally facilitate such an office-holder to realise assets. In these cases, the order will frequently contain terms which in some way go towards protecting the interests of local creditors. An order in aid may also be granted so as to enable the liquidator to perform his investigative functions, such as exercising the power to interview directors or officers, or to have them examined before a local court.

The concept of an order in aid is widely known in common law jurisdictions and some, notably England, have specific statutory provisions identifying the foreign jurisdictions whose liquidators or other such officers will be assisted by this procedure.

13.2.2   Local winding-up proceedings

Some jurisdictions also have the concept of liquidating the affairs of a branch of a foreign corporation. This procedure involves the local court ordering a full liquidation of the company in the relevant jurisdiction. This procedure will not always facilitate the liquidation of the main company as it will generally mean the realisation of assets for the benefit of local creditors, with only the surplus, if any, being remitted to the 'main liquidator'.

13.2.3   Other issues

Because different jurisdictions throughout the world have different approaches to the recognition of foreign insolvency procedures, it is extremely difficult to predict the efficiency of an insolvency assignment having cross-border implications. A difficult example for Ireland is examinership. Once a petition for the appointment of an examiner is presented to the High Court, the company is deemed to be under the protection of the court, a concept known under the US equivalent Chapter Eleven procedure as the 'automatic stay'. Frequently the automatic stay is critical to the ongoing survival of the company on a going-concern basis. However, if the company has a business and assets located in jurisdictions which will not recognise or give effect to the automatic stay, the ongoing survival of the company may be prejudiced by the actions of local creditors, such as repossession of trading premises or other assets. Similarly, it will be necessary to know at the outset that if a scheme of arrangement is proposed and confirmed by order of the High Court, it can be rendered binding on all interested parties, including foreign creditors. As a matter of Irish law, such a scheme will bind all creditors regardless of their place of origin. However, it will still be a matter for the relevant foreign law as to whether creditors are precluded from disregarding the scheme and pursuing local remedies in their own jurisdiction. An Irish court will be reluctant to make an order where there is doubt as to whether it can be enforced.

The issues described above arise where the assets and activities of the company in other jurisdictions are those of the company itself, whether arising directly or through a branch. If the company has incorporated a subsidiary in other jurisdictions, as will commonly be the case, that subsidiary is a separate legal identity which is liable to be subject entirely to the insolvency procedures which govern companies in that jurisdiction. The interest and rights of a liquidator of a parent company are confined to those of a shareholder. This can mean in certain cases that the 'parent liquidator' would himself initiate steps to have the subsidiary company placed in liquidation under the relevant local laws. The principal continuing interest of the parent liquidator will be to await the remittance of any surplus from the local liquidator.

Finally, it is worth noting that the concept of a floating charge, common in Ireland and the UK, is not recognised in some jurisdictions. This means that a receiver appointed pursuant to such a charge will often not be recognised in other jurisdictions. This creates particular difficulties, and is not addressed by the EU Insolvency Regulation.

13.3 Effect in Ireland of foreign insolvency proceedings

Many jurisdictions approach the issue of recognition of foreign insolvency proceedings from the point of view of reciprocity and orders in aid are sometimes granted in cases where the courts of the foreign state concerned also make such orders under a corresponding provision.

Section 250 of CA 1963 provides that an order made by a court of any country recognised for the purposes of that section, and made for or in the course of winding up a company, may be enforced by the High Court in the same manner in all respects as if the order had been made by the High Court itself. Thus the court will recognise such a foreign order. The only country in respect of which the necessary ministerial order has been made for the purpose of this section is Great Britain and Northern Ireland. Section 250 has recently been amended so that it does not apply in relation to an order made by a court of a state to which the EU Insolvency Regulation applies.

As far as restructurings are concerned, s 36 of the Companies (Amendment) Act 1990 provides similarly that any order made by a court of any country recognised for the purpose of that section and made for or in the course of reorganisation or reconstruction of a company may be enforced by the High Court. No recognition order has yet been made under this section.

The nearest equivalent of these sections in the context of personal bankruptcies is s 142(1) of the Bankruptcy Act 1988, which expressly provides that the High Court and its officers may act in aid of any court in the Isle of Man or the Channel Islands, at the request of such a court, in any bankruptcy matter before such court, and that the High Court shall have like jurisdiction and authority as in the case of a bankruptcy originating under its own original jurisdiction. Section 142 further provides that the government may by order extend this provision to any other jurisdiction where the government is satisfied that reciprocal facilities to that effect will be afforded by that jurisdiction. (Originally this section included orders made by a court in Northern Ireland, England and Wales and Scotland. This has been deleted and recognition of bankruptcy orders made in those states is governed by the EU Insolvency Regulation.)

It will always be necessary to examine the particular rules which apply to any jurisdiction where a foreign insolvency office-holder seeks to be recognised in this jurisdiction.

13.4 International rules on cross-border insolvencies

Historically, there has been very little harmonisation of insolvency law throughout Europe or worldwide. This is largely explained by the fact that although insolvency in many jurisdictions is largely a matter of company law, it is characterised also by principles based on other disciplines such as the laws of property and equity and certain regulatory controls. Because the insolvency laws are not uniform, it has proved difficult to harmonise substantive laws and there are no regulations or conventions (except those applying to insurance undertakings) which attempt to do so. However, efforts have been made to establish a regime for the improved efficiency and effectiveness of the conduct of cross-border insolvencies in the European Union. The result of these efforts is contained in Council Regulation No 1346/2000, which will be dealt with in further detail below.

The United Nations Commission on International Trade Law (UNCITRAL) has adopted a Model Law on Cross-Border Insolvency. The model law is designed to provide uniform legislative provisions to deal with cross-border insolvency and to promote the objectives of:

(a)   co-operation between the courts and competent authorities involved in cases of cross-border insolvency;

(b)   fair and efficient administration of cross-border insolvency that protects the interests of all creditors and other interested persons, including the debtors;

(c)   protection and maximisation of the value of the debtors' assets; and

(d)   facilitation of the rescue of financially troubled businesses.

The UNCITRAL Model Law has not yet been adopted by Ireland. Therefore, for cases between Ireland and states outside the EU, the issues discussed earlier in this Chapter still arise.

13.5   Council Regulation (EU) No 1346/2000 on Insolvency Proceedings

The entry into force of the Regulation on 31 May 2002 brought an end to a prolonged vacuum in EU law relating to insolvency, marked by the absence of co-ordinated international approach to the recognition of insolvency proceedings.

The Brussels Convention on Jurisdiction of Courts and Enforcement of Judgments in Civil and Commercial Matters expressly excluded:

> bankruptcy proceedings relating to winding up of insolvent companies and other legal persons, judicial arrangements, compositions and analogous proceedings (Article 1).

A similar exclusion is contained in Regulation No 44/2001 on Jurisdiction and the Recognition and Enforcement of Judgments in Civil and Commercial Matters, which entered into force on 1 March 2002 (Article 1.2).

Several bi-party or multi-party Conventions existed on this subject, principally between countries with close geographic, economic and financial ties, for example between Belgium and France, between Belgium and The Netherlands, between Germany and Austria, and between the Nordic States. Ireland was not a party to any such Conventions.

The Regulation is not an attempt to harmonise substantive laws, but establishes a regime for the improved efficiency and effectiveness of the conduct of cross-border insolvencies. This is achieved by providing for cross-border recognition and enforcement of basic orders such as the appointment of liquidators and other insolvency office-holders, and of remedies typically invoked in insolvency proceedings. It also establishes a regime for the management of asset realisation and the processing of creditor claims in multi-jurisdictional cases.

Whilst harmonisation is not the objective, the Regulation contains some important substantive provisions which achieve a form of limited harmonisation for individual cases by the mandatory application of the laws of the Member State in which insolvency proceedings are opened (*les concursus*).

13.6   Scope of the Regulation

The Regulation is expressed to apply to:

> Collective insolvency proceedings, which entail the partial or total divestment of a debtor and the appointment of a liquidator (Article 1).

The Annex to the Regulations stipulates for each jurisdiction the category of proceedings which this includes. In the case of Ireland, these are listed as meaning compulsory winding up, bankruptcy, administration in bankruptcy of the estate of persons dying insolvent, winding up in bankruptcy of partnerships, creditors' voluntary winding up (with confirmation of a court), arrangements under the control of the court which involve the vesting of all or part of the property of the debtor in the official assignee for realisation and distribution, and company examinership. Whilst the Regulation provides for 'creditors' voluntary winding up (with confirmation of a court)', the concept of voluntary liquidation in Ireland generally means, by definition, that there has been no court order. The Corporate Insolvency Regulations (SI 333/2002) establish a procedure whereby such a liquidator can apply to have his appointment confirmed by a certificate of the Master of the High Court, thereby bringing it within the scope of the Regulation.

The term 'liquidator' is defined as 'any person or body whose function is to administer or liquidate assets of which the debtor has been divested or to supervise the administration of his affairs' (Article 2). The Annex lists those persons for each Member State. In the case of Ireland, it means a liquidator, official assignee, trustee in bankruptcy, provisional liquidator or examiner.

Receivership is also excluded from the Regulation. In Ireland and the United Kingdom receivership is frequently regarded as a form of insolvency practice. This is because the most common form of receivership in commercial practice is the receiver appointed under a modern bank debenture containing a floating charge over all the assets of the borrowing company. In truth, such an appointment is no more than the enforcement by one creditor of his security over defined assets and therefore is not a 'collective insolvency proceeding' such as the Regulation is intended to embrace. While such receiverships are common in Ireland, they are relatively unknown in many EU Member States. Therefore recognition of such appointments can be problematic in some EU jurisdictions.

The Regulation does not apply to insolvency proceedings concerning insurance undertakings, credit institutions or collective investment undertakings. Insurance undertakings are the subject of a separate Directive, 2001/17/EC. Credit institutions are subject to Directive 2001/24/EU.

Where the Regulation uses the term 'debtor', this means the entity the subject of insolvency proceedings, whether it be a natural or legal person, corporate or non-corporate. (This contrasts with Irish domestic company law, which applies only to companies formed under the Companies Acts.)

13.7   Jurisdiction and 'main' proceedings

The cornerstone of the jurisdictional regime is established by Article 3. Article 3.1 provides that the courts of the Member State in which the centre of a debtor's main interests is situated shall have jurisdiction to open insolvency proceedings. This will be the main state for primary proceedings, or the 'State of the opening of proceedings'.

The Regulation does not define the term 'centre of main interests' (COMI). Article 3.1 states only that in the case of a company or legal person, the place of the registered office shall be presumed to be the centre of its main interests in the absence of proof to the contrary. This is a rebuttable presumption.

The only other guidance is to be found in paragraph (13) of the Preamble, which states that:

> The centre of main interests should correspond to the place where the debtor conducts the administration of his interests on a regular basis and is therefore ascertainable by third parties.

The establishment of the location of the COMI of the debtor (company or natural person) is critical in every case where a debtor has assets in more than one Member State. This is because where the proceedings are opened in the state of the COMI, they have the universal effect within the EU afforded by the Regulation and the insolvency process is governed by the laws of the state of the COMI.

Identification of COMI has been the subject of a number of reported cases. The leading case is the case of *Eurofood IFSC Limited* Case C–341/04, ECJ 2/5/2006. This case concerned a company incorporated in Ireland, which was a wholly owned subsidiary of the Italian food conglomerate Parmalat s.p.a. The function of Eurofood was to administer financing facilities for trading companies in the Parmalat group. The company had four directors, being two executives of the Parmalat group based in Italy, and two professionals (a lawyer and a banker) based in Ireland. It was not disputed that many of the broad commercial policy decisions relating to the transactions of the company were taken in Italy. However, the key issue of fact was where the company 'administered its interests on a regular basis ... ascertainable by third parties'. The court was satisfied that in so far as the administration of the company's affairs was concerned, all the evidence showed that this was in Ireland and, accordingly, found that the COMI was in Ireland. In the judgments of both the Supreme Court of Ireland and of the European Court of Justice, there was debate about cases where a company incorporated in one state finds itself largely influenced in decision-making by a parent company located in another Member State. The European Court held as follows:

> where a debtor is a subsidiary company whose registered office and that of its parent company are situated in two different Member States, the presumption laid down in the second sentence of Article 3.1 of the Regulation, whereby the centre of main interests of that subsidiary is situated in the Member State where its registered office is situated, can be rebutted only if factors which are both objective and ascertainable by third parties enable it to be established that an actual situation exists which is different from that which location of that registered office is deemed to reflect. That could be so in particular in the case of a company not carrying out any business in the territory of the Member State. By contrast, where a company carries on its business in the territory of the Member State where its registered office is situated, the mere fact that its economic choices are or can be controlled by a parent company in another Member State is not enough to rebut the presumption laid down by that Regulation.

There have been many cases, both before and after *Eurofoods*, in which the relevant courts have found that the COMI is located in a Member State other than the state of incorporation of the debtor. All the circumstances and facts are taken into account in making such findings, and a petition for the opening of such proceedings is required to detail the evidence supporting the assertion of COMI, particularly where it is being asserted that the presumption based on the location of the registered office can be rebutted.

13.7.1   Territorial proceedings

Article 3.2 provides that where the centre of a debtor's main interest is situate within the territory of any Member State, the courts of another Member State have jurisdiction to open insolvency proceedings against that debtor if it possesses an establishment within the territory of that other Member State. The effect of such proceedings is restricted to the assets of the debtor located in the territory of the second Member State. These are therefore called 'territorial insolvency proceedings'. If proceedings have already opened in the main state, these 'territorial proceedings' will be 'secondary' and therefore subordinate to the 'main proceedings'.

The intention is that territorial insolvency proceedings will only be opened outside the 'main' state after the opening of main proceedings and thus will be 'secondary' to the main proceedings. There are, however, two circumstances in which territorial proceedings can be opened without insolvency proceedings opening in the main state (Article 3.4):

(a) where main insolvency proceedings cannot be opened because the conditions for doing so in the main state cannot be satisfied; and

(b) where territorial proceedings are requested by a creditor in the second Member State within which the debtor has the necessary establishment, or where the creditor's claim arises from the operation of that establishment.

The potential for abuse by the opening of insolvency proceedings in a multiplicity of jurisdictions, causing duplications of administrative expenses and loss of value for creditors generally, is addressed by the requirement that for the opening of any territorial proceedings, the debtor has an establishment within the relevant territory. The term 'establishment' is defined as 'any place of operations where the debtor carries out a non-transitory economic activity with human means and goods' (Article 2). This limits the scope for forum shopping, because the mere presence of assets, however great or small their value, in a Member State other than the main state, will not be sufficient to enable the courts of such a state to exercise insolvency jurisdictions on a territorial basis.

13.8 Recognition of insolvency proceedings

Chapter II establishes the rules for recognition of insolvency judgments. Any judgment opening insolvency proceedings handed down by a court of a Member State which has jurisdiction under the Regulation shall be recognised in all the other Member States from the time it becomes effective in the state of opening of the proceedings (Article 16). Thus the appointment of a liquidator shall be recognised in other Member States without any further formalities. This extends also to not only the order appointing a liquidator, but also the powers of the liquidator, being the powers conferred on him by the laws of the main state.

The liquidator's appointment is evidenced by a certified copy of the original decision appointing him or any other certificate issued by the court which has jurisdiction. He may exercise all those powers which derive from his appointment, including the power to remove the debtor's assets from the territory of any Member State in which they are situate, subject to special rules concerning rights *in rem*. If territorial proceedings have been opened in another state or if asset preservation measures have been taken, the main liquidator must respect those proceedings in relation to the assets in that territory.

Article 21 provides for the publication by a liquidator of notice of his appointment in the Member State in which he has been appointed, and in any relevant Member State. The notice must state whether he is a 'main' liquidator or a 'secondary' liquidator.

Such publication is particularly important in the context of third parties honouring obligations to the debtor. Article 24 provides that where an obligation has been honoured in a Member State for the benefit of a debtor who is subject to insolvency proceedings opened in another Member State when it should in fact have been honoured for the benefit of the liquidator in those proceedings, the person honouring the obligations is deemed to have discharged the obligation only if he was unaware of the opening of the insolvency proceedings. If the appointment has first been advertised in that Member State, the third party is presumed to have been aware of the opening of the proceedings and the onus will fall on him to prove otherwise.

Recognition extends not only to judgments concerning the opening of insolvency proceedings and appointment of liquidators, but also to judgments concerning the course and closure of insolvency proceedings and compositions approved by the court. Such judgments may be enforced by the procedure described in Regulation No 44/2001 (relating to civil and commercial judgments generally).

13.8.1   Insolvency judgments

The rule of recognition, without further formalities, applies also to 'judgments deriving directly from the insolvency proceedings and which are closely linked with them, even if they were handed down by another court'.

This is a significant substantive provision which extends recognition and enforcement beyond such basics matters as the asset swelling remedies, notably fraudulent preference challenges (CA 1963, s 286); invalidation of floating charges (CA 1963, s 288); the power of a liquidator to apply to the court for the return of assets improperly transferred by the company (CA 1990, s 139); and the power of the court to order a company to contribute to the debts of a related company (CA 1990, s 140) or to order the pooling of assets of related companies where both are in liquidation (CA 1990, s 141). It will also extend to remedies affecting officers of the insolvent company, such as declarations of personal liability for the debts of the company grounded on fraudulent or reckless trading (CA 1963, s 297) or on failure to keep proper books of account of the company (CA 1990, s 204); liability for misfeasance (CA 1963, s 298); and the power of the court to summons persons for examination before the court and to order the return of assets (CA 1963, s 245).

Before the Regulation came into force, the limited ability to enforce many of these remedies against foreign parties or foreign resident directors (all being excluded from the Brussels Convention) had confined the range of remedies available to liquidators. Thus the Regulation greatly improves this aspect of insolvency practice as far as EU-resident parties and the recovery of assets within other Member States are concerned.

One would also expect that orders restricting the directors of an insolvent company from being appointed as directors or officers or being concerned in the management of a company unless they meet certain capital requirements or disqualifying directors absolutely from so acting (CA 1990, Pt VII) will be recognised and enforced under the regulation on the grounds that such orders are judgments 'deriving directly from the insolvency proceedings and which are closely linked with them'.

There are some provisions of Irish company law which, although 'closely linked' with insolvency proceedings, are perhaps not 'deriving directly' from them. For example, s 251 of CA 1990 provides that certain of the provisions of the Companies Acts which previously only applied where a company was being wound up, may be applied where a company is insolvent but is not being wound up and the reason or principal reason why it is not being wound up is the insufficiency of its assets. The provisions which can be applied in such circumstances include the following:

(a)   the power of the court to order the return of assets improperly or fraudulently transferred (CA 1990, s 139);

(b)   the power of the court to order a company to contribute to the debts of related companies (CA 1990, s 140);

(c)   criminal and civil liability of officers where the company's failure to keep proper books of account contributes to the inability of the company to pay its debts (CA 1990, ss 203 and 204);

(d)   the power of the court to order inspection of books and papers by creditors and contributories;

(e)   the power of the court to summon persons for examination before the court and make orders for return of assets (CA 1963, s 245);

(f)   power to arrest an absconding contributory (CA 1963, s 247);

(g)   liability for fraudulent and reckless trading (CA 1963, s 297); and

(h)   liability of officers for misfeasance (CA 1963, s 298).

Section 251 of CA 1990 is a far-reaching provision which is being invoked more frequently, principally in some cases by the Director of Corporate Enforcement. Undoubtedly a judgment under this section would be 'closely linked' with insolvency proceedings. However, it is questionable whether in the absence of the opening of insolvency proceedings as defined in the Regulation they 'derive directly' from insolvency proceedings. They are, therefore, outside the scope of the Regulation.

13.9   *Lex concursus*

Article 4 declares that the law applicable to insolvency proceedings and their effects shall be that of the Member State within the territory in which such proceedings are opened, known as the 'State of opening of proceedings'. This is the concept of the *lex concursus*. It is one of the most important features of the Regulation in that it governs not only laws relating to procedural matters, but many of the substantive rules which affect the conduct of insolvency proceedings. Article 4 lists the principal such matters. The most important are those concerning the ascertainment of assets and liabilities of the debtor, including:

(a)   the treatment of assets acquired and liabilities incurred after the opening of the insolvency proceedings;

(b)   the respective powers of the debtor and the liquidator;

(c)   the conditions under which set offs may be invoked;

(d)   the effects of insolvency proceedings on current contracts to which the debtor is a party;

(e)   the effects of the proceedings brought by individual creditors (with the exception of law suits pending);

(f)   the rules governing the lodging, verification and admission of claims;

(g)   the rules governing the distribution of proceeds from the realisation of assets, the ranking of claims and the rights of creditors who have obtained partial satisfaction after the opening of insolvency proceedings by virtue of a right *in rem* or through a set off;

(h)   rules concerning the costs and expenses incurred in the insolvency proceedings; and

(i)   rules relating to voidness and voidability or enforceability of legal acts detrimental to all the creditors.

This mandatory choice of law is the closest one finds to a harmonisation of laws, in that the *lex concursus* will govern all these issues in the liquidation of any one debtor company. Where the insolvency proceedings are commenced in the state where the debtor has its centre of main interests, those rules have effect throughout the EU. Therefore, the Regulation will enable those who have dealings with a debtor whose centre of main interest is within the EU to know the substantive legal provisions by which their rights would be determined in the event of the debtor's insolvency. In doing so, counterparties should not assume that the place of the registered office determines this issue (see **13.7** above) and should satisfy themselves on the location of the COMI.

13.9.1   Special choice of law

There are a number of special choice of law rules by way of exceptions to the principle of determination according to the *lex concursus*. These concern such matters as:

(a)   rights *in rem* in respect of assets belonging to the debtor which are situated within the territory of another Member State at the time of the opening of the proceedings (Article 5);

(b)   the right of creditors to claim set off where such is permitted by the laws governing the creditor's claim but perhaps not by the *lex concursus* (Article 6);

(c)   the rights of the seller of goods under reservation of title and the rights of purchasers of goods (Article 7);

(d)   issues concerning immoveable property are governed solely by the law of the Member State within which the property is situate (*lex situs*) (Article 8);

(e)   the effects of insolvency proceedings on parties to a payment system or settlement system or to a financial market are governed by the law of the Member State applicable to that system or market (Article 9);

(f)   issues concerning employment contracts are governed solely by the law of the Member State applicable to the contract of employment (Article 10); and

(g)   issues concerning rights to immoveable property, a ship or an aircraft subject to registration in a public register are determined by the law of the Member State under the authority of which the register is kept (Article 11).

Whilst the *lex concursus* governs rules concerning voidness, voidability or unenforceability of acts detrimental to all creditors, this is subject to the exception that the *lex concursus* shall not apply where the person who benefited from an act detrimental to the creditors proves that the act is subject to the law of a Member State other than that of the state of opening of the proceedings and that law does not allow any means of challenging that act in the relevant case (Article 13). This exception is not intended to permit other states to apply their own standards to transactions under scrutiny, but it must be shown that their laws do not permit such a challenge in any circumstances whatsoever.

13.10   Secondary insolvency proceedings

Chapter III provides that the opening of proceedings in the debtor's centre of main interests will permit the opening in another Member State of secondary insolvency proceedings without the debtor's insolvency being examined in that other state. The secondary insolvency proceedings can only be opened in another state where the debtor has an establishment. Such proceedings are territorial in effect. This means that they are restricted to the assets of the debtor situated in the territory of the second Member State.

Secondary insolvency proceedings under Chapter III must be 'winding-up proceedings'. The definition of 'winding-up proceedings' is more limited than 'insolvency proceedings'. Winding-up proceedings are proceedings involving only the realisation of assets of the debtor. They do not include proceedings for a reorganisation. The Annex to the Regulation defines winding-up proceedings and, in the case of Ireland, examinership is excluded.

Whilst primacy is given to the main proceedings, the law applicable to secondary proceedings is the law of the Member State within which those secondary proceedings are opened. This is most critical in such aspects as the priority and ranking of claims, the effects on contracts and the potential for challenge to transactions based on laws relating to such matters as voidable preferences. However, those laws of the 'second state' only apply in relation to the realisation and distribution of the assets within that state.

Secondary proceedings may be requested by a liquidator in the main proceedings or any other person or authority empowered to request the opening of insolvency proceedings under the law of the Member State within which the secondary proceedings are requested. Typically this would enable such proceedings to be commenced on the application of either the liquidator in the main proceedings or a creditor or other interested party in the relevant second state.

The Regulation imposes a system for communication and exchange of information between the 'main' liquidator and the 'secondary' liquidator. Article 31 provides that the liquidators shall be duty-bound to communicate information to each other and to co-operate with each other. They must immediately communicate any information which may be relevant to the other proceedings, in particular the progress made in lodging and verifying claims and all measures aimed at terminating the proceedings. The secondary liquidation must give the main liquidator an 'early opportunity of submitting proposals on the liquidation or the use of assets in the secondary proceedings'.

The court which has opened secondary proceedings can stay the process of liquidation in those proceedings on the request of the main liquidator. In doing so it may require the main liquidator to take measures to guarantee the interests of creditors in the secondary proceedings. Such a stay can be rejected only if it is manifestly of no interest to the creditors of the main proceedings. A stay may be for a period of up to three months and can be extended for similar periods (Article 33).

A creditor may lodge his claim in the main proceedings and in any secondary proceedings. Each liquidator shall then lodge in the other proceedings claims which have already been lodged in his liquidation provided that doing so advances the interests of the creditors concerned. Each liquidator is empowered to participate in the other proceedings on the same basis as a creditor, in particular by attending creditors' meetings (Article 32).

Although secondary proceedings must be 'winding-up' proceedings and therefore cannot be commenced as proceedings for a reorganisation or rescue plan, if the law governing the secondary proceedings permits the closure of such proceedings without liquidation of the debtor but by a rescue plan, composition or comparable measure, the main liquidator can propose such a measure. Closure of the secondary proceedings by such a measure can only become final with the consent of the main liquidator. If the main liquidator refuses his consent, the measure can become final only if the financial interests of the creditors in the main proceedings are not affected by the measure. It is difficult to envisage circumstances in which the main liquidator would withhold his consent unless the interests of the creditors in the main liquidation are impaired. In effect, therefore, the main liquidator enjoys a veto over any such plan.

Where the secondary proceedings result in a surplus after payment of all claims allowed under those proceedings, the second liquidator must transfer that surplus to the main liquidator.

13.11 Information and treatment of creditors

The Regulation establishes a procedural regime for the lodgment of claims and information to creditors and for equality of treatment of creditors generally.

Article 39 permits any creditor in a Member State other than the state of opening of the proceedings, including the tax authorities and social security authorities of Member States, to lodge claims in the insolvency proceedings.

This provision enshrines the basic principle of equality of treatment for creditors, regardless of their state of residence or business attachment. Most importantly, it overrides the widely practised exclusionary rule of private international law whereby the courts of one state refuse to enforce the revenue or other public laws of other sovereign states.

Article 20 contains two important provisions to preserve the fundamental rule of equal treatment of creditors:

(a) Where, after the opening of insolvency proceedings in the state of the debtor's main centre of interests, a creditor obtains by any means total or partial satisfaction of his claim on assets of the debtor situated in the territory of another Member State, he must return those assets to the liquidator.

(b) Where a creditor obtains a dividend in the course of insolvency proceedings in any state, whether it be the primary or a secondary state, he can only share in dividends in other insolvency proceedings where creditors of the same ranking have, in those other proceedings, obtained an equivalent dividend.

13.12 Public policy

A Member State can refuse to recognise insolvency proceedings or judgments of another Member State where doing so would be 'manifestly contrary to that State's public policy, in particular its fundamental principles or the constitutional rights and liberties of the individual' (Article 26). As far as concerns recognition of the appointment of liquidators and the basic process of asset realisation and distributions to creditors, it is difficult to envisage, at least from an Irish point of view, measures which would offend public policy or the Constitution. However, one must anticipate that certain aspects of the investigative and enforcement process could face scrutiny under this Article, either under the Irish Constitution or similar fundamental laws in other Member Sates. For example, s 8 of the Companies (Amendment) Act 1990, which governs examinership law and practice in Ireland, contained a provision to the effect that if an officer or agent of the company or other person refused to produce to the examiner any book or document or answer any question put to him by the examiner, the examiner could certify that refusal to the court and the court would then conduct an enquiry and punish the offender in like manner as if he had been guilty of contempt of court. That provision was based on a similar provision of CA 1990, which was later held to be unconstitutional (*Desmond v Glackin (No 2)* [1993] 3 IR 67). Therefore, amending legislation in 1999 deleted the reference to contempt of court and provides that the court can 'make any order or direction it sees fit' (Companies (Amendment) (No 2) Act 1999). Similarly, s 297 of CA 1963, which provides for personal liability of any directors found party to fraudulent trading, was the subject of a constitutional challenge in 1997 (*O'Keefe v Ferris and Others* [1997] 3 IR 463 (SC)), albeit an unsuccessful challenge. Therefore one must expect that different mechanisms for enquiry and for compelling the provision of information originating in different Member States will encounter challenges from time to time against the fundamental laws in other Member States.

13.13 Conclusion

As a Regulation adopted by the EU Council, this measure has force of law effective from 31 May 2002. Several aspects of the Regulation has been problematic in practice. However, the fundamentals of the Regulation improve the efficiency and effectiveness of cross-border insolvency proceedings and widen the scope of the asset swelling and other remedies available to liquidators.

The Regulation does not legislate for groups of companies. Therefore, its effects are limited to the assets and affairs of each distinct company, including branches in separate states. Accordingly, there will be 'group' cases where the administration of the insolvency will be conducted through the network of subsidiary companies.

The Regulation has been used effectively to open main insolvency proceedings in one jurisdiction, for all companies in a group, thereby applying a uniform insolvency regime to the conduct of the insolvency proceedings. This can only be done if all the relevant companies can be found properly to have their COMI in the one jurisdiction.

INDEX

All references are to heading numbers

A

Acting in good faith

examinerships, and, 9.1.4

'Acts' of bankruptcy

generally, 12.1.3

Advertisements

appointment of liquidators, and, 3.8.1

creditor's petitions, and, 3.5.1.4

proof of debt, and, 3.11.3

Agent of company

liquidators, and, 4.4.4.3

receivers, and, 7.4

Appeals

bankruptcy, and, 12.2.2.3

Appointment of agents

liquidations, and, 4.4.4.1

receivership, and, 7.3.3.2

Appointment of employees

receivership, and, 7.3.3.2

Appointment of examiner

generally, 9.1.9

notification, 9.1.10

Appointment of liquidator

advertisement, 3.8.1

filing notices, 3.8.2

introduction, 3.8

service of notice, 3.8.3

statement on company correspondence, 3.8.4

Appointment of receiver

contract, under, 7.1

court, by, 7.1.1

date of commencement, 7.2.2

effect, 7.6

introduction, 7.2.1

notification, 7.5

purpose, 7.2.1

validity assessment checklist, 8.12

Arrangements with creditors

outside control of court, 12.4.2

under control of court, 12.4.1

Assessed taxes

preferential debts, and, 2.3.3.1

Asset swelling powers

action against directors, 4.5.8

contribution orders, 4.5.7.1–4.5.7.2

failure to keep proper books and records, 4.5.8.2

floating charges, 4.5.6

fraudulent conveyance, 4.5.1

fraudulent disposal of property, 4.5.2

fraudulent preference, 4.5.3

fraudulent trading, 4.5.8.1

introduction, 4.5

payment made by insolvent company, 4.5.4

pooling orders, 4.5.7.3

post-liquidation disposal of assets, 4.5.5

reckless trading, 4.5.8.2

B

'Balance sheet' test

tests for insolvency, and, 1.2

Bankruptcy

'acts' of bankruptcy, 12.1.3

appeals, 12.2.2.3

arrangements with creditors
    outside control of court, 12.4.2
    under control of court, 12.4.1

bankruptcy petition, 12.2.2.2

bankruptcy summons, 12.2.2.1

composition after bankruptcy
    creditors' meeting, 12.7.1
    introduction, 12.7

creditor's proceedings
    appeals, 12.2.2.3
    background, 12.2.1
    introduction, 12.2.2
    petition, 12.2.2.2
    summons, 12.2.2.1

debtor's position
    background, 12.3
    petition, 12.3.1

definition, 12.1.1

disabilities of bankrupt, 12.5.1

EU Regulation (EC/1346/2000), 12.10

historical background, 12.1.2

insolvent deceased estates, 12.9

introduction, 12.1

meaning, 1.1

offences, 12.5.2

overview, 1.1

petition, 12.2.2.2

post-bankruptcy issues
    disabilities of bankrupt, 12.5.1
    offences, 12.5.2

proceedings
    appeals, 12.2.2.3
    background, 12.2.1
    introduction, 12.2.2
    petition, 12.2.2.2
    summons, 12.2.2.1

receivers and managers, 12.8

summons, 12.2.2.1

winding up of estate, 12.6

C

Capital gains tax

preferential debts, and, 2.3.3.1

Carrying on business

liquidators' powers, and, 4.4.4.2

receivers' powers, and, 7.3.2.2

'Cash flow' test

tests for insolvency, and, 1.2

Company's petition

compulsory liquidation, and, 3.5.2

Composition after bankruptcy

creditors' meeting, 12.7.1

introduction, 12.7

Compromise of litigation

receivers' powers, and, 7.3.2.4

Compromises

approval, 9.2.1

examinership, and
    generally, 9.2.4
    introduction, 1.2.5

introduction, 9.2

Revenue, and
    ability to compromise, 9.2.3
    general position, 9.2.2

selection of classes of members and
creditors, 9.2.2

winding-up, and, 9.2.5

Compulsory liquidation

appointment of agent, 4.4.4.3

appointment of liquidator
    advertisement, 3.8.1
    filing notices, 3.8.2
    introduction, 3.8
    service of notice, 3.8.3
    statement on company
    correspondence, 3.8.4

appointment of solicitor, 4.4.4.1

asset swelling powers
    action against directors, 4.5.8
    contribution orders, 4.5.7.1–4.5.7.2
    failure to keep proper books and
    records, 4.5.8.2
    floating charges, 4.5.6
    fraudulent conveyance, 4.5.1
    fraudulent disposal of property, 4.5.2
    fraudulent preference, 4.5.3
    fraudulent trading, 4.5.8.1
    introduction, 4.5
    payment made by insolvent company,
    4.5.4
    pooling orders, 4.5.7.3
    post-liquidation disposal of assets,
    4.5.5
    reckless trading, 4.5.8.2

Compulsory liquidation (contd)

carrying on the business, 4.4.4.2

commencement, 3.4

company's petition, 3.5.2

contributories' meetings, 3.8.7

costs, 2.3.1

creditors' meetings, 3.8.7

creditor's petition

    advertisement, 3.5.1.4

    defences, 3.5.1.6

    demand letter, 3.5.1.1

    generally, 3.5.1

    hearing, 3.5.1.5

    issue, 3.5.1.2

    notice of intention to liquidate, 3.5.1.1

    service, 3.5.1.3

    substitution of creditor, 3.5.1.7

CRO filings, 3.14

debts to employees under contract, 2.3.2

defences, 3.5.1.6

demand letter, 3.5.1.1

effect on officers of company, 3.7

Examiner's Office meetings, 3.9

first sitting of court, 3.10

generally, 1.2.3

introduction, 3.1

issue of notice to proceed, 3.8.8

jurisdiction of court, 3.2

liquidators

    And see **Liquidators**

    appointment, 3.8–3.8.8

    CRO filings, 3.14

    discharge, 3.13

    duties, 4.3.1–4.3.6

    effect, 3.7

    powers, 4.4–4.5

    qualifications, 4.2

    types, 4.1

locus standi, 3.3

notice of intention to liquidate, 3.5.1.1

notice to proceed, 3.8.8

official liquidators, 3.1

order of payments

    costs in court liquidation, 2.3.1

    debts to employees under contract, 2.3.2

    generally, 2.3

    preferential debts, 2.3.3–2.3.3.2

overview, 1.2.3

petitioners, 3.3

preferential debts, 2.3.3–2.3.3.2

priority of payment of debts, 3.11.1

procedure, 3.5

proof of debt

    adjudication of claims, 3.11.4

    advertising for creditors, 3.11.3

    claims admissible to proof, 3.11.2

    generally, 3.11

    priority of payment, 3.11.1

remuneration of liquidator, 3.13

service

    creditor's petition, 3.5.1.3

    notice of appointment of liquidator, 3.8.3

    order on company's bankers, 3.8.5

substitution of creditor, 3.5.1.7

Confirmation of proposals

examinerships, and, 9.1.20

Contracts

examinerships, and

    during protection, 9.1.15

    pre-protection, 9.1.14

Contractual set-off

rules as to priorities, and, 2.2.2

Contributories' meetings

compulsory liquidation, and, 3.8.7

Contribution orders

liquidators' powers, and, 4.5.7.1–4.5.7.2

Corporate insolvency

And see **Winding up**

compulsory liquidation, 1.2.3

creditors' voluntary liquidation, 1.2.2

examination, 1.2.5

introduction, 1.2

members' voluntary liquidation, 1.2.1

receivership, 1.2.4

Corporation tax

preferential debts, and, 2.3.3.1

Costs and expenses

examinerships, and, 9.1.21

order of payments in liquidation, and, 2.3.1

Creditors

distribution and realisation of assets, and, 2.1.2

Creditors' meetings

composition after bankruptcy, and, 12.7.1

compulsory liquidation, and, 3.8.7

examinerships, and, 9.1.17

Creditor's petitions

And see **Compulsory liquidation**

advertisement, 3.5.1.4

defences, 3.5.1.6

demand letter, 3.5.1.1

generally, 3.5.1

hearing, 3.5.1.5

issue, 3.5.1.2

notice of intention to liquidate, 3.5.1.1

service, 3.5.1.3

substitution of creditor, 3.5.1.7

Creditors' voluntary liquidation

accountants', fees, 6.7.4

convening creditors' meeting, 6.7.2–
6.7.2.1

creditors' meeting, 6.9

dissolution, 6.10

employees, 6.4

existing contracts, and, 6.3

final meeting, 6.10

generally, 6.1

introduction, 1.2.2

liquidators

> *And see Liquidators*
>
> asset swelling measures, 4.5–4.5.8
>
> duties, 4.3.1–4.3.6
>
> introduction, 4.1
>
> powers, 4.4–4.4.7
>
> qualifications, 4.2

miscellaneous provisions, 6.11

moneys received, 6.6

notice of creditors' meetings, 6.7.2.1

overview, 1.2.2

proxy, 6.7.2.1

remuneration of liquidators, 6.10

representing company, 6.13

representing creditors, 6.12

required steps, 6.7–6.7.4

reservation of title, 6.5

resolution to wind up company, 6.7.3

rules of the superior courts, and, 6.8

shares as consideration for sale of
company property, 6.10

solicitors' fees, 6.7.4

'solvency', 6.2

statement of affairs, 6.7.1

vacancy in office of liquidator, 6.10

CRO filings

compulsory liquidation, and, 3.14

Cross-border insolvency

effect of foreign proceedings in Ireland,
13.3

EU Insolvency Regulation (No 1346/
2000)

> conclusion, 13.13
>
> generally, 13.5
>
> information to creditors, 13.11
>
> insolvency judgments, 13.8.1
>
> jurisdiction, 13.7
>
> *lex concursus*, 13.9–13.9.1
>
> 'main' proceedings, 13.7–13.7.1
>
> public policy, 13.12
>
> recognition of insolvency proceedings,
> 13.8–13.8.1
>
> scope, 13.6
>
> secondary insolvency proceedings,
> 13.10
>
> special choice of law, 13.9.1
>
> territorial proceedings, 13.7.1
>
> treatment of creditors, 13.11

extraterritorial effect of Irish orders and
appointments

> generally, 13.2
>
> local winding-up proceedings, 13.2.2
>
> orders in aid, 13.2.1
>
> other issues, 13.2.3

international rules, 13.4

introduction, 13.1

receivership, and, 7.8

UNCITRAL Model Law, 13.4

D

Debentureholder

receivers, and, 7.4

Defences

compulsory liquidation, and, 3.5.1.6

Demand letters

compulsory liquidation, and, 3.5.1.1

Directions

examinerships, and, 9.1.5

Directors

compulsory liquidation, and, 3.7

disqualification orders

> applicants, 11.13
>
> automatic disqualification, 11.11
>
> costs, 11.10
>
> discretion of court, and, 11.12
>
> duration, 11.15
>
> enforcement, 11.16.1–11.16.2

Directors (contd)

disqualification orders (contd)
    generally, 11.9
    introduction, 10.7
    period of disqualification, 11.15
    time limits for applications, 11.14
  duties and liabilities
    acting in interests of creditors, 10.5
    advising directors, 10.8
    disqualification orders, and, 10.7
    failure to keep proper books of
    account, 10.3
    fraudulent preferences, 10.4
    fraudulent trading, 10.2.1
    interests of creditors, 10.5
    introduction, 10.1
    keeping proper books of account, 10.3
    misfeasance, 10.6
    reckless trading, 10.2.2
    restriction orders, and, 10.7
  examinerships, and, 9.1.12
  restriction orders
    acting honestly, 11.3.1
    acting responsibly, 11.3.2
    applicants, 11.2.2
    applications, 11.2.1–11.2.2
    consequences, 11.8.1–11.8.3
    costs, 11.5–11.6
    defending applications, 11.3–11.3.3
    enforcement, 11.16.1–11.16.2
    generally, 11.1
    introduction, 10.7
    investigation costs, 11.6
    just and equitable, 11.3.3
    legal costs, 11.5
    obligations of non-executive director,
    11.4
    relief, 11.7

Directors' duties and liabilities

acting in interests of creditors, 10.5
advising directors, 10.8
disqualification orders, and, 10.7
failure to keep proper books of account,
10.3
fraudulent preferences, 10.4
fraudulent trading
  generally, 10.2.1
  introduction, 10.1
interests of creditors, 10.5
introduction, 10.1
keeping proper books of account, 10.3

misfeasance, 10.6
reckless trading
  generally, 10.2.2
  introduction, 10.1
restriction orders, and, 10.7

Disabilities

bankruptcy, and, 12.5.1

Disposal of assets post-liquidation

liquidators' powers, and, 4.5.5

Disqualification orders

applicants, 11.13
automatic disqualification, 11.11
costs, 11.10
discretion of court, and, 11.12
duration, 11.15
enforcement, 11.16.1–11.16.2
generally, 11.9
introduction, 10.7
period of disqualification, 11.15
time limits for applications, 11.14

Distribution of assets

effect of winding up on creditors and third
parties, 2.1.2
proof of debts, 2.1.3
role of liquidator, 2.1.1

E

Employees' debts

order of payments in liquidation, and,
2.3.2

**EU Insolvency Regulation (No 1346/
2000)**

bankruptcy, and, 12.10
conclusion, 13.13
generally, 13.5
information to creditors, 13.11
insolvency judgments, 13.8.1
jurisdiction, 13.7
lex concursus, 13.9–13.9.1
'main' proceedings, 13.7–13.7.1
public policy, 13.12
receiverships, and, 7.8
recognition of insolvency proceedings,
13.8–13.8.1
scope, 13.6
secondary insolvency proceedings, 13.10
special choice of law, 13.9.1
territorial proceedings, 13.7.1
treatment of creditors, 13.11

Examination

generally, 1.2.5

order of payments, 2.5

Examiner's Office meetings

compulsory liquidation, and, 3.9

Examinerships

acting in good faith, 9.1.4

affidavit verifying contents of petition, 9.1.3

appointment of examiner

    generally, 9.1.9

    notification, 9.1.10

confirmation of proposals, 9.1.20

contracts, and

    during protection, 9.1.15

    pre-protection, 9.1.14

costs and expenses, 9.1.21

creditors' meetings, 9.1.17

directions, 9.1.5

directors' powers, and, 9.1.12

effect of petition

    generally, 9.1.6

    provisional liquidator, on, 9.1.8

    receiver, on, 9.1.7

examiners

    appointment, 9.1.9–9.1.10

    costs and expenses, 9.1.21

    powers, 9.1.11

    remuneration, 9.1.21

good faith, and, 9.1.4

guarantees, and, 9.1.18

hire agreements, and, 9.1.19

interim examiners, 9.1.5

leases, and, 9.1.19

members' meetings, 9.1.17

members' powers, and, 9.1.13

order of payments, 2.5

overview, 1.2.5

payment of pre-petition debts, 9.1.16

petition

    affidavit verifying contents, 9.1.3

    effect of presentation, 9.1.6–9.1.7

    generally, 9.1.2

    good faith, and, 9.1.4

petitioners, 9.1.1

pre-protection contracts, 9.1.14

priorities, and, 2.5

provisional liquidators, and, 9.1.8

receivers, and, 9.1.7

remuneration of examiners, 9.1.21

report to the court, 9.1.20

revocation, 9.1.22

schemes of arrangement, and, 9.2.4

Extraterritorial effect of Irish orders and appointments

generally, 13.2

local winding-up proceedings, 13.2.2

orders in aid, 13.2.1

other issues, 13.2.3

F

Failure to keep proper books and records

liquidators' powers, and, 4.5.8.2

Fiduciary duties

liquidators, and, 4.3.1

Floating charges

liquidators' powers, and, 4.5.6

Fraudulent conveyance

liquidators' powers, and, 4.5.1

Fraudulent disposal of property

liquidators' powers, and, 4.5.2

Fraudulent preference

liquidators' powers, and, 4.5.3

Fraudulent trading

liquidators' powers, and, 4.5.8.1

G

Good faith

examinerships, and, 9.1.4

Guarantees

examinerships, and, 9.1.18

H

Hire agreements

examinerships, and, 9.1.19

I

Income tax

preferential debts, and, 2.3.3.1

Incorporation of subsidiary

receivers' powers, and, 7.3.3.3

Insolvency

meaning, 1.2

Insolvency set-off

rules as to priorities, and, 2.2.2

Insolvent deceased estates

bankruptcy, and, 12.9

Interim examiners

examinerships, and, 9.1.5

International insolvency

effect of foreign proceedings in Ireland, 13.3

EU Insolvency Regulation (No 1346/ 2000)

    conclusion, 13.13

    generally, 13.5

    information to creditors, 13.11

    insolvency judgments, 13.8.1

    jurisdiction, 13.7

    lex concursus, 13.9–13.9.1

    'main' proceedings, 13.7–13.7.1

    public policy, 13.12

    recognition of insolvency proceedings, 13.8–13.8.1

    scope, 13.6

    secondary insolvency proceedings, 13.10

    special choice of law, 13.9.1

    territorial proceedings, 13.7.1

    treatment of creditors, 13.11

extraterritorial effect of Irish orders and appointments

    generally, 13.2

    local winding-up proceedings, 13.2.2

    orders in aid, 13.2.1

    other issues, 13.2.3

international rules, 13.4

introduction, 13.1

receivership, and, 7.8

UNCITRAL Model Law, 13.4

J

Judgment mortgages

rules as to priorities, and, 2.2.4

Jurisdiction of court

compulsory liquidation, and, 3.2

L

Leases

examinerships, and, 9.1.19

Liquidation

compulsory liquidation

    And see **Compulsory liquidation**

    generally, 3.1–3.14

    introduction, 1.2.3

creditors' voluntary liquidation

    And see **Creditors' voluntary liquidation**

    consequences, 5.5

    generally, 6.1–6.10

    introduction, 1.2.1

    miscellaneous provisions, 6.11–6.13

    overview, 5.1

introduction, 1.2.1–1.2.3

liquidators

    And see Liquidators

    asset swelling measures, 4.5–4.5.8

    duties, 4.3.1–4.3.6

    introduction, 4.1

    powers, 4.4–4.4.7

    qualifications, 4.2

members' voluntary liquidation

    And see **Members' voluntary liquidation**

    consequences, 5.5

    generally, 5.2–5.4

    introduction, 1.2.1

    miscellaneous provisions, 6.11–6.13

    overview, 5.1

order of payments

    costs in court liquidation, 2.3.1

    debts to employees under contract, 2.3.2

    generally, 2.3

    introduction, 3.11.1

    preferential debts, 2.3.3–2.3.3.2

voluntary liquidation

    And see **Voluntary liquidation**

    common provisions, 6.11

    consequences, 5.5

    creditors', 6.1–6.10

    introduction, 1.2.1–1.2.2

    members', 5.2–5.4

    overview, 5.1

Liquidators

administrative duties

    compulsory liquidation, 4.3.3.2

    creditors' voluntary liquidation, 4.3.3.3

    generally, 4.3.3

    members' voluntary liquidation, 4.3.3.1

appointment

    advertisement, 3.8.1

    effect, 3.7

Liquidators (contd)

appointment (contd)

 filing notices, 3.8.2

 introduction, 3.8

 persons qualified, 3.6

 service of notice, 3.8.3

 statement on company

 correspondence, 3.8.4

appointment of agent, 4.4.4.3

appointment of solicitor, 4.4.4.1

asset swelling powers

 action against directors, 4.5.8

 contribution orders, 4.5.7.1–4.5.7.2

 failure to keep proper books and

 records, 4.5.8.2

 floating charges, 4.5.6

 fraudulent conveyance, 4.5.1

 fraudulent disposal of property, 4.5.2

 fraudulent preference, 4.5.3

 fraudulent trading, 4.5.8.1

 introduction, 4.5

 payment made by insolvent company, 4.5.4

 pooling orders, 4.5.7.3

 post-liquidation disposal of assets, 4.5.5

 reckless trading, 4.5.8.2

carrying on the business, 4.4.4.2

CRO filings, 3.14

discharge, 3.13

duties

 administrative, 4.3.3

 fiduciary, 4.3.1

 general, 4.3.2

 policing, 4.4.7

 procedural, 4.3.3

 statutory, 4.3.3

fiduciary duties, 4.3.1

general duties, 4.3.2

policing powers and duties, 4.4.7

powers

 appointment of agent, 4.4.4.3

 appointment of solicitor, 4.4.4.1

 asset swelling, 4.5

 carrying on the business, 4.4.4.2

 generally, 4.4

 not requiring court sanction, 4.4.4

 official liquidators' functions, and, 4.4.2

 pending hearing of petition, 4.4.1

 policing, 4.4.7

 requiring court sanction, 4.4.3

 sale of assets, 4.4.4.4

 specific, 4.4.6

 voluntary liquidations, in, 4.4.5

powers in voluntary liquidations

 approval in creditors' liquidation, 4.4.5.2

 approval in members' liquidation, 4.4.5.1

 introduction, 4.4.5

 not requiring approval, 4.4.5.3

 restrictions on exercise, 4.4.5.4

 liquidators' remuneration, 4.4.5.5

provisional liquidation, in, 4.4.1

qualifications, 4.2

realisation of assets, and

 generally, 4.3.6

 introduction, 2.1.1

remuneration

 generally, 4.4.5.5

 official liquidators, 3.13

sale of assets, 4.4.4.4

specific powers, 4.4.6

statutory duties

 administrative nature, of, 4.3.3

 creditors, to, 4.3.5

 members, to, 4.3.4

 realise assets, to, 4.3.6

types, 4.1

Local rates

preferential debts, and, 2.3.3.1

Locus standi

compulsory liquidation, and, 3.3

M

Managers

bankruptcy, and, 12.8

Members' meetings

examinerships, and, 9.1.17

Members' powers

examinerships, and, 9.1.13

Members' voluntary liquidation

consequences, 5.5

declaration of solvency, 5.2.1

failure to file resolution and/or declaration, 5.4

final meeting, 5.2.7

generally, 5.2

independent report, 5.2.3

introduction, 1.2.1

Members' voluntary liquidation (contd)
liquidators
   And see Liquidators
   asset swelling measures, 4.5–4.5.8
   duties, 4.3.1–4.3.6
   generally, 5.3
   introduction, 4.1
   powers, 4.4–4.4.7
   qualifications, 4.2
meetings, 5.2.6
notices, 5.2.6
overview, 1.2.1
resolution to wind up company, 5.2.4
shares as consideration for sale of company property, 5.2.5
statement of assets and liabilities, 5.2.2
summoning general meeting, 5.2.5
vacancy in office of liquidator, 5.2.5

Mortgages

rules as to priorities, and, 2.2.4

N

Notice of intention to liquidate

compulsory liquidation, and, 3.5.1.1

Notice to proceed

compulsory liquidation, and, 3.8.8

O

Offences

bankruptcy, and, 12.5.2

Officers of company

compulsory liquidation, and, 3.7

Official liquidators

introduction, 3.1
remuneration, 3.13

Order of payments

examination, in, 2.5
liquidation, in
   costs in court liquidation, 2.3.1
   debts to employees under contract, 2.3.2
   generally, 2.3
   preferential debts, 2.3.3–2.3.3.2
receivership, in, 2.4

P

Pari passu **rule**

rules as to priorities, and, 2.2.1

Payments made by insolvent company

liquidators' powers, and, 4.5.4

Personal insolvency

And see **Bankruptcy**

arrangements with creditors, 12.4
composition after bankruptcy, 12.7
debtor's position, 12.3
insolvent deceased estates, 12.9
introduction, 12.1
post-bankruptcy issues, 12.5
proceedings, 12.2
receivers and managers, 12.8
winding up of estate, 12.6

Petition

bankruptcy, and, 12.2.2.2

Petitioners

compulsory liquidation, and, 3.3
examinerships, and, 9.1.1

Pooling orders

liquidators' powers, and, 4.5.7.3

Post-liquidation disposal of assets

liquidators' powers, and, 4.5.5

Preferential creditors

receivership, and, 8.6.3

Preferential debts

compulsory liquidation, and, 2.3.3–2.3.3.2
order of payments in liquidation, and
   generally, 2.3.3
   rates, 2.3.3.1
   salaries, 2.3.3.2
   taxes, 2.3.3.1
   wages, 2.3.3.2
rates, 2.3.3.1
salaries, 2.3.3.2
taxes, 2.3.3.1
wages, 2.3.3.2

Priorities

compulsory liquidation, and, 3.11.1
judgment mortgages, 2.2.4
order of payments in examination, 2.5
order of payments in liquidation
   costs in court liquidation, 2.3.1
   debts to employees under contract, 2.3.2
   generally, 2.3
   introduction, 3.11.1
   preferential debts, 2.3.3–2.3.3.2

Priorities (contd)

order of payments in receivership, 2.4

pari passu rule, 2.2.1

retention of title

    incorporation of clause, 2.2.3.2

    purpose, 2.2.3.1

    validity, 2.2.3.3

set off, 2.2.2

Proof of debt

compulsory liquidation, and

    adjudication of claims, 3.11.4

    advertising for creditors, 3.11.3

    claims admissible to proof, 3.11.2

    generally, 3.11

    priority of payment, 3.11.1

generally, 2.1.3

Provisional liquidators

examinerships, and, 9.1.8

powers, 4.4.1

R

Rates

preferential debts, and, 2.3.3.1

Realisation of assets

effect of winding up on creditors and third parties, 2.1.2

liquidators' powers, and, 4.3.6

proof of debts, 2.1.3

role of liquidator, 2.1.1

Receivers

advice before appointment

    acceptance of appointment, 8.2.7

    appointment, 8.2.5

    debentures not providing for receivers, 8.2.2

    eligibility to act, 8.2.1

    fees, 8.2.4

    indemnity, 8.2.3

    notice of appointment, 8.2.6

    prior charge-holders, and, 8.2.8

    remuneration, 8.2.4

    resources, 8.2.9

advice following appointment

    acceptance of appointment, 8.3.2

    deed of appointment, 8.3.1

    insurance, 8.3.5

    notice to company of appointment, 8.3.4

    publication of notice of appointment, 8.3.3

    removal, 8.3.7–8.3.8

    resignation, 8.3.7

    restrictions, 8.3.8

    rival appointments, and, 8.3.6

agent of company, as, 7.4

appointment

    advice, and, 8.2.5

    contract, under, 7.1

    court, by, 7.1.1

    date of commencement, 7.2.2

    effect, 7.6

    introduction, 7.2.1

    notification, 7.5

    purpose, 7.2.1

    validity assessment checklist, 8.12

appointment of agents, 7.3.3.2

appointment of employees, 7.3.3.2

bankruptcy, and, 12.8

carrying on business, 7.3.2.2

compromise of litigation, 7.3.2.4

cross-border insolvency, and, 7.8

debentureholder, as, 7.4

duties, 7.3.1

effect of appointment

    company, on, 7.6.1

    directors, on, 7.6.2

examinerships, and, 9.1.7

function, 7.3.1

implied powers

    employ agents, to, 7.3.3.2

    employ employees, to, 7.3.3.2

    generally, 7.3.3

    hive down, to, 7.3.3.3

    incorporate subsidiary, to, 7.3.3.3

    insure, to, 7.3.3.1

    repair, to, 7.3.3.1

incorporation of subsidiary, 7.3.3.3

liability, 7.7.1

meaning, 7.1

powers

    absence of specific clause, in, 7.3.6

    carrying on business, 7.3.2.2

    compromise litigation, to, 7.3.2.4

    debenture deed, under, 7.3.2.1–7.3.2.4

    employ agents, to, 7.3.3.2

    employ employees, to, 7.3.3.2

    generally, 7.3.2

    hive down, to, 7.3.3.3

    implication, by, 7.3.3

    incorporate subsidiary, to, 7.3.3.3

    insure, to, 7.3.3.1

    introduction, 7.3.1

Receivers (contd)

powers (contd)

   repair, to, 7.3.3.1

   sale, of, 7.3.2.3, 7.3.4

   take possession, to, 7.3.2.1

   use of seal, 7.3.5

qualifications, 7.7.2

remuneration

   advice, and, 8.2.4

   generally, 7.7.3

resignation

   advice, and, 8.3.7

   generally, 7.7.4

sale of property, 7.3.2.3, 7.3.4

statutory basis, 7.1.2

taking possession, 7.3.2.1

types, 7.1

use of seal, 7.3.5

Receivers and managers

bankruptcy, and, 12.8

Receivership

advising contractors, 8.5

advising creditors

   introduction, 8.6

   preferential creditors, 8.6.3

   secured creditors, 8.6.1

   special creditors, 8.6.2

advising directors

   directors' statement of affairs, 8.8.1

   proceedings, 8.8.3

   suspension of powers, 8.8.2

advising employees

   action against receiver, 8.10.2

   continuity of employment, 8.10.4

   introduction, 8.10

   preferential payouts, 8.10.3

   receivers appointed under debenture, 8.10.1

   transfer of employment, 8.10.4

advising guarantors, 8.9

advising liquidator appointed to company

   connected persons, 8.7.6

   effect on receiver's agency, 8.7.2

   effect on receiver's appointment, 8.7.1

   effect on receiver's duties, 8.7.4

   effect on receiver's powers, 8.7.3

   floating charges, 8.7.5

   fraudulent preference, 8.7.9

   introduction, 8.7

   rule in Clayton's case, 8.7.8

   time of creation of charge, 8.7.7

advising potential receiver

   acceptance of appointment, 8.2.7

   appointment, 8.2.5

   checklist, 8.13

   debentures not providing for receivers, 8.2.2

   eligibility to act, 8.2.1

   fees, 8.2.4

   indemnity, 8.2.3

   notice of appointment, 8.2.6

   prior charge-holders, and, 8.2.8

   remuneration, 8.2.4

   resources, 8.2.9

advising receiver after appointment

   acceptance of appointment, 8.3.2

   deed of appointment, 8.3.1

   insurance, 8.3.5

   notice to company of appointment, 8.3.4

   publication of notice of appointment, 8.3.3

   removal, 8.3.7–8.3.8

   resignation, 8.3.7

   restrictions, 8.3.8

   rival appointments, and, 8.3.6

advising shareholders, 8.9

advising suppliers, 8.5

appointment of receivers

   contract, under, 7.1

   court, by, 7.1.1

   date of commencement, 7.2.2

   effect, 7.6

   introduction, 7.2.1

   notification, 7.5

   purpose, 7.2.1

   validity assessment checklist, 8.12

Director of Corporate Enforcement, and

   disciplinary findings, 8.4.3

   notifications, 8.4.1

   production of books and records, 8.4.2

effect

   company, on, 7.6.1

   directors, on, 7.6.2

existence of company, 8.1.1

existence of debenture, 8.1.2

generally, 1.2.4

introduction, 7.1

order of payments, 2.4

overview, 1.2.4

Receivership (contd)

sale of company or assets
    checklist, 8.14
    generally, 8.11
    hive down, 8.11.1
scope of debenture, 8.1.2

Reckless trading

liquidators' powers, and, 4.5.8.2

Remuneration

examinerships, and, 9.1.21
liquidators, and
    generally, 4.4.5.5
    official liquidators, 3.13
receivers, and, 7.7.3

Resignation

receivers, and, 7.7.4

Restriction orders

acting honestly, 11.3.1
acting responsibly, 11.3.2
applicants, 11.2.2
applications, 11.2.1–11.2.2
consequences, 11.8.1–11.8.3
costs, 11.5–11.6
defending applications, 11.3–11.3.3
enforcement, 11.16.1–11.16.2
generally, 11.1
introduction, 10.7
investigation costs, 11.6
just and equitable, 11.3.3
legal costs, 11.5
obligations of non-executive director, 11.4
relief, 11.7

Retention of title

incorporation of clause, 2.2.3.2
purpose, 2.2.3.1
validity, 2.2.3.3

Revocation

examinerships, and, 9.1.22

Rules as to priorities

judgment mortgages, 2.2.4
order of payments in examination, 2.5
order of payments in liquidation
    costs in court liquidation, 2.3.1
    debts to employees under contract, 2.3.2
    generally, 2.3
    preferential debts, 2.3.3–2.3.3.2

order of payments in receivership, 2.4
pari passu rule, 2.2.1
retention of title
    incorporation of clause, 2.2.3.2
    purpose, 2.2.3.1
    validity, 2.2.3.3
set off, 2.2.2

S

Salaries

preferential debts, and, 2.3.3.2

Sale of property

receivers' powers, and, 7.3.2.3, 7.3.4

Schemes of arrangement

approval, 9.2.1
examinership, and
    generally, 9.2.4
    introduction, 1.2.5
introduction, 9.2
Revenue, and
    ability to compromise, 9.2.3
    general position, 9.2.2
selection of classes of members and creditors, 9.2.2
winding up, and, 9.2.5

Seal of company

receivers' powers, and, 7.3.5

Secured creditors

receivership, and, 8.6.3

Service of documents

compulsory liquidation, and
    creditor's petition, 3.5.1.3
    notice of appointment of liquidator, 3.8.3
    order on company's bankers, 3.8.5

Set off

rules as to priorities, and, 2.2.2

Solicitors

liquidators' powers, and, 4.4.4.1

Substitution of creditor

compulsory liquidation, and, 3.5.1.7

Summons

bankruptcy, and, 12.2.2.1

T

Taking possession

receivers' powers, and, 7.3.2.1

Taxes

preferential debts, and, 2.3.3.1

Third parties

distribution and realisation of assets, and, 2.1.2

V

Voluntary liquidation

common provisions, 6.11

consequences, 5.5

creditors' voluntary liquidation

    accountants', fees, 6.7.4

    convening creditors' meeting, 6.7.2–6.7.2.1

    creditors' meeting, 6.9

    dissolution, 6.10

    employees, 6.4

    existing contracts, and, 6.3

    final meeting, 6.10

    generally, 6.1

    miscellaneous provisions, 6.11

    moneys received, 6.6

    notice of creditors' meetings, 6.7.2.1

    proxy, 6.7.2.1

    remuneration of liquidators, 6.10

    representing company, 6.13

    representing creditors, 6.12

    required steps, 6.7–6.7.4

    reservation of title, 6.5

    resolution to wind up company, 6.7.3

    rules of the superior courts, and, 6.8

    shares as consideration for sale of company property, 6.10

    solicitors' fees, 6.7.4

    'solvency', 6.2

    statement of affairs, 6.7.1

    vacancy in office of liquidator, 6.10

introduction, 5.1

liquidators' powers

    approval in creditors' liquidation, 4.4.5.2

    approval in members' liquidation, 4.4.5.1

    introduction, 4.4.5

    not requiring approval, 4.4.5.3

    restrictions on exercise, 4.4.5.4

liquidators' remuneration, 4.4.5.5

members' voluntary liquidation

    consequences, 5.5

    declaration of solvency, 5.2.1

    failure to file resolution and/or declaration, 5.4

    final meeting, 5.2.7

    generally, 5.2

    independent report, 5.2.3

    liquidators, 5.3

    meetings, 5.2.6

    miscellaneous provisions, 6.11

    notices, 5.2.6

    resolution to wind up company, 5.2.4

    shares as consideration for sale of company property, 5.2.5

    statement of assets and liabilities, 5.2.2

    summoning general meeting, 5.2.5

    vacancy in office of liquidator, 5.2.5

overview, 1.2.1–1.2.2

Voluntary liquidators

And see **Liquidators**

approval

    creditors' liquidation, 4.4.5.2

    members' liquidation, 4.4.5.1

introduction, 4.4.5

not requiring approval, 4.4.5.3

restrictions on exercise, 4.4.5.4

liquidators' remuneration, 4.4.5.5

W

Wages

preferential debts, and, 2.3.3.2

Winding up

compulsory liquidation

    And see **Compulsory liquidation**

    generally, 3.1–3.14

    introduction, 1.2.3

creditors' voluntary liquidation

    And see **Creditors' voluntary liquidation**

    consequences, 5.5

    generally, 6.1–6.10

    introduction, 1.2.1

    miscellaneous provisions, 6.11–6.13

    overview, 5.1

introduction, 1.2.1–1.2.3

liquidators

    And see **Liquidators**

    asset swelling measures, 4.5–4.5.8

    duties, 4.3.1–4.3.6

    introduction, 4.1

    powers, 4.4–4.4.7

    qualifications, 4.2

Winding up (contd)

members' voluntary liquidation
   And see **Members' voluntary liquidation**
   consequences, 5.5
   generally, 5.2–5.4
   introduction, 1.2.1
   miscellaneous provisions, 6.11–6.13
   overview, 5.1
schemes of arrangement, and, 9.2.5
voluntary liquidation

And see **Voluntary liquidation**
   common provisions, 6.11
   consequences, 5.5
   creditors', 6.1–6.10
   introduction, 1.2.1–1.2.2
   members', 5.2–5.4
   overview, 5.1
Winding up of estate
bankruptcy, and, 12.6